THE INTUITIVE DIMENSIONS OF ADMINISTRATIVE DECISION MAKING

Stephen H. Davis
Patricia B. Davis

A SCARECROWEDUCATION BOOK

The Scarecrow Press, Inc.
Lanham, Maryland, and Oxford
2003

A SCARECROWEDUCATION BOOK

Published in the United States of America
by Scarecrow Press, Inc.
A Member of the Rowman & Littlefield Publishing Group
4501 Forbes Boulevard, Suite 200, Lanham, Maryland 20706
www.scarecroweducation.com

PO Box 317
Oxford
OX2 9RU, UK

British Library Cataloguing in Publication Information Available

Library of Congress Cataloging-in-Publication Data
Davis, Stephen H. (Stephen Hunt), 1949–
  The intuitive dimensions of administrative decision making / Stephen H.
Davis, Patricia B. Davis.
      p. cm.
"A ScarecrowEducation Book."
Includes bibliographical references (p.   ) and index.
  ISBN 0-8108-4619-5 (pbk. : alk. paper)
  1. School management and organization—Decision making. 2. Intuition. I.
Davis, Patricia B. (Patricia Blackwell), 1946– II. Title.
LB2806 .D32 2003
371.2—dc21

                                                          2002013864

∞™ The paper used in this publication meets the minimum requirements of
American National Standard for Information Sciences—Permanence of Paper
for Printed Library Materials, ANSI/NISO Z39.48-1992.
Manufactured in the United States of America.

CONTENTS

TABLES AND FIGURE

TABLES

FIGURE

PREFACE

There is no question that intuition is an extraordinary dimension of human cognition, possessed and used by virtually everyone at one time or another. Neither is there much doubt that as organizations become more complex, so do the decisions faced by managers and leaders. As these decisions become more complex, the ability to solve them through rational/analytical means alone becomes increasingly difficult. Principals and aspiring administrators need to know that their intuitions have the potential to assist them in making good decisions under complex and stressful conditions. Although we agree that one can't teach intuition as one might teach a child to read, we can raise awareness about the intuitive experience, its value in aiding the decision-making process, and the kinds of strategies that may prove useful in nurturing one's intuitive skills. The kinds of rational decision theories and models frequently being taught in graduate programs are of limited use in the field, particularly with the complex problems and dilemmas commonly faced by principals. Principals often don't have the time or the information to make decisions without the use of heuristic processes like intuition. Intuitive skills cannot be built like some kind of cognitive construction project, but they can be polished and used to enhance, and in some cases replace, rational/analytical decision approaches.

Our interest in the topic of intuitive decision making evolved through more than fifty years of collective experiences as school administrators and as professionals in higher education. Through our experiences in the field and conversations with dozens of school administrators, it became clear that there is a growing disconnection between how principals are being taught to make decisions and how decisions are actually made on the job. We recalled from our own experiences as principals and superintendents that many of the most challenging problems were solved not through extensive analysis but through gut feelings, educated hunches, and intuitions. Importantly, more often than not, our intuitions were correct!

In our explorations of the literature on administrative decision making, we looked for studies that emphasized qualitative rather than quantitative approaches to decision making. We found very few. Instead, the literature continues to emphasize normative or prescriptive approaches to decision making that focus on highly analytical and deliberative ways of thinking. Such approaches may work well with certain kinds of well-structured problems, but are rarely applied to the kinds of problems that pose the greatest risks to principals and their schools.

So, with these issues in mind, we set out to examine just how principals go about using their intuitions on the job and to determine the relative effectiveness of intuitively and rationally derived decisions. Our quest involved an extensive review of the literature in the fields of rationalist philosophy, problem solving and decision making, intuitive thinking and decision making, and the neuroscience of decision making. It also involved a two-tiered study of ninety public school principals in Contra Costa County, California. From this study came rich and insightful descriptions of how principals used their intuitions to help resolve their most perplexing decisions. As a result of our investigations into the literature and experiences of principals, we were able to develop thirty key ideas and principles pertaining to the issue of developing, activating, and using one's intuition to become a more effective decision maker.

We hope the book proves to be of value to anyone who currently occupies a position of leadership in educational administration or who aspires to do so in the future. We also hope that those who teach in administrative preparation programs will consider what we have to say about effective decision making in schools. Good decision making is at the heart of good leadership. To be effective decision makers, principals must be able to employ a broad array of decision-making tools and strategies. We believe that intuition is one such tool that has been largely overlooked and undervalued by scholars interested in decision making as well as practitioners in the field.

In the introduction, we introduce three short stories about school leaders and their experiences with three very different, yet equally challenging, problems. We go on to discuss in chapter 1 how Western society continues to value highly rational and analytical approaches to problem solving and decision making, even in the face of mounting evidence that such approaches have limited value in the day-to-day turbulence of organizational life. In chapter 2, we take a close look at the paradox between problem solving and decision making as they have evolved through empirical research and as they are practiced in complex organizations. We point to an important and recent shift in scholarly interest from prescriptive models of decision making to what is commonly referred to as naturalistic decision making (i.e., how decisions are actually made in the field). From this new strand of research, there has been growing interest in examining the subtle and nuanced aspects of decision making. Such efforts have included studies about tacit knowledge, heuristic thinking, and intuition. Most research in these areas, however, has occurred in private sector environments or in public sectors outside the field of education (such as medicine, law enforcement, and the military). In chapter 3, we take a concentrated look at the topic of intuition—what it means, how it works, how it is experienced, and how it has been studied. In chapter 4, we provide an overview of how research has unlocked many of the mysteries of the brain-mind and how we have come to better understand how thoughts, feelings, and behaviors are linked to certain neuroscientific principles, structures, and processes. In chapter 5, we provide the results of our own research on intuitive decision making, including how principals responded to a popular survey on intuitive decision making and in-depth interviews with six highly intuitive principals. We were surprised at how powerful and pervasive intuition was in principals' efforts to resolve complex and important professional problems. Finally, in chapter 6, we synthesized the findings from our research with the research and literature of others in an attempt to construct a set of common principles and concepts about intuitive thinking and effective decision making.

We are very grateful to the ninety principals who responded to our survey and especially to those six principals who agreed to participate in follow-up interviews. Without their contributions and wonderful insights, this book would not have been possible. Although we would like nothing better than to acknowledge each one by name, we will respect their privacy in the interests of confidentiality. Their stories and experiences were heartfelt, often deeply personal, and extremely sensitive. And through their stories, we were able to capture the essence of what it means to be an intuitive decision maker.

We are also deeply grateful to Dr. Weston Agor from the University of Texas, El Paso, who pioneered much of the early research on intuition and managerial decision making. Dr. Agor provided us with numerous documents, survey materials, references, and sage advice as we worked through the various stages of this project.

INTRODUCTION

We begin this book with three short stories that serve as parables for better understanding the decision dilemmas and contexts faced by school leaders almost every day. We offer these stories to establish the point that real world administrative decision making rarely conforms to popular theories about, or expectations for, analytical planning and rational thinking. Our stories also set the stage for a more detailed discussion about the incongruity between increasing demands for rational/analytical leadership and real-world administrative decision contexts and challenges.

MARSHA'S DILEMMA

It was 8.55 A.M. and principal Marsha Mahan was double-checking her schedule for the day before leaving the office to conduct one final classroom observation of Peter Allen, a second-year probationary English teacher. Marsha's schedule was pretty typical for a Wednesday—Peter Allen's observation, several meetings to attend or lead (both on and off campus), phone calls and e-mail messages to return, various administrative forms and reports to complete, and an after-school activity to supervise. Even if everything went as planned, Marsha knew

that the typical workday also brought with it a number of unanticipated problems and challenges. Above all else, school leadership was
a people business, and when dealing with people Marsha knew enough
to expect the unexpected. She also knew that during the course of a
typical workday she would be called upon to make a wide range of
decisions: some that would be routine and relatively unimportant,
some that would be complex and extremely important, and several that
would fall somewhere in between routine and complex.

Marsha was especially concerned about the upcoming observation of
Peter Allen. He was approaching the end of his second year of probationary status, and Marsha had just a few days to make a final decision
about whether to recommend the renewal of his contract and tenure.
She had not anticipated waiting this long to make such a critical decision, but given the hectic pace of her job, she simply didn't have enough
time to observe all of the teachers who were due for formal evaluations
this year.

Peter Allen had started out as a promising young teacher, fresh out of
a teacher-training program at the local state university. Marsha hired
him knowing that he would be a work in progress. Nevertheless, she had
high hopes that with careful mentoring he would turn out to be a fine
teacher in a couple of years or so. Unfortunately, it didn't work out that
way. Only twenty-four years old, Peter had a serious problem maintain-
ing a professional relationship with his students. He seemed far more interested in being perceived as a buddy to his students than as an adult
role model. Several complaints from parents, and even from a few colleagues on the staff, had alerted Marsha to the issue several months earlier. Not surprisingly, Peter's biggest problem was his lack of classroom
control. Quite simply, his students were loud, rude, and frequently off
task. There were times when the noise was so bad that other teachers in
his classroom wing called the office to complain. Marsha had spent quite
a bit of time with Peter during the current school year observing his
classes and making suggestions for improvement. To date, nothing she
had done had made much difference.

What really vexed Martha, however, was the fact that Peter was exceptionally knowledgeable in his subject matter and was very creative in
designing his lessons and course curricula. Moreover, he was a very nice
young man who appeared eager to please. Marsha felt a significant de-

gree of responsibility for Peter's professional development and, given her busy schedule, she felt guilty for not giving him the attention he needed to be successful. This was going to be an extremely important classroom observation and a very tough decision.

Marsha had just a couple of minutes before the start of Peter's second-period class, so she quickly grabbed a pen and notepad and reached to open her office door. As she did, she heard a loud and angry woman's voice in the outer office. Although the exact words were difficult to understand, it was clear to Marsha that the woman was extremely upset with one of the secretaries. Marsha opened the door and began to walk in the direction of the front desk. Suddenly, without warning, the front door to the main office burst open and in stumbled two disheveled boys escorted by physical education teacher Marv Adams. Marv held them firmly by the arms and sat them down in the lobby chairs directly behind the shouting woman.

A quick glance at the two boys revealed that they had been in a fight of some sort. One boy's nose was bleeding while the other had a welt the size of an egg under one eye. The boys were extremely agitated, and it was all that Marv could do to keep them under control. Undeterred by the interruption, the woman continued to berate the secretary. Meanwhile, the clock ticked ceaselessly toward 9:00 A.M. and the start of Peter Allen's class.

Marsha had several decisions to make, and she had to make them quickly. There certainly was no time for in-depth analysis or lengthy reflection. The situations demanded immediate action. In essence, Marsha needed to act before she could think. However, Marsha knew that a wrong decision with any one of the three dilemmas that confronted her could easily exacerbate things. And, in a people business, once problems got out of control they often took on a life of their own, magnifying to several times their original intensity (March 1994). Fortunately, Marsha was very skilled at her job. Intuitively, she knew what to do almost as soon as she stepped into the main office. She quickly separated the two boys and arranged for supervision, asked the angry parent if she would please step into her office, and sent the secretary to Peter's classroom to inform him that she would be late.

Sound familiar? Almost anyone who has occupied a position of leadership or authority in schools can identify with Marsha's decision dilemmas.

We've run this scenario by dozens of school and district office administrators in recent years and virtually every response goes like this: "So,
what else is new? We deal with stuff like this every day!"

The point of this little vignette is not to underscore the complexities
and challenges of the principal's job. Those are well-established facts
(Ubben and Hughes 1997). Rather, the point is that the nature of school
leadership is such that decisions like Marsha's are commonplace and require a highly refined and efficient decision-making process that leaves
little time for careful deliberation and rational analysis (Hanson 1996;
March 1994).

DARLA'S SECRET

Marsha's dilemmas represent only a portion of the difficult decisions
regularly faced by school leaders. Take, for example, the extremely sensitive situation that confronted high school vice principal Dan Charles.
Dan was in his fourth year as the vice principal in charge of student discipline and counseling services at Central High School. Although in his
early thirties, Dan had handled just about every kind of student problem imaginable. He had a real knack for getting to the bottom of seemingly unresolvable problems. Dan seemed to have a sixth sense about
when a student, or a teacher for that matter, was or was not telling the
truth or revealing all of the relevant facts.

One morning around 8:20, Dan heard a loud knock on his office
door. Before he could rise from his desk, the door opened and in came
Ken Colt, a tenth-grade English teacher, with student Darla Campbell
firmly in tow. Mr. Colt's first words were, "I've had it up to here with
Ms. Campbell's profane outbursts and disruptive behavior. I want her
out of my class permanently."

Dan directed Darla to sit in the adjoining waiting room and then mo-
tioned for Mr. Colt to sit down and explain what had happened. According to Mr. Colt, Darla had come to class with red eyes and in an extremely agitated mood. She repeatedly ignored his requests to take her
seat, and when she finally did, wouldn't stop pestering the boy sitting in
front of her. When Mr. Colt admonished her again for her disruptive behavior, she responded with a profane comment heard by the entire class.

That, apparently, was the last straw. According to Mr. Colt, Darla had been a problem all semester. His long list of disciplinary referrals to Dan's office confirmed this.

Dan thanked Mr. Colt and told him that he would take care of the situation. Dan's next move was to talk with Darla. As she entered his office, Dan's first impression was that Mr. Colt had been right on. Darla's eyes were indeed red, and she was clearly agitated and restless. In response to Dan's questions about the incident, Darla simply looked away and said nothing. Dan interpreted Darla's uncooperative attitude as an admission of guilt and began to reach for the phone to call her mother.

As Dan picked up the receiver, something didn't feel right. He couldn't put his finger on what was troubling him, but he had a hunch that there was more to this situation than either he or Mr. Colt knew. On a gut feeling, his first call went not to Mrs. Campbell but to Rick Meade, the school's liaison officer with the juvenile probation department.

Fortunately, Rick was in his office and answered the phone. No sooner had Dan identified himself than Rick exclaimed, "Dan! Boy, am I glad you called. I was just about to call you about one of your students, Darla Campbell." Dan's gut feeling turned out to be correct as Rick described how Darla had been sexually assaulted by her drunken father the night before and that the police were on their way to arrest him as they spoke. Rick also asked Dan to keep Darla in the office until officials from Child Protective Services could pick her up. According to Rick, Darla's mother had come home late in the evening to find the assault in progress and notified the police once her husband had gone to work early that morning.

Under the circumstances, Dan knew that kicking Darla out of class, or perhaps school, was quite possibly the worst thing he could do. But how did Dan make the decision to call the probation officer? Certainly not through careful deliberation or lengthy analysis. He simply had an intuitive feeling that something wasn't right. He couldn't explain why, but somewhere from the depths of his subconscious mind came a signal—a sense of unease that caused him to take a different course of action than the situation, on its surface, appeared to call for.

As with the dilemmas faced by Marsha Berry, we ran this tale by several school leaders. Once again, we heard that decisions like this happen all the time in public schools. One principal responded, "Don't ask me to explain why or how, but sometimes I just know what to do."

Just knowing what to do is a surprisingly common attribute among experienced professionals in just about any industry or organization. Moreover, it appears that the higher one climbs up the management ladder, the more apt one is to take decisive action without relying on ponderous analytical processes (Dreyfus and Dreyfus 1986). We will talk more about this later.

Let's take one more look at a decision dilemma faced by a school leader. In this situation, the dilemma arose not prior to, or as a crisis was unfolding, but after a long and carefully crafted process of analysis and rational deliberation.

THE BILINGUAL PROGRAM

Superintendent Josh Winters should have been ecstatic. He had just completed what he hoped would be the last of a long series of meetings with parents, teachers, community activists, and members of the school board over the development of a bilingual program for the district's Hispanic student population. The solution to this issue was a long time in coming and the product of hotly contested beliefs about the merits of bilingual education. As a superintendent, Josh was well aware of the political nature of school district leadership. However, nothing in his several years of leadership experience had prepared him for the intensity of the political pressure prompted by the district's efforts to establish a bilingual program. The issue had deeply divided the community and had generated the very real threat of a formal complaint filed by a local political advocacy group with the U.S. Department of Education, Office of Civil Rights.

The issue had simmered for years before a small group of Hispanic parents came forward with their concern about the lack of a bilingual program in the district, despite the fact that over 30 percent of the students were non- or limited-English speakers.

The latest meeting had been held with a group of teacher representatives from throughout the district and several Hispanic parents. The teachers had pretty much dominated the meeting. They presented a proposal that would implement a districtwide sheltered English program that fell far short of the transitional bilingual program advocated by the parents and their supporters. The teachers had clearly done their homework, citing numerous studies and scholarly commentaries that supported their position. Their arguments were quite persuasive and, as a result, the Hispanic parents in attendance remained relatively silent. Both Josh and the teachers interpreted their silence as general acceptance of the plan.

In his heart, Josh believed that the real reason the teachers opposed a bilingual program was primarily financial. The resources needed to hire qualified teachers and to purchase appropriate books and materials for the bilingual program would reduce the district's general fund budget and, thus, would reduce the chances of much in the way of a pay raise for next year. Nevertheless, their presentation this evening was compelling and very logical. The teachers had covered almost every possible angle in coming up with a rational solution. Up to this point in time, Josh had been torn on the issue and didn't have any strong feelings one way or the other. He desperately hoped that the series of meetings would result in a consensual agreement among all involved.

As Josh left the meeting, however, he had a nagging feeling that something wasn't quite right. He couldn't put his finger on anything specific, but something just didn't feel right. Although he needed time to reflect on his feelings of unease, he was under tremendous pressure from the community and board of education to come up with a solution. In fact, his job later in the evening was to present the board of education with his final recommendation during a much anticipated public meeting of the board.

In the forty-five minutes or so remaining before the board meeting, Josh decided to take a walk. Walking always seemed to relax Josh and gave him a chance to distance himself from the problems and dilemmas of the job. Thirty-five minutes later, Josh returned to the district office and took his place at the head of the boardroom. He had made his decision. He would not recommend the teachers' plan. He hadn't worked out all of the key points in his head yet, but he simply knew that the teachers' plan wouldn't fly with the board or the Hispanic community. More importantly, it just wasn't going to meet the needs of the students. Tonight, he would ask the board for a postponement until he had a chance to thoroughly and rationally frame his position. He knew that asking for a postponement was risky, but in his gut he knew it was the right thing to do.

Josh's dilemma illustrates yet another aspect of administrative decision making and problem solving. Oftentimes, a very logically and rationally constructed action plan simply doesn't feel right. Even in the face of overwhelming evidence to the contrary, Josh knew something that the others didn't. He just couldn't articulate how he knew. The point here is that administrative decision making often requires more than a logical construction of facts and figures. In most complex decision dilemmas, there are intangible issues, subtle nuances, and qualitative judgments that shape our perspectives and choices.

The three vignettes described above underscore the well-established fact that executive decision making is fraught with complexities, uncertainties, ambiguities, and unanticipated hazards. A great irony of organizational leadership is that despite such challenges, there are enormous pressures placed upon leaders in most Western societies to be highly logical, analytical, and rational thinkers. The need for rational, or analytical, thinking is undeniably an important management attribute. In fact, it is generally true that a leader's ability to sift through the chaff and clutter of complex problems requires a sensible, logical, and orderly mind. However, the paradox faced by leaders of complex organizations like public schools is that often the opportunity to apply cool, deliberative, and rational solutions to difficult problems and dilemmas is defeated by their frequency, intensity, urgency, and political complexity. As a result, leaders must resort to other forms of decision making such as limited rationality, heuristics, or intuitive judgment just to keep up with the relentless pace and demands of the job.

We believe that to fully understand the dynamics of this paradox it is important to examine the principles and premises of both rational and intuitive thinking. Although in the extreme they exist on opposite ends of what many psychologists would describe as a cognitive continuum, they most often function in concert with one another. As we will discuss in greater depth later in the book, intuition and rationality generally play codependent roles in most complex administrative decision-making processes. Because of this, and because of the culture of rationality that permeates most Western societies, we will begin our journey through the intuitive dynamics of administrative decision making by examining the evolution of rational thinking, its benefits and risks to contemporary organizational leadership, and its relevance in complex decision making.

❶

THE TYRANNY OF RATIONALITY

Acquaintance with the details of fact is always reckoned, along with their reduction to system, as an indispensable mark of mental greatness.

—William James

RATIONAL TRADITIONS

Among the most prominent qualities of Western civilization is its passion for rationalism and empirical inquiry (Morris 1990). According to the *Philosophical Dictionary* (2001), rationalism is defined as an "epistemological theory that significant knowledge of the world can best be achieved by a priori means." In essence, this means that the rationalist seeks to acquire knowledge and truth through the power of reason, or analytic thought. The capacity of the mind to think with deliberate and structured rationality is a trait unique to humans and underscores the high levels of esteem granted to those who can apply the principles of logic and analytical reasoning to the solution of complex problems and dilemmas (Miranda 2001).

For centuries, conceptions of the rational mind have permeated man's efforts to better understand the nature of knowledge, of truth, of his place in the world, and of his relationships with God, the state, and fellow men. Although an in-depth examination of rationalist philosophical thought is beyond the scope of this book, a brief overview of how rationalist thinking has evolved over time is important for understanding how and why the preoccupation with analytical problem solving and decision making has become so deeply entrenched in Western organizations and educational institutions.

More than two thousand years ago, Plato described the capacity to reason (i.e., a priori knowledge) as a more reliable method than sensory experience in determining truth, knowledge, and reality. According to Plato, and to future generations of rationalist philosophers, the senses were overly subjective and subject to tremendous interpretive variations among individuals. As a result, the senses were considered to be unreliable, imprecise, and too difficult to quantify in any consistent way. In his efforts to explain the essence of reality, Plato proposed the notion of a permanent eternal order (i.e., fundamental principles and truths) that exists beyond the sensory confirmation of the common man. He was, perhaps, the first of the great Western thinkers to propose the idea that virtually all knowledge could be reduced to mathematical models (Brown 2001).

However, it was Plato's prized pupil, Aristotle, whose explanation of the principles of rationality provided an enduring conceptual framework for understanding rationalist thinking that has survived to this day. The concept of "Aristotelian logic," which includes the concepts of empiricism, scientific observation, and inductive reasoning, continues to serve as the foundation of the Western scientific method. Like Plato, Aristotle believed that theoretical and scientific thinking provided the true path to knowledge, truth, and human happiness (Hocker 2001; Taylor 2001).

The origins of modern rationalist philosophy can be traced to the Age of Enlightenment during the seventeenth and early eighteenth centuries. During this period, "traditional sources of certainty—particularly religion and philosophy—came under attack simultaneously" (Gigerenzer and Todd 1999, 6). Notions of unbounded rationality yielded to a new pragmatic rationality expressed through various calculations of probability. One example of this can be found in Pascal's wager that even though the probability of the existence of God might be small, it was infinitely wiser (and thus more rational) to forego worldly pleasures on the chance that eternal salvation was worth the sacrifice (Gigerenzer and Todd 1999).

Widely regarded as the father of modern rationalist thought, French philosopher René Descartes led the "Cartesian" movement to redefine man's role in a rapidly changing social order. Like Plato and Aristotle before him, Descartes maintained that truth could only be revealed through the process of reason and rational thought. He also believed that there existed a fundamental knowledge that could only be revealed through logic and mathematical deduction (*Internet Encyclopedia* 2001; Bombardi 2001).

Conceptions about the supremacy of the rational mind were exemplified by Descartes's radical proposition, "I think, therefore I am" (Jones 2001, 1). From this perspective, man's capacity to examine the world through the prism of logic and analytical thinking was seen as a more authentic pathway to genuine truth and knowledge than that which could be experienced through the senses. In this way, the Cartesians differed from the eighteenth-century English empiricists such as Locke, Berkeley, and Hume who argued that knowledge and truth could only be acquired through revelations generated from sensory experience (i.e., a posteriori reasoning) and were the product of deductive, rather than inductive, reasoning (McCormick 2001; Owens 1995).

Other important Cartesian rationalists of the era included Dutch philosopher Benedict Spinoza and German philosopher/mathematician Gottfried Wilhelm von Leibniz. Spinoza explored the nature and origins of the human mind and human emotion while Leibniz championed the theory that the principles of reasoning could be reduced to mathematical calculations which he described as an algebra or calculus of thought (Gigerenzer and Todd 1999; Jones 2001).

Seventeenth- and eighteenth-century philosophers were driven primarily by the deeply ingrained religious, political, and cultural influences of the era. They wrestled with the emerging, and rather disquieting, philosophical tension between man as a free thinker with natural rights, man as a subject of God and his divine interventions, and man as a subject of the state (Arsham 1996). A prevailing belief among philosophers

of this era was that God, truth, and knowledge were inextricably combined and that the very essence of reason was rooted in the principles of
Christian theology.

The Cartesian rationalist method was largely founded on four key
laws, or propositions, all of which continue to figure prominently in
Western thinking today. First, the Cartesians argued that man should
"accept nothing as true which is not clear and distinct." Second, it is best
to "analyze a problem into its parts and discuss it part-by-part." Third,
thoughts should be "arranged from simple to complex as the order of
study." And fourth, "enumerations must be full and complete and nothing must be omitted" (*Internet Encyclopedia* 2001, 2). As we will see in
the next chapter, these propositions provided the conceptual framework
for virtually all of the normative decision-making models of the twentieth century.

The evolution of modern rationalist theory continued through the
eighteenth- and nineteenth-century works of such prominent philosophers as Immanuel Kant, Georg Hegel, and Émile Durkheim. Kant argued that true knowledge was the product of the interaction between
certain absolute concepts and ideas about the world and the accumu-
lated experiences of the individual. It was Kant's belief that an individual's experience contributes to the capacity to reason, to understand,
and to judge a priori truths (McCormick 2001).

Hegel, perhaps the best-known German philosopher of his time, is
most remembered today for his theory of how the development of self-
knowledge and social progress were the products of a dialectic (cyclical)
process. However, like so many of his rationalist contemporaries, Hegel
also believed man's pursuit of absolute truth represented the highest
form of consciousness (*Microsoft Encarta* 2001).

Durkheim, a nineteenth-century French sociologist, was profoundly
influenced by the social, economic, and political changes induced by
the industrial revolution. He argued that the scientific method could be
applied to virtually all problems (e.g., religion and morality) and would
result in logical and accurate solutions (Jones 1986).

Well into the nineteenth century, the vast majority of the rationalist
literature was confined to various philosophical propositions about
man, religion, and society. The core beliefs of the rationalists however,
continued to revolve around the idea that truth and knowledge were

constructed upon certain absolute or universal propositions separate from an individual's life experiences or sensory perceptions. The essence of rationalist thinking was that one could only come to know truth and acquire knowledge through mental reasoning.

As noted above, the advent of the industrial revolution reshaped Western societies with unprecedented speed and intensity. Within a few short years, Western economies began to shift away from cottage industries and toward large, mechanized, factory systems. With this shift came a host of unprecedented management challenges relating to the organization and control of human resources, concepts of mass production, notions of operational and fiscal efficiencies, cultivation of mass markets, distribution of products, and the identification of the attributes of effective managerial behavior.

In the United States, the influx of immigrants from the European continent created an ample labor force, but one that required training, organization, and direction. Thus, by the turn of the century, social and economic conditions in the United States were ideal for the application of rationalist approaches to management and organizational structure. It was also during this time that rationalist thinkers began to seek and apply more pragmatic (rather than theoretical) solutions to the complex problems generated by the exploding industrialization of society.

At the dawn of the twentieth century, three men emerged as giants of organizational and economic rationalism: Frederick Taylor, Max Weber, and Henri Fayol. They lived during a time when the principles of scientific rationalism were being shaped and honed by such notable scientists, economists, logicians, and pragmatic philosophers as Charles Darwin, Herbert Spencer, William James, and a bit later by John Dewey and Bertrand Russell. The works of Taylor, Weber, and Fayol, however, had an especially powerful influence on managerial and organizational structure, operations, and thinking that has continued into the twenty-first century.

For nearly one hundred years, the ideas developed by Taylor, Weber, and Fayol defined the modern era of organizational behavior. Their emphasis on objective, standardized, and scientifically sound techniques for analyzing organizations and implementing change provided a framework for organizational design and leadership the vestiges of which continue to shape virtually all kinds of private and public organizations today.

Taylor was a former machine shop laborer who later became a mechanical engineer and then an engineering consultant in the late 1800s. Confronted and perplexed by the complexities and inefficiencies inherent within the emergent nineteenth-century workplace entities referred to as organizations, Taylor devised a number of scientific principles on how to maximize productivity, minimize waste, and increase human and capital efficiencies. Taylor's time and motion studies epitomized the rationalist philosophy of the time. Through the careful planning, scheduling, structuring, controlling, organizing, and standardizing of the work of factory workers, Taylor maintained that organizations could maximize production and, ultimately, profits. His book *The Principles of Scientific Management*, published in 1911, had a profound influence on the management and organization of private businesses and public agencies (like schools) throughout Europe and the United States (Greenberg and Baron 1997). According to Taylor, the goal of scientific management was

> to prove that the best management is a true science, resting upon clearly defined laws, rules, and principles, as a foundation. And further to show that the fundamental principles of scientific management are applicable to all kinds of human activities, from our simplest individual acts to the work of our great corporations, which call for the most elaborate cooperation. And, briefly, through a series of illustrations, to convince the reader that whenever these principles are correctly applied, results must follow which are truly astounding. (Owens 1995)

The work of Max Weber, a German sociologist and economist, in many ways paralleled that of Frederick Taylor. Like Taylor, Weber's primary interest was dedicated to the rationalization of Western culture by increasing human mastery over natural and social environments. As a sociologist, Weber was particularly concerned with the development of modern social structures within complex industrialized societies. It was Weber who provided a comprehensive framework for understanding organizational bureaucracy that endured throughout the twentieth century. The idea behind bureaucratic structure was directly linked to the growing need in Western nations for the coordination and control of large numbers of people. Weber's concept of bureaucracy will strike any reader who is familiar with the structure and organization of public schools as immediately recognizable. For example, Weber's bureaucratic organization included a chain of command, written rules of conduct and standardized procedures, the specialized division of labor, impersonal relationships between management and labor, promotion based on achievement, and the efficient attainment of organizational goals (Elwell 1996).

Weber also conceived of two primary forms of rationality. The first, which he termed "zweckrational," represented carefully reasoned technocratic thinking and the application of rationally chosen means to achieve worthwhile goals. The second form of rationality Weber referred to as "wertrational," or value-oriented rationality. This represented the most dangerous form of rationalism because of the subjective nature of values. The wertrational process all too often resulted in the use of rational means to pursue an irrational or immoral goal. Hitler's extermination of the Jews is a graphic example of wertrationalism in action (Elwell 1996). According to Weber, Western societies of the late nineteenth and early twentieth centuries were becoming increasingly zweckrational, a debatable assumption when viewed through the retrospective lens of modern history.

One final note about Weber: Although he has been described by many scholars as the capitalist's Marx, Weber had deep concerns about the dehumanizing potential of the zweckrational society. He feared that that the overregulation and bureaucratization of society would most certainly constrain human creativity and limit human potential. Moreover, he believed that the zweckrational society would eliminate the importance of charisma as an attribute of effective leadership. Interestingly, much of the popular literature on organizational leadership today underscores this point exactly. Consider, for example, the archetypical manager who runs the organization by the book, who is primarily concerned with following standard operating procedures, and who lacks the imagination and courage to initiate change. Most people who have worked in complex and highly bureaucratic organizations can identify with Weber's concerns.

The third giant of the scientific management movement was a French industrialist named Henri Fayol. Whereas Taylor was concerned primarily with the structure and organization of the workplace and workers, Fayol's attention was directed at the roles and functions of management.

In his comprehensive theory of administration, Fayol proposed that effective management required five key managerial functions:

1. Plan and forecast future actions.
2. Organize the structural, material, and human resources of the enterprise.
3. Command and maintain purposeful activity among employees.
4. Coordinate and unify the activities and efforts of employees.
5. Control organizational operations and tasks according to established policies.

Fayol went on to describe fourteen principles for organizational design and administration. As with Weber's elements of the bureaucratic organization, much of Fayol's thinking continues to shape and describe the administrative structure of public schools (Jarris 2001). His fourteen principles included

1. The specialized division of management labor.
2. Management authority and responsibility for organizational productivity.
3. Discipline.
4. Unity of command.
5. Unity of direction (e.g., top-down).
6. The subordination of individual interests to the goals of the organization.
7. Remuneration of staff based on performance, skills, and qualifications.
8. Centralization of authority.
9. Clear lines of authority.
10. Order.
11. Equity.
12. Stability of tenure.
13. Initiative.
14. Esprit de corps.

The ideas of Taylor, Weber, and Fayol redirected the esoteric postulates of rationalist philosophy to the development of concrete and practical guidelines for industrial society. Our current conceptions of bureaucracy and scientific management are direct descendents of the ideas generated by these men—ideas, we might add, that were originally shaped to meet the needs of a burgeoning industrial economy and a highly stratified society characterized by large numbers of poor and undereducated European immigrants.

As the twentieth century unfolded, the rationalist philosophical movement made room for other, more progressive philosophical approaches such as pragmatism, idealism, analytic philosophy, existentialism, and phenomenology. However, during the post–World War II years, rational historicists such as Kuhn, Lakatos, and Laudan continued to advance the idea that good theories of rationality also fit the model of empirical science (*Stanford Encyclopedia of Philosophy* 2001). Without question, the imprint made by the rationalist tradition has permeated virtually every facet of institutional life in Western society.

RATIONAL EXPECTATIONS

Nowhere has the Western devotion to rationalism been stronger than in America. Suffused with a "can do" spirit, the American culture prizes those who can get things done. Individuals who accomplish tasks, make decisions quickly, and solve problems efficiently, accurately, and analytically are held in high esteem. There is a prevailing notion in the collective American psyche that rational problem solving represents one of man's highest callings. This idea is especially prevalent in the realm of organizational management. Long-standing faith in the efficacy of scientific management underscores widely held beliefs that the most effective managers are highly rational, charismatic, all knowing, and in command of the various problems, people, and issues faced by their organizations.

More than ever before, managers today are expected to make decisions on the basis of clear and systematic lines of reasoning and carefully delineated problem-solving steps (Cappon 1994; Gaynor 1998; Peters and Waterman 1982). Moreover, the advent of computer technology has increased expectations that management decisions and actions will be data driven and shaped by the use of quantitative analyses and sophisticated information systems (Arsham 1996; Bolman and Deal 1997; Owens 1995). The national preoccupation with computers and their immense capacity to process information has created an expectation that management decisions will be precise, immediate, and optimal. The theory is that since computers can scan through literally thousands of calculations in mere seconds (or less), they can quickly and efficiently provide optimal solutions to even the most complex and confounding organizational problems (Cuban 2001; Drake and Roe 1999; Dreyfus and Dreyfus 1986).

The continuous drive to develop new technologies and to apply scientifically tested solutions to virtually every aspect of daily life exemplifies the almost theistic devotion to rational thinking in this country. Our long established national self-identity as a pioneering people has provided a historical framework for rationally induced breakthroughs in medicine, space exploration, communication systems, transportation, military technology, entertainment, and so on. This phenomenon was greatly accelerated by Cold War pressures to outperform the Soviet Union militarily and economically, and spurred on by the belief that new scientific knowledge could create wealth, improve human life, solve social problems, and achieve national goals (Owens 1995).

Although human relationships are largely qualitative in nature, we often go to great lengths to explain and interpret them through quantitative or numerical methods. A critical human trait, it seems, is the ability to understand, compare, and manipulate numbers. Even qualitative problems and issues are frequently reduced to measurable scales and computations. For example, in describing an aesthetic experience (such as a work of art, music, taste, a movie, etc.), it is common practice to ask a person to rate the experience from one to ten. Of course, the difficulty with attempts to quantify subjective experience in this way is that the same numbers might mean different things to different people. Likewise, numerical rating scales fail to account for subtleties and nuances in individual experiences, feelings, and dispositions. Nevertheless, we are a people obsessed with quantifying, measuring, comparing, and manipulating data of all kinds (Arsham 1996).

Our system of law is a prime example of hyperrationality in action. Efforts to ensure equal and procedurally fair treatment for all citizens have resulted in the most overregulated and procedurally encumbered legal system in the world. Laws, statutes, codes, and administrative regulations abound in this country and are indicative of a national preoccupation with order, control, and the application of rational systems. Proponents of ra-

tionality maintain, with arguable justification, that such efforts are necessary in order to provide consistency, predictability, and equality in a plu-
ralistic society (Howard 1996).

As we noted above, the influence of rational thinking has had a profound influence in the shaping of American organizational life. From
businesses to schools and to other public institutions, we have become
fervent devotees of the bottom line, of quantifiable data, and of statistical and numeric representations of success or failure. For example, the
concept of operations research (OR) emerged during the Second World
War and quickly spread to nearly every segment of American organizational life (Arsham 1996). Through OR, managers and administrators
could use "statistics, optimization models, information models, computer simulations, and linear programming" to improve organizational
performance, product quality, and human efficiencies (Robbins 1997,
554). During the same period, management scholars like Herbert Simon, Peter Drucker, and Victor Vroom developed a series of normative
decision-making models around the theory that optimal decisions would
occur if and when managers applied certain prescribed techniques and
strategies (Owens 1995; Yukl 1994). The appeal of such rational strategies lies largely with the timeworn notion that we can bring order, structure, predictability, optimization, efficiency, and control to the world if
we apply the right kind of dispassionate logic and calculative analysis.
According to this theory, problems and dilemmas, like car engines, once
reduced to their component parts, can be scrubbed clean from contam-
inants and reassembled to ensure optimum performance.

Despite nearly two decades of research on the qualities and attributes of more enlightened, value-driven leaders (some refer to this as
transformational leadership), as well as research on the growing complexity of organizational leadership, graduate schools and management
training programs continue to emphasize traditional vestiges of nineteenth-century scientific rationalism (Agor 1986; Bolman and Deal
1997; Brown 1990; Rowan 1986). According to Bennis and Nanus
(1985, 219) management education overrelies on "mechanistic pseudo-
rational theories which raise dangerous assumptions about the clarity of
goals, the viability of alternatives, the use of technology and its consequences, and the reliability of information." Nevertheless, there is
ample evidence that the job market continues to place a premium on

hiring college graduates who possess strong quantitative skills. In fact, the demand for such skills is likely to continue to expand as the impetus for data-driven decisions and the availability of data to managers increases (Arsham 1996).

Reports such as those described above raised our level of concern about the kind of decision-making training being provided to prospective school administrators. Since most accounts of graduate training programs referred to graduate schools of business, we decided to take a look for ourselves at the kinds of management training programs being offered by graduate schools of education. To do this, we picked up a copy of the year 2000 edition of the *U.S. News and World Report College Rankings*. From this, we selected the top twenty schools of education. We then accessed each university website and examined its course offerings in the field of educational administration. What we found merely confirmed what we had learned about business schools: virtually every course offered on the topic of administrative decision making emphasized analytic, logical, and/or quantitative methods. Not one course could be found that emphasized naturalistic, descriptive, holistic, heuristic, or intuitive decision making. We find this sadly ironic in view of the fact that most problems and decisions faced by school administrators are far too complex to be effectively addressed through rational/analytical approaches alone. We will say more about this later.

Our public schools are living laboratories of scientific rationalism. The rationalist legacy is evidenced by such practices and policies as grade levels, standardized testing, teacher credentialing, class periods, salary schedules, board policies, the bureaucratic structure of management, budgeting, curriculum standards, instructional methods, personnel classification systems, and strategic planning. The list goes on and on. Rational choice theories continue to serve as the basis for our definitions of effective learning and quality schools. Such theories are embedded in our applications of progressive discipline, IQ tests, outcome-based instruction, curricular articulation, behavioral objectives, lesson plans, and performance evaluations. According to Owens (1995, 175), "Many people, including educational administrators and school board members, tend to persist in the belief that more rigorous application of [rational decision-making practices] is essential to improving organizational performance."

There is also a prevailing belief among many educational leaders and policymakers that corporate business models can and should be applied to education. For example, management concepts such as Management by Objective, Zero-Based Budgeting, Strategic Planning, Total Quality Management, Centralization and Decentralization, Restructuring, and Reengineering were all adopted by schools from the private sector with rather modest results (Deal and Peterson 1994; Sergiovanni 1996). Many critics of public schools, however, maintain that they are often ill equipped or unwilling to embrace change or new ideas about management until the wave of innovation has long passed beyond the private sector. As a result, basic school structures and traditional beliefs about leadership have become deeply entrenched within the organizational culture of most schools and school systems (Sergiovanni 1996).

There is little question that school leaders feel the pressure to be highly rational actors. For one thing, literature regarding effective schools casts principals as supremely and practically rational. Arguably, the same could be said for superintendents. A prevailing (and dubious) assumption within this body of literature portrays the principal as a person who can predict and control people, events, and various management processes (Hanson 1996). Such assumptions are compounded by the fact that different people and different interest groups have different sets of expectations for the principal. The political contexts and challenges of school leadership have been the bane of principals for decades. However, the level of political turbulence today is exacerbated by both the self-serving polarization of school stakeholders and the expectation that technological solutions to complex problems will result in instantaneous feedback and highly rational outcomes (Davis and Hensley 1999; Drake and Roe 1999). Ask virtually any school leader who has used e-mail, and he is likely to report that the volume, diversity, and intensity of correspondence from school constituents has consumed ever-increasing chunks of time—time that otherwise could be spent observing teachers and interacting with students. E-mail, by the way, has provided very little, if any, relief to the overwhelming volume of letters, reports, and memos regularly received by principals during a typical school day. The pressures on managers and leaders to be effective and efficient decision makers are such that a failure to solve problems often leaves a "debris of disappointment, cynicism, and feelings of guilt" (Cuban 2001, 16).

Rational expectations are deeply embedded within the various policy mandates directed at public schools across the country. For example, in California, as in most other states, standards for administrative behavior now focus on such concepts as accountability, performance outcomes, and data-based decision making. The California Commission on Teacher Credentialing, in concert with the State Leadership Academy and the Association of California School Administrators, has recently developed a revised set of professional standards for administrators. Standard 3 states that to be effective, administrators must "utilize the principles of systems management, organizational development, problem-solving, and (data-based) decision-making techniques." A similar statement has been issued by the University Council on Educational Administration, a national organization of professors of educational administration (Drake and Roe 1999). In California, the state legislature recently passed a school accountability law that rewards or punishes schools on the basis of between-school aggregate comparisons of student performance on the norm-referenced SAT 9 achievement test. In fact, the law even provides for the dismissal of principals in consistently underperforming schools.

As a result of pressures like these, school leaders have become preoccupied with planning, goal setting, standard operating procedures, performance assessments, the allocation of rewards and/or sanctions, and normative decision making processes (Deal and Peterson 1994). The unfortunate side effect of such pressures is that many principals are fast becoming more interested in advancing school performance-rating scales, following the rules, and self-preservation than they are in finding new and exciting ways to break the mold of traditionalist thinking. Bold and proactive school leaders who take calculated risks and who strive to find innovative and creative ways to expand student learning are being replaced by administrative caretakers constrained by an ever-increasing array of rules, regulations, standards, and rational prescriptions for student success and school effectiveness.

Bolman and Deal (1997, 265) made a wonderful statement about the illusionary expectations of rational management. We feel that it provides an especially pertinent perspective to our concerns about the preoccupation with rational/analytic models of effective leadership and decision making.

Led to believe that they should be rational and on top of it all, managers become confused and bewildered. They are supposed to plan and organize, yet they find themselves muddling and playing catch-up. They want to solve problems and make decisions. But problems are ill-defined and options murky. Control is an illusion and rationality an afterthought.

Despite such concerns, there is little question that the synthesis of scientific inquiry, democracy, and a free-market economy has created the wealthiest and most advanced nation on Earth. For these things, most Americans are justifiably grateful. It is also important to acknowledge that rational approaches to organizational structure and management are critical to the smooth, equitable, and efficient operation of public schools. There are simply too many issues and tasks that require carefully reasoned analysis to ignore. However, in the passionate embrace of rationality, school leaders often fail to recognize that most organizational problems and dilemmas are messy, complex, ill defined, and not easily resolved through algorithmic reason or the application of syntactic rules (Miranda 2001). The day-to-day challenges of school leadership (or most organizational leadership for that matter) are rarely aligned with or conducive to hypothetical-deductive thinking.

There is little doubt that we live in a society that embraces and frequently benefits from rational thinking and analytic decision making, especially among top-level managers and leaders. In fact, much of the literature on organizations is based upon the assumption that planning, structure, control, and systematic management approaches lead to greater productivity and efficiency. Organizational scholars and practitioners continue to be consumed with finding the optimal combinations of planning, structure, control, and systematic management in an effort to increase organizational effectiveness and quality (Bolman and Deal 1997; Peters and Waterman 1982). We would be among the first to argue that the application of rational/analytical approaches to certain organizational problems and issues can lead to effective (if not optimal) decisions. But just how rational are complex organizations such as schools? How much control do school leaders really have? And what about managers and leaders? To what extent do rational/analytical models of decision making represent what they actually do, and how useful are such models in guiding them through the day-to-day demands of the job? A closer look at just how modern organizations really work and how managers really manage will help to put the theories and expectations of rationality into perspective.

MANAGING COMPLEX ORGANIZATIONS: RATIONALITY VERSUS REALITY

Organizations today come in all shapes and sizes. The sheer volume and diversity of organizational types and structures is such that it has become increasingly difficult to make generalizations about them or about the characteristics and attributes of the managers who lead them. Bolman and Deal (1997) aptly describe this phenomenon in their comparison of McDonald's restaurants and Harvard University. Both are large and multilayered organizations, but with very different goals, technologies, structures, means of production, and outcomes. Rational systems of management and production work far better at McDonald's than at Harvard. From San Francisco to Paris, a Big Mac is still a Big Mac. The ingredients are the same, the methods of production are the same, and the standard operating procedures from restaurant to restaurant are the same. As an organization, McDonald's has developed a formula for success that, when transplanted from one location to another, almost always works the same. The need for creative or intuitive decision making is relatively small given the highly structured, standardized, and predictable processes that are adhered to by McDonald's managers throughout the world.

Harvard University, on the other hand, is anything but regimented, rule driven, or standardized. Dozens of academic departments, each with its own internal goals, technologies, and organizational systems, operate independently from one another. Professors, known for their highly specialized skills and unique perspectives, exert enormous influence over what is taught and how it is taught. In contrast, administrators possess proportionately less influence over the behaviors and actions of professors than managers at McDonald's do over cooks, dishwashers, and front-counter salespeople. Important decisions are often made through processes that may include negotiation, manipulation, compromise, and coalition building. There are rarely optimum solutions to complex problems because information is often lacking or biased, because right or wrong answers are dependent upon particular values or points of view, and because all possible alternatives simply cannot be identified.

McDonald's and Harvard University are both large and enormously successful organizations. Harvard, however, is by far the more complex of the two. It is no coincidence that rational models of behavior and decision making are better suited to organizations with simple technologies, standard operating procedures, and predictable outcomes.

Human service organizations like Harvard and public schools are especially complex for a number of reasons. First, in human service organizations, goals and objectives are often unclear, vague, and subject to differing interpretations among stakeholders. Second, in human service organizations, individual and group values, needs, preferences, and demands vary and fluctuate. In addition, interpersonal and intergroup conflicts and competition for power and influence reflect a growing diversity among stakeholders in American organizations and underscore the often turbulent nature of civic participation in a democratic society. Third, in human service organizations, technologies that underlie the various organizational outputs and products are often poorly understood and used inconsistently by employees. For example, in schools, teaching represents a form of technology that is very complex and not always uniformly understood or practiced in consistent ways by different teachers (unlike the machine technology that churns out one Big Mac after another). Fourth, in human service organizations, problems are often not transparent. That is to say, problems are rarely simple and often possess no clear solution. Once again, when the machine technology of a McDonald's restaurant breaks down, the solution is often quickly and accurately diagnosed and implemented (e.g., a new burner is needed for the grill). In schools, however, when a disproportionate number of students fail a particular teacher's class or fail to progress normally on norm-referenced tests of academic skills, it is often extremely difficult, if not impossible, to pinpoint a particular teaching method as the prime culprit. The collection of variables that interact to influence student learning (e.g., teaching, curriculum, peer influence, parent influence, gender, ethnicity, campus climate) are simply too numerous and amorphous to track and repair like a faulty burner on a grill.

Most complex organizations (including schools) of the late nineteenth and early twentieth centuries were characterized as closed systems.

That is, they were tightly structured and controlled environments with little interest in external environments, trends and influences, or public participation. Ideas about social justice, diversity, equity, and environmental sensitivity were either unknown to managers or perceived as superfluous to the fundamental mission of the organization (Hanson 1996; Owens 1995). Likewise, schools and school administrators were considered to be apolitical and impervious to the pressures of special interest groups or to the thrusts and parries of political life in the broader community (Davis and Hensley 1999). Thus, safe and secure in their isolationist cocoons, many complex organizations lumbered through the twentieth century with little concern for the outside world. Rational systems of organization and control, applied through the tenets of scientific management, were widely practiced by virtually all kinds of complex organizations and especially schools.

Of course, during the last quarter of the twentieth century, rising public concerns about social justice, equity, ethical behavior, democratic participation, and environmental issues began to break down the walls of organizational isolationism. Riding on a wave of post–World War II prosperity, unprecedented productivity, and rapid changes in consumer demands, corporate America slowly opened its doors to the outside world. Schools were no exception to this phenomenon.

Today, most complex human service organizations are open systems. As such, they are often contradictory, ambiguous, surprising, and turbulent places that must contend with continually changing environments and technologies characterized by "constant streams of fragmented and multiple demands lacking coherence and follow-through" (Bennis 1989; Fullan 1997, 7; March 1994). To survive, complex organizations must adapt quickly to increasing demands for choice, quality, and socially responsible policies and practices (Krabuanrat and Phelps 1998). According to Greenberg and Baron (1997, 52), the "informating of the workplace" has created organizational environments characterized by infinite connections to global resources, by rapid and nearly limitless channels of communication, and by the replacement of manual tasks with technological processes and solutions. The continual evolution of technology often makes human skills and competencies obsolete almost as quickly as they are acquired. Furthermore, organizations today often measure success according to short-term gains rather than long-term growth and stability. The recent wave of accounting scandals by such prominent icons of the corporate world as Enron and Arthur Anderson underscores a myopic view of the future held by some organizations. It has also unveiled a disturbingly callous and tawdry aspect of organizational leadership that appears to be more interested in the appearance of short-term profitability and in the accrual of personal wealth by a few highly ranked executives—wealth gained, we might add, at the expense of the financial security of thousands of lower-level employees and stockholders.

Such dynamics generate increasing pressures on managers to act quickly and decisively, often without time for reflection or deep deliberation (Cuban 2001; Krabuanrat and Phelps 1998). Not surprisingly, as organizations have become increasingly receptive to and interactive with external environments, rational systems of control and decision making have become less useful.

A core problem faced by most complex organizations is how to cope with uncertainty. Organizational events and activities are often nonlinear and do not always unfold according to neatly developed plans or models (Hanson 1996). Goals and technologies have become increasingly complex and fluid, and it has become increasingly difficult to connect causes with effects or actions with outcomes (Owens 1995). Moreover, power has become increasingly distributed throughout modern organizations. This is especially true in schools where collective bargaining agreements and various interest groups and coalitions have increased the ability of employees, parents, and community members to directly influence school policies and practices (Fullan 1997).

Such descriptions are somewhat ironic in view of the fact that organizations were invented over a hundred years ago for the purpose of bringing order and predictability to the challenges created by new technologies, an expanding workforce, and the industrialization of Western economies. Organizations provided much needed structure and control over increasingly complex tasks, environments, and people. To a significant degree, they continue to do so today. However, over the years, we have come to view organizations not as static and monolithic entities but as dynamic and organic social systems. A major struggle for managers and leaders in organizations of all kinds is how to reconcile the tension between the enduring paradigms of scientific management and bureaucratic control with the often chaotic, tumultuous, and unpredictable qualities of organizations, their members, and their external constituents.

Organizational life in Western societies is governed by what Bennis (1989, 102) refers to as a "left-brain culture." A left-brain culture is one that is driven by logic, analysis, technical skills, and administrative control. Bennis argues that because modern organizations are so complex and difficult to control, what is needed is more right-brain qualities such as conceptual thinking, imagination, and intuition. We will talk more about right- and left-brain thinking in chapter 3. However, it is important to note that what Bennis is really saying is that rational approaches to organizational structure and management by themselves are unable to fully resolve the complex nature of the problems and dilemmas faced by human service organizations.

Schools are arguably the most complex of all human service organizations. According to Hanson (1996, 142), schools are besieged by "interacting spheres of influence." Values, preferences, problems, solutions, skills, interests, and demands descend upon the typical school from a continually shifting array of individuals and groups, each with fluctuating degrees of influence and power. Although school administrators work hard to bring order and structure to organizational chaos and turbulence, schools continue to be a "mixture of structured and unstructured activities, formal and informal procedures, and controlled and autonomous behaviors" (Hanson 1996, 81).

Schools are simultaneously loose and tight. At any given time, there are elements under the direct control of school administrators and other elements that are not. For example, in times of crisis (like a fire on campus), administrators are usually able to implement predetermined procedures that are adhered to by all teachers and most students. In contrast, despite intricate evaluation systems and carefully delineated curriculum guidelines, once inside the classroom, most teachers have considerable latitude in terms of what is taught and how. Administrators call this phenomenon the logic of confidence. That is to say, even though most principals might think they know what is going on in classrooms during a typical school day, they spend very little time actually observing teachers in action.

The loose/tight paradox can also be seen in the way schools are structured. Most schools are comprised of subunits (such as grade levels or

academic departments) that often have very little or no interaction with
one another. Collaboration and interaction among subunits varies according to the particular attributes, goals, and requirements of common
projects or political coalitions. For example, in most high schools, the
drama department rarely interacts with the math department. Likewise,
social studies generally has little to do with physical education, science
with foreign language, and so on. In light of this, schools require leaders who can simultaneously frame common, schoolwide goals while supporting the individual needs and objectives of vastly different subunits
within the organization. Traditional systems of bureaucratic control, organizational structure, and rational decision making may work some of
the time and with parts of the school, but generally cannot be effectively
applied to all parts of the school at the same time.

So where does this leave managers and school principals? Are they really rational actors who can, through the application of carefully targeted
strategies and techniques, exert control over the goals, behaviors, values,
attitudes, and outcomes of organizations and their members? The answer to that question is both yes and no. Clearly there are times and situations where a company president's or school principal's vision or powers of analysis can provide the catalyst for organizational change and
individual growth. However, a closer look at the nature of organizational
management and school leadership raises serious questions about the viability of the paradigm that casts leaders as supremely rational actors.

Rational behavior is not serendipitous, spontaneous, or accidental.
Rather, it is purposeful, focused, and logical. To thoroughly diagnose the
nature of a problem and to carefully weigh and consider all possible options is a painstaking and time-consuming process. As we will discuss in
more detail in chapter 2, few managers are able to employ this kind of
rational thinking. Instead, managers rely on various abbreviated or truncated forms of rational analysis. The more experienced a manager becomes, the more likely she is to rely on heuristic or intuitive decision
making processes (Agor 1986).

Reflect for a moment on Marsha's dilemma. Confronted with three
important decision events (two of which were spontaneous and completely unplanned), Marsha needed to take immediate action on each.
Although the consequences of making a poor decision with the angry
parent and the combative boys could be severe, Marsha had no time

to carefully analyze each situation, consider all possible alternatives, or to identify the best solution among all possible solutions. Instead, she had to think in action. As she took action, her thinking evolved accordingly. As an experienced principal, Marsha had, over the years, acquired a broad repertoire of similar experiences and decisions. As a result, she knew what to do almost without thinking. Was Marsha's decision making the product of rational analysis? Not in the traditional meaning of the term. Were her actions the result of her intuition? Perhaps. Were the outcomes of her actions logical and rational? Most likely. The chances are that Marsha actually relied on a combination of intuitive/heuristic thinking and quasi-rational analysis, drawing upon her large warehouse of knowledge and past experiences to guide her decision process almost as quickly as she was confronted with the events themselves. In fact, because of her vast experience, Marsha was able to produce sensible and logical decisions without having to rely on highly structured and time-consuming analysis.

Like Marsha, for most managers and leaders, a typical workday consists of few breaks in the workload, a wide variety of fragmented and paradoxical activities and requests for assistance, and numerous disjointed conversations. Work is frequently interrupted by relatively trivial issues and concerns that often require (or result in) rapid mood shifts. The constant flow of problems means that managers must simultaneously attend to numerous tasks, few of which ever capture the manager's full attention. School principals have been described as "victims of the moment." The intensity, immediacy, and physical proximity of problems faced by school administrators often result in principals being dragged into the "crisis of the moment" (Deal and Peterson 1994; Fullan 1997, 37).

In this whirlwind of activity, managers and principals have little time for reflection or careful analysis, and decision processes are often characterized by short bursts of emotionally charged and disorderly thinking. Most decisions are the product of holistic and relational thinking rather than ordered and structured processes. Despite tremendous pressure to be rational and logical, in deciding what to do next, most managers "operate mostly on the basis of intuition—hunches and judgments based on prior experience" (Bolman and Deal 1997, 266). Moreover, most managers prefer quick closure to organizational problems and prefer to act upon concrete information, even if such information is inaccurate or incomplete. In fact, gossip, speculation, or hearsay is often preferred over abstract data or extensive and highly detailed analyses (Mintzberg 1973, 1976; Yukl 1994).

Interestingly, the typical high school principal attends to nearly 150 separate tasks each day (Mintzberg 1980). Assuming most principals work at least ten hours per day, that averages out to approximately four minutes per task. Clearly, most tasks and problems receive very little time for in-depth analytical thinking or deliberation.

Ironically, like their counterparts in the private sector, school principals are taught to emphasize planning, establish measurable goals and objectives, and facilitate systematic and planned change. They also tend to favor structured management approaches such as Management by Objectives, Total Quality Management, and Strategic Planning (Deal and Peterson 1994).

Not surprisingly, among many principals, a tension exists between the technical and expressive aspects of the job. Most successful principals are able to apply analytical and structured management approaches when necessary. However, they also understand the power of symbolic behaviors, metaphorical descriptions, rituals, and storytelling (Bolman and Deal 1997; Deal and Peterson 1994). They recognize that effective leadership is both a science and an art and that good decision making is not necessarily dependent upon the application of dispassionate rational processes. According to Bennis (1989, 103), leaders must have both "administrative and imaginative skills." Deal and Peterson (1994, 5) describe this as having a "different eye." A different eye. Imaginative skills. Right-brain thinking. Intuition. No matter how the phenomenon is defined, it is almost universally understood that the most effective leaders are far more than dispassionate analysts. There is a decidedly qualitative element to their behaviors and decision making that can't be measured or quantified.

THE LIMITS OF RATIONALITY

As we have argued, the limited utility of seeking rational solutions to complex organizational problems poses serious challenges to those leaders who tenaciously adhere to the tenets of scientific management. Highly structured and rational approaches work particularly well in simple, routine, and predictable organizational settings like McDonald's.

Such approaches work less well in complex, novel, and unpredictable human service organizational settings like Harvard University or public schools (Kenneth et al. 1997).

The truth is that most human problems cannot be resolved through algorithmic reasoning. The Cartesian theory of detached, objective reason simply fails to capture many of the features of intentional behavior. Moreover, it ignores several of the critical qualities that make us human. For most of us, the search for meaning and truth is a hybridized mixture of passion, sentiment, interpretation, metaphoric imagining, faith, and linear thinking (Harbort 1997; Miranda 2001; Sergiovanni 1996). The preoccupation among many managers with hyperrational thinking represents a heartless philosophy that does not value experimentation, abhors mistakes, is inflexible and unresponsive, and denigrates the importance of human values (Peters and Waterman 1982).

Theories of rational choice tend to assume that all preferences have equal value and deserve equal consideration. According to Stanford professor James March (1994, 192), however, rational theories of choice simply don't "match the contradictions, inconsistencies and fuzziness of reality." In the real world, the nature of any given problem is often in question; information about the problem is often incomplete and unreliable; and individual values, preferences, and interpretations often vary considerably (Bennis and Nanus 1985). Austrian economist Haus-Herman Hoppe (1997, 51) argues that in an uncertain and often surprising world, we simply cannot predict all of our future actions or their outcomes. According to Hoppe,

> Apart from the laws of propositional logic, arithmetic, and causality, however, all other knowledge about the external world is uncertain. We do not and cannot know with certainty what kinds of objects and object-qualities exist, how many units of what physical dimensions there are, and what quantitative cause-and-effect relationships exist between various magnitudes of various objects. All of this must be learned from experience. Moreover, experience is invariably past experience, that of past events. It cannot reveal whether or not the facts and relationships of the past will also hold in the future.

The works of Daniel Goleman (1995) and Herbert and Stuart Dreyfus (1986) underscore the fact that human intelligence is far more than calculative rationality. According to Goleman, quantifiable measurements of intelligence (e.g., IQ) account for only about 20 percent of the factors that determine life success. He notes that other characteristics, such as self-motivation, persistence, impulse control, delayed gratification, empathy, hope, and the ability to manage one's mood and stress, all interact to produce functional, emotionally intelligent, and successful individuals.

Dreyfus and Dreyfus (1986) argue that the application of calculative rationality is most effective for beginners, not experts. Beginners generally lack the broad repertoire of experiences and knowledge possessed by experts. As a result, they must construct a framework of propositions, situational responses, and decision processes that over time become automatic and even intuitive. Since all of us are experts at some things and beginners at others, we tend to apply a continuum of cognitive and sub-cognitive processes ranging from highly analytical to highly intuitive, depending upon our level of expertise with the situation or task at hand. According to Dreyfus and Dreyfus (1986, 205), however, the advent of the computer age has resulted in a growing indifference to "genuine know-how, wisdom, and good judgment." They argue that "to confuse the common sense, wisdom, and mature judgment of the expert with today's artificial intelligence, or to value them less highly, would be a genuine stupidity."

There is truth to the old saying that one's first impressions are usually the best. In general, the longer one consciously deliberates about one's preferences and judgments, the less accurate and predictive they become. This is because as we contemplate and wrestle with a problem, personal preferences, motivation levels, frustration, uncertainty, second guessing, and time pressures begin to seep in and contaminate our ability to apply objective, dispassionate, and calculative analysis (Bargh and Chartrand 1999). Most of us who occupy, or have occupied, leadership positions are well aware that paralysis by analysis is a very real occupational hazard.

Most scholars in the field of organizational theory and leadership assert that for the last twenty-five years or so, most American organizations and public institutions have entered into a new postmodern era. Today, scholarly focus has shifted from studying theories of bureaucratic control and scientific management to a far more complex framework constructed around interacting and competing values, beliefs, and concerns about social equality, the distribution of power, workplace diversity, and qualitative assessments of organizational behavior.

So where does that leave us in terms of understanding the role of rational thinking in school leadership? The answer is a bit of a mixed bag. While we can't deny the importance of rational approaches in the solution of routine and well-defined problems, its usefulness in resolving complex problems is limited. Despite this, there is evidence that school administrators are under considerable pressure to apply analytical and rational methods in their responses to increasingly complex educational issues.

We conclude chapter 1 with a question posed by Michael Fullan (1997, 6): "What does a reasonable leader do when faced with impossible tasks?" In chapter 2, we examine this question by looking at a number of concepts and propositions about the very essence of leadership—decision making and problem solving.

2

PROBLEM SOLVING AND DECISION MAKING: THE ESSENCE OF LEADERSHIP

At the heart of educational practice is decision making. All practitioners at one time or another must act. To act they must choose.

—Larry Cuban

If Mintzberg's (1980) account of a typical day in the life of a high school principal is indeed accurate, there is little doubt that most principals are awash in problems, dilemmas, and decisions. As former superintendents and principals, we can attest to the unrelenting pace of the job and to the feeling that once the principal steps on campus his mental circuits are on full alert. Like boxers waiting for the opening bell, the principal's gloves are always up and the feet are constantly moving, even when the opponent has yet to enter the ring. One incontrovertible aspect of the job is to expect the unexpected. To survive, the principal must be ever vigilant and agile.

The stories of Marsha Mahan, Dan Charles, and Josh Winters are prime examples of how problem-solving and decision-making events can quickly and unexpectedly capture a leader's time and attention. Even after an extensive decision-making process, new insights or aspects of the problem can surface to create a whole new series of decisions. There is a decidedly nonlinear aspect to many educational problems, and most principals have little, if any, time to reflect on the mechanics of their decisions. We asked several principals to explain exactly how they go about making tough decisions. One principal responded, "I don't know exactly. I just do it." Another stated, "It depends on the situation. I don't follow a script." And a third principal said, "I have all these decision-making binders. You know, turtle wadding. I can't even remember the names of some of those models."

So how well do the theories of rationality match real-world decision contexts and the processes used by school leaders? To what extent is it possible, or even desirable, to frame problem-solving and decision-making activities around models of rational choice? In the real world, just how do leaders and managers solve complex problems and make decisions? In this chapter, our answers to these questions provide a framework for understanding how intuitive thinking has become an increasingly important tool for leaders in complex human service organizations.

WHAT'S THE PROBLEM?

Dan Charles knew he had a problem the moment he saw Ken Colt escorting Darla Campbell into his office. With Darla's history of poor behavior, Dan's first reaction upon hearing Mr. Colt's version of events was almost automatic: call Darla's mother, explain the situation, request a parent conference, and suspend Darla for three days—an exasperating but routine situation that Dan, in his capacity as school disciplinarian, had handled time and time again. From Dan's initial perspective, this was a simple problem with a clear solution. However, his conversation with the probation officer changed things somewhat. What at first seemed like a routine behavioral problem took on an entirely new dimension. Suspending Darla no longer seemed like the best response. Other alternatives now surfaced, thus complicating Dan's decision choices. In this situation, getting a clear and accurate definition of the real problem was not only difficult but crucial to its successful resolution.

Still, there were only a few plausible options open to Dan. He could suspend Darla for three days, come up with an alternative form of discipline, or let the matter drop. There were no clear decision rules to follow now. It would be up to Dan's best judgment as to which response to implement. Moreover, as new information about the problem emerged,

Dan's goal shifted from one that focused on following the school's standard operating disciplinary procedures to one that focused more on ensuring Darla's physical and emotional well-being.

Nevertheless, the problem was still relatively containable and was not likely to adversely affect other students, teachers, or the school as a whole. Without question, it was a nasty problem—but it was still a problem that, given Dan's experience, could be quickly managed.

Josh Winters, on the other hand, faced a far more formidable situation. He had to make a critical decision about how to best meet the learning needs of a growing number of limited- and non-English speaking students. In this case, there wasn't anything close to an optimal solution. Individual goals, preferences, values, and beliefs among teachers, fellow administrators, and the public were far too diverse and emotionally charged to allow for a decision that all parties would readily agree upon. In addition, the stakes were very high educationally, fiscally, and politically. Josh's problem was anything but routine or simple. No degree of analysis could provide a solution that would guarantee an optimal result. Josh was not even sure that the root problem could ever be identified with absolute clarity. There were so many variables in play that could influence how students learn that it was impossible to know for certain which program would best meet the needs of English language learners. Josh would have to trust his intuition on this one.

So here we have two very serious but very different problems in terms of structure, clarity, viable options, and organizational risk. Interestingly, the less complex of the two problem scenarios was also under the most time pressure. Dan had to make a decision about Darla very quickly while Josh could postpone his decision for a while. For most principals, the bilingual problem would have been the more complex of the two. However, for a principal who was highly experienced in working with programs for English language learners, the problem faced by Josh might have been a reasonably simple one to resolve. It all depends on one's perspective, knowledge, experience, and level of skill. A complex problem for one principal could be a routine problem for another (Funke and Frensch 1995).

According to Stanford professor Larry Cuban (2001), there is no objective definition of a "problem." It really depends on how a problem is framed, and that, in turn, depends upon the perceptions, competencies, backgrounds, and personal attributes of the problem solver. According to Karl Weick (1995, 89) "Problems are conceptual entities that are designed rather than discovered." That is to say, problems are created as a result of the unique perspectives, experiences, and interpretations of the individuals affected by them (Tannenbaum and Schmidt 1958). Despite this, it is generally true that most problems represent a gap between what currently is and what ought to be. Moreover, the gap must matter and it must be hard to close (Cuban 2001; Weick 1995). As we described above, there is a difference between simple and complex problems, or as Cuban describes them, "tame" and "wicked" problems. And, although what appears to be a simple problem for one principal could be comparatively complex for another, there are several generally agreed-upon characteristics of what constitutes a complex problem.

Complex problems are typically ill defined, ambiguous, novel, and risky, and present unclear or multiple solutions. They often require more time and effort to resolve and are defined less by the task features than by the interaction between task features and the problem solver's personal characteristics. With complex problems, goals and objectives often change over time, usually as the problem-solving process unfolds. Sometimes the problem transforms itself in the course of exploring solutions. Such was the case with Dan Charles as he grappled with Darla Campbell's situation. What at first appeared to be a classroom behavior problem evolved into something far more ominous as the details of Darla's ordeal at the hands of her father became known. In addition, analytical data is generally of little use in resolving most complex problems, and facts and information are often limited or distorted according to the particular perspectives of the fact/information givers and interpreters. It is not unusual for complex problems to be conflict laden, as there are typically a variety of competing values, preferences, beliefs, demands, and needs at stake. Finally, for many stakeholders, their interests in resolving a problem generally contain a considerable degree of emotional and/or personal investment. Once again, consider Josh Winters's dilemma. Deciding on how to best address the needs of the non- and limited-English language speakers was rife with conflicting beliefs and values among many school stakeholders. There was no way Josh could resolve this problem without upsetting someone (Cuban 2001; Funke and Frensch

1995; Morris 1990; Owens 1995; Payne, Bettman, and Johnson 1997; Simon 1986; Weick 1995; Yukl 1994).

If principals only had to deal with one complex problem at a time, then that would be challenging enough considering the highly political and turbulent nature of public school administration—but the reality is that complex problems often come in droves. It is rare to find a principal who is not simultaneously managing several complex problems in various stages of completion or multiple problems over a very narrow time frame (Wagner 1991).

Cuban (2001) describes the kinds of complex situations faced by the typical school principal as dilemmas rather than problems. From Cuban's perspective, a problem is a relatively structured event that can, through appropriate and focused effort, be solved. A dilemma, however, is so complicated and contentious that a solution that simultaneously and fully satisfies all stakeholders is impossible to find. As a result, dilemmas can only be managed. We are reminded of the old saying that a decision that upsets all stakeholders equally is often the best a manager can hope for.

NOT ALL PROBLEMS ARE CREATED EQUAL

Problems in complex human service organizations like schools come in different forms and contexts. Moreover, they tend to exist along a continuum that ranges from highly structured and well-defined problems to poorly structured and ill-defined dilemmas (Smith and Piele 1997; Ubben and Hughes 1997). Although differences in problem-solver expertise, values, and beliefs mitigate problem complexity, when these factors are removed from the equation, several common problem dimensions, types, and categories emerge.

To begin, most problems vary according to the extent to which they affect all components or functions of an organization (breadth), the number and layers of individuals within the organization (depth), and the degree to which they represent a particular class or genre of similar problems (generality). The stories of the three principals provided at the beginning of this book are good examples of this. Recall that Marsha Mahan was confronted with three almost simultaneous problems—how to manage an angry parent, two boys who had been in a fight, and an important classroom observation of an at-risk probationary teacher. None of the situations contained the ability to reach deeply within or broadly throughout the school. The parent situation was an incident-specific conflict that did not extend beyond the main office and the principal's secretary. Likewise, the situations involving the fighting boys and the observation of the at-risk teacher were similarly contained. In contrast, Josh Winters's bilingual education dilemma was more far-reaching, affecting virtually every operational component of the school. It also reached deeply throughout the personnel infrastructure of the school (e.g., teachers and staff would assume new roles and responsibilities; training and the commitment of resources would affect most employees and academic programs).

Most likely, Marsha's experiences with the angry parent and the two fighting boys closely approximated other similar situations (i.e., generality). Certainly, Marsha's years of experience in managing conflicts and hostile parents helped her to develop mental schemas of such situations and effective heuristic strategies for their resolution. As a result, she knew intuitively that she had a high probability of arriving at a successful outcome in both situations even before she became directly engaged in them.

However, in Josh's case, the ambiguity, novelty, and complexity of the bilingual issue were such that he had few, if any, prior experiences that could come close to approximating the problem context, structure, or solution options. In this situation, Josh was flying solo. Each decision along the way was taking him through new and uncharted territory.

According to Smith (1997), virtually all problems have structural elements consisting of participants, goals, constraints, means, causes, and related knowledge. However, as we mentioned above, not all problems are alike. Smith describes seven types or categories of problems most often found in complex organizations like schools.

1. Cannibalization. This occurs when some decision or organizational activity becomes successful at the expense of another. Take, for example, Dan's problem with Darla. In order to meet Darla's needs (which were critically important), Dan had to violate standard operating procedures for handling students who misbehave in class.

By not suspending her, Dan did the right thing for Darla at the expense of sending a strong message to other students that defiant and disruptive behavior would be dealt with firmly and consistently.

2. Chicken and Egg. A problem is created when, in order to get Y one must first have X. Conversely, in order to get X one must also have Y. Josh was faced with a serious chicken-and-egg dilemma. In order to successfully implement a new bilingual program, he would need supplemental funding from the U.S. Department of Education. Likewise, in order to become eligible for supplemental funding, Josh's district would have to demonstrate its willingness and readiness to implement an approved bilingual program.

3. Cost-Benefit Displacement. In this common scenario, one party benefits from a decision while another party pays. Josh was faced with yet another dilemma where in order to qualify for federal funding, he had to allocate a certain proportion of the school district's general fund toward the implementation of a bilingual program. Because this was a tight budget year, in order to do this, he had to reduce funding for a number of programs such as library books, staff development, and capital outlay.

4. Falling between Two Stools. Given the complexity and extremely high political sensitivity attached to the bilingual issue, if Josh tried to satisfy too many people who held divergent goals and viewpoints, he would run the risk of satisfying no one (ergo, falling between two stools).

5. Responsibility-Authority Split. This all-too-common dilemma surfaces when a manager is responsible for solving a problem but has no authority for accomplishing the tasks necessary to do so. As principal, Marsha was responsible for evaluating the performance of new teachers such as Peter Allen. Although it was her job to build a persuasive and legally sound case against retaining an incompetent teacher, she had absolutely no authority to dismiss that teacher. Only the school board could make that decision. By missing her scheduled observation of Peter Allen, Marsha knew she was increasing the risk that her recommendation to dismiss him from probationary employment would fall on deaf ears.

6. Slippery Slope. Any school leader knows that making an exception to the rule runs the risk of creating a new precedent. By not

suspending Darla for her defiant and disruptive behavior, Dan vi-
olated an established school rule. In doing so, he could make it
more difficult to justify suspending another student for the same,
or similar, behavior in the future, particularly if the student and
her parent got wind of his handling of Darla's case and chal-
lenged him on his inconsistent disciplinary measures.

7. Thrashing. Thrashing occurs when an administrator places an in-
ordinate emphasis on task management rather than task outcome.
This is precisely what may have gotten Josh into trouble. In his effort to empower the teaching staff and school principal by giving
them the green light to devise a plan for meeting the needs of non-
and limited-English speaking students, he failed to provide them
with clear decision parameters or a set of goals upon which a decision should be based. Josh was more concerned with the process
than the product. As a result, when they came up with an unac-
ceptable action plan, he had to short circuit the process and inject
an autocratically derived solution, much to the chagrin of the
teachers, principal, and several parents. In doing so, Josh lost a
great deal of trust and confidence in his leadership.

Complex problems rarely exist in neatly packaged bundles. In fact, the
examples described above underscore the fact that what may seem like a
relatively straightforward solution to a difficult situation can easily create
a chain reaction of other, unanticipated problems. This is exactly what
Cuban (2001) means when he describes "wicked problems" as being
dilemmas that can only be managed, not solved.

PROBLEM FRAMING: DEVELOPING PERSPECTIVE

As we mentioned earlier, what may seem like a complex problem for one
principal may be a relatively routine problem for another. Although expertise, or lack thereof, unquestionably explains much about this paradox, the way in which an individual frames problematic situations may
be equally important (Beach 1997; Dreyfus and Dreyfus 1986).

Problem framing involves the process of embedding an observed
event or situation in a context that gives it meaning. Similar to the de-

velopment of a mental schema, problem framing creates an image of the situation that is held up against the vast and complicated tapestry of the problem solver's life experiences, personality attributes, emotional states, intellectual abilities, perspectives, prejudices, and many other idiographic variables. Thus, problem framing is both a conscious and an unconscious process (March 1994; Tenbrunsel et al. 1999). The threads of an individual's personal tapestry can align themselves in an infinite array of combinations to create meaning out of the meaningless and to make sense out of the non-sensible. Problem framing is also influenced by a manager's level of confusion or ignorance pertaining to the situation. The confused manager's focus is on interpreting data, while the ignorant manager's focus is on acquiring more data. A critical problem for many managers, however, is the tendency to frame problems retroactively. That is, they often reframe a problem in order to fit their solutions to it (Weick 1995). Those of us who have spent time leading and observing complex organizations often refer to this phenomenon as the "ready, fire, aim" syndrome.

According to Cuban (2001), knowing how to effectively frame problems is the first step toward problem solving. He maintains that, despite the subjective forces that can influence the framing process, there are four key steps to consider when problem framing. First, the problem solver should identify the personal, professional, organizational, and societal values at play within the situation. Second, compromises or heuristic ways to address the problem should be identified. Third, all values should be listed and evaluated (including the problem solver's). And fourth, the situation should be reframed according to the rank order of values (Cuban 2001, 17).

An important and closely related component of the framing process is how a problem is diagnosed. Weick (1995, 9) calls this "problem setting." This involves the "process of naming the things the problem solver will attend to and the context in which they will be attended to." To accomplish this task effectively, the problem solver must determine three important aspects of the turbulence created by the problem situation—its intensity, its focus, and its source. In other words, how intense is the turbulence? Who or what is the target of the turbulence? And who or what is the source of the turbulence (Hanson 1996)?

Josh's bilingual problem can help put these ideas into context. The teachers' proposal to establish a sheltered English program was quite creative, cost effective, and persuasive. However, as Josh reflected upon the proposal, his intuition cautioned him to take a closer look at its viability. A number of things just didn't feel right. As a result of his intuition, Josh took some time alone to reconsider the situation and wound up reframing the problem entirely. It suddenly dawned on him that the teachers' proposal would satisfy their needs and interests, but would deprive the non- and limited-English speaking students of what he believed could be a more effective educational program. In addition, the proposal would undoubtedly inflame the Hispanic community while raising the risk of being confronted with a formal complaint lodged with the U.S. Department of Education's Office of Civil Rights. Josh felt the need to consider the community values on this matter and to weigh them against his own beliefs about quality educational practice for all students. He also reconsidered the forces, targets, and sources of turbulence that had already arisen over this issue and projected how these factors could play out if, in fact, he were to override the teachers' plan. Josh arrived at the conclusion that the trade-off was in the best interests of students and the organization. He could withstand the pressures and expressions of disappointment from the faculty. These would, in all likelihood, pass over time. With assistance from a federal bilingual development grant, Josh could also weather the demands placed on the district's budget. However, he would have a far greater and ominous challenge in store for himself and the school district if he were to alienate the rapidly growing Hispanic community.

The process of reframing helped Josh to redefine the problem from one that was vested in addressing the particular needs and interests of the teachers to one that posed a serious obstacle to the learning needs of all students. Josh's dilemma also underscores the importance and potential power of problem framing. The way in which a problem is framed not only influences the quality of potential solutions but can shape the problem solver's perception of the problem as being a threat or an opportunity. When problems are seen as threats, the tendency is to search for solutions that will avoid conflict or harm. When seen as opportunities, the focus shifts from what things to avoid to what things to address. Problem solving becomes less reactive and more proactive, less constrained and more creative (Pashiardis 1994; Simon 1986).

THE NATURE OF COMPLEX PROBLEM SOLVING

The term *problem solving* is often used interchangeably and erroneously with the term *decision making*. This is especially true when assessing the attributes of a complex, or wicked, problem. Problem solving is a much broader phenomenon that encapsulates all of the tensions, turbulence, goals, strategies, agendas, preferences, demands, complexities, and potential outcomes of a problematic event. Decision making, on the other hand, is the specific process that an individual or group engages in to solve a problem. The solution to Josh's bilingual problem, for example, would require several independent decisions, many of which would unfold over time. In addition, there was little doubt in Josh's mind that regardless of the eventual solution selected, other unanticipated problems and consequences of his decision would emerge, thus creating an entirely new set of dilemmas to deal with.

Research in the field of complex problem solving tends to center around three key domains. The first, personal factors, includes the examination of the problem solver's cognitive abilities, emotions, and motivations. The second, situational determinants, looks specifically at the task demands of the problem and the degree to which its various components and elements are observable and clearly understood (transparency). The study of system characteristics makes up the third domain. Here, the researcher is primarily concerned with the content of the problem and its stability over time (Sternberg and Frensch 1991). Most research in complex problem solving is performed through either single case studies or experimental design. Single case studies generally involve cognitive modeling approaches or phenomenological analyses of the problem solver's experience during the problem-solving process. Experimental approaches most often involve the manipulation of closely controlled problematic situations and the assessment of problem-solver behaviors and strategies. Such assessments are frequently compared with various normative models that represent ideal behaviors and strategies (Funke and Frensch 1995; Simon 1986).

Complex problems are complex precisely because their resolution generally requires a series of decisions, some that are related, and some that are not (Razik and Swanson 2001; Simon 1986). In addition, for a problem to be complex, a number of factors must be considered. First, the problem must be nontransparent. That is, all of the variables (e.g., goals, issues, options, predicted outcomes) are not known, or not known with clarity. Second, the problem contains multiple goals and/or conflicting goals. Goals often change during the process of problem solving. Third, there are several elements or components to the problem, many of which are tightly connected (thus increasing complexity). Finally, the problem is subject to dynamic developments (i.e., spontaneous, unplanned events or phenomena) (Funke and Frensch 1995.)

Complex problem solving is a multistep activity that seeks to overcome gaps between a given state (or situation) and a desired goal state. For individual problem solvers, such activities frequently include the development of mental representations, or schemas, of a problem's successful resolution. The process of envisioning outcomes often involves the use of heuristic strategies to simplify problem variables and to decrease the anxiety that accompanies the dissonance between the problem and the desired goal state (Morris 1990; Simon 1986). In addition, multiple barriers often cause problem solvers to seek approximate rather than optimal solutions. Complex problems in human service organizations are rarely solved through linear or formulaic processes, and solutions are subjected to variations in stakeholder preferences, demands, goals, skills, knowledge, and motivations. Unanticipated environmental influences, fluctuations in the problem structure, competing resources, shifting allocations of power, and time-delayed effects add complexity to the task of reaching optimal solutions. Therefore, problem solvers often settle for an outcome that doesn't perfectly match their mental schemas of the optimal solution. As a result, progress toward reaching a solution may be difficult, if not impossible, to evaluate (Cappon 1994; Funke and Frensch 1995; Patterson 1993; Sternberg and Frensch 1991).

Solving complex problems requires the efficient interaction between the problem context, the task requirements, and the problem solver's cognitive, emotional, and social skills and knowledge. As we noted earlier, this can be an idiosyncratic process since no two problem solvers share the same cognitive, emotional, or social attributes. A closer look at the anatomy of a complex problem reveals several internal and external factors that influence how these variables interact. Internal factors are those that pertain to the problem solver's level of experience, cognitive attributes (e.g., knowledge, learning style), and noncognitive attributes (e.g., self-confidence, motivation). External factors consist of the problem structure (e.g., task complexity, task transparency), problem context (e.g., degree of familiarity), and environmental factors (e.g., feedback loop, expectations, demands).

Most people do not use predefined pathways in the quest to resolve complex problems. In fact, people tend to move back and forth between problem-solving steps, and often skip steps. Most complex problems involve a recursive and episodic process whereby the problem solver often moves forward, backward, and laterally through problem-solving steps. Sometimes these processes occur simultaneously (Cuban 2001; Wagner 1991). Frequently, the problem itself is reframed as the process unfolds. "Goals evolve and change during action, which means that both the existing and the desired state are fluid. Gaps open and close, widen and narrow" (Weick 1995, 88). Oftentimes, problem solving is strictly intuitive in nature and is accomplished in ways that defy explanation or description (Wagner 1991). Later, we will examine in depth the role of intuition in decision making and the surprising degree to which leaders rely upon intuition to help them resolve their most challenging problems.

PROBLEM SOLVING AND DECISION MAKING: WHAT'S THE DIFFERENCE?

One could think about problem solving and decision making as an artist would think about the tools of the trade. Whereas problem solving would represent the frame and canvas, decision making would represent the brush and paint. Leadership is decision making; that's what leaders do. Mintzberg's (1976) portrayal of the typical day in the life of a school principal revealed a hectic, fragmented, and rapidly changing environment where literally dozens of decision events occur throughout the workday. Some decision events are planned, but many are not. Depending upon the decision context, task requirements, or environmental demands, organizational decision making involves the actions of a single individual or a group. Since we are primarily interested in decision making by individual school principals, we will make only periodic references to group decision making.

As we pointed out earlier, decision making is really a subset of problem solving. With very simple or routine problems, making a decision and problem solving are synonymous events. We offer a couple of examples from our own leadership experience.

Problem: There has been a reduction in the deferred maintenance budget. As a result, there will be enough money to either recarpet the faculty room or to replace worn-out classroom drapes. Decision: The principal makes a decision to put off recarpeting the faculty lounge for a year and replace the drapes. Problem solved.

Problem: All application materials for an eleventh-grade English teaching position were due on June 30. On July 1st, the principal paper-screens applicants. Three very highly qualified applicants have not submitted completed application packets. In one case, the application materials are missing two letters of reference. In another case, a formal copy of the candidate's graduate school transcripts is missing. In the third case, the transcripts are in, as are the letters of reference, but the application form is missing. The principal is faced with the problem of determining how to deal with three qualified applicants who have missed the deadline for submitting all application materials. Decision: The principal decides that to be fair and consistent, and to protect the district legally, she must exclude all candidates with incomplete application materials from advancing to the first round of interviews. Problem solved.

In complex situations, however, the act of making a decision may have a limited, or even no, effect on solving the problem. For example, when Dan decided not to formally suspend Darla, his decision certainly eliminated another, comparatively trivial, source of worry for Darla, but it had no influence on the overarching problem of how to help her overcome the devastating effects of the preceding night's events. Neither did Dan's decision make life any easier for Mr. Colt, who had been verbally abused by Darla in front of thirty students. In fact, by making the right decision for Darla, Dan may have damaged Mr. Colt's standing in the eyes of the other students.

Understanding how executive decisions are made in complex organizations has been a very popular topic of interest for researchers. Over the past fifty years or so, the field of decision research has included a wide range of disciplinary perspectives, including theories of economic choice, political science, bureaucracies and leadership, games, military science, and theories about cognition and neuropsychology (Harvey, Bearley, and Corkrum 1997). Despite the expanding range and scope of empirical research, there is no universally endorsed or overarching, theoretical framework used by researchers to study decision making. Not surprisingly, it has not been possible to describe a universal sequence of events leading to perfect decisions. Complicating the practical application of research in this field is the fact that most traditional decision research has involved the use of inexperienced people, such as college students, who are engaged in laboratory tasks where contextual, or situational, factors play a limited role (Goldstein and Hogarth 1997; Pashiardis 1994; Smith, 1997; Zsambok, 1996).

In the years immediately following World War II, scholars began to examine organizational decision making in depth. From these early research efforts, prescriptive theories about how managers could reach optimal decisions emerged. Much of the early research focused on models of economic choice and subjective expected utility (Simon 1986). Attempts to determine how managers could make important executive decisions that would result in the best possible payoffs with minimal risks were built upon the long-standing rationalist belief that the right logico-mathematical modeling and analysis could provide optimal outcomes. In the 1950s, theories of expected utility expanded to a line of empirical research that examined how people calculate probabilities in order to maximize the potential of a positive decision outcome. In essence, it was presumed that individuals acted out of self-interest and that important decisions were made on choices that were consistent with predictions of maximizing one's self-interest (Tenbrunsel et al. 1999).

About the same time, new questions about the limits of human analytic capacity led to Herbert Simon's (1986) theory of limited, or bounded, rationality. For over two decades, notions of limited rationality dominated most research in the field of organizational decision making. It continues to do so today (March 1994). However, in the late 1960s, and throughout the rest of the twentieth century, a slow shift occurred in the research agenda. Rather than trying to find precise analytic approaches toward reaching optimal, or even satisfactory, decisions, many scholars redirected their efforts toward describing how managers actually make decisions on the job. This new naturalistic approach to decision research shifted scholarly attention to the study of real-world decision making embedded within a wide range of idiographic factors. Naturalistic decision research placed less emphasis on the quantitative analysis and predictive attributes of leadership behavior and more emphasis on the qualitative aspects of the decision-making process.

Researchers in the field of naturalistic decision making examine such fuzzy concepts as ways of knowing, feelings, emotions, common sense, tacit knowledge, heuristic thinking, and intuition (Owens 1995). In addition, naturalistic approaches to decision making acknowledge and explore the complexities of human perceptions, the dimensions of conscious and subconscious mental processes under varying degrees of stress and sensory stimulation, imagination, sense making, ambiguous problem characteristics, individual reflections, phenomenological experiences, and judgments (Hogarth and Kunreuther 1997; Smith 1997; Weick 1995). Today, most scholars agree that naturalistic decision research informs and adds contextual dimension to normative models of decision making. Neither approach adequately explains how effective leaders make decisions, but together the blending of research foci has provided more holistic and comprehensive descriptions of decision making in complex organizations.

DECISION CATEGORIES, TYPES, AND CONTEXTS

Most scholars of decision making in complex organizations describe two major categories of decisions: programmed decisions and nonprogrammed decisions. These categories have also been described as vigilant and hypervigilant, or tame and wicked, decisions. Programmed decisions are those that are simple, routine, highly structured, repetitive, habituated, familiar, lower level, and quantitative in nature. Logical-analytical approaches often work best when making programmed decisions. Time constraints rarely limit or inhibit the decision maker's ability to apply analytical decision methods. Nonprogrammed decisions, on the other hand, are novel, unfamiliar, ambiguous, complex, nonsystematic, and qualitative in nature. Analysis and dispassionate logic are often of little use in resolving nonprogrammed problems and decisions. Instead, decision makers generally rely on limited rationality, heuristics, or intuition (or some combination of these). Moreover, time pressures can constrain the decision maker's ability to apply highly analytical decision approaches. There may be a need to decide quickly, without a great deal of time for careful reflection or deliberation (Cuban 2001; Greenberg and Baron 1997; Johnston, Driskell, and Salas 1997; Miller, Hickson, and Wilson 1999; Pashiardis 1994; Razik and Swanson 2001; Ubben and Hughes 1997). It is possible, however, to have a programmed decision with time constraints or a nonprogrammed decision without time constraints. Although time pressure is a variable that can exacerbate task complexity, it is usually not, in and of itself, important enough to cause one to classify a decision as programmed or nonprogrammed. It is also important to note that the quality requirements of a decision can influence its level of complexity, as can the level of experience and skill of the decision maker.

In theory, simple problems generally require programmed decisions. Conversely, complex problems generally require nonprogrammed decisions. However, in reality, problems and decisions are rarely one or the other. They tend to exist on a continuum from the very simple to the highly complex and often contain a mixture of simple and complex characteristics. For example, Josh's bilingual problem is, on the whole, quite complex. In order to resolve the dilemma, Josh must make a series of decisions, some that are quite simple and routine (like notifying school board members of his decision to postpone taking action on the teachers' proposed ESL program), and some that are quite complex (like deciding on the goals, structure, and curricular elements of a sound bilingual program). Some of Josh's more routine decisions could be made by carefully weighing the pros and cons of a particular approach or by making thoughtful predictions about potential outcomes. His most difficult decision, however, was to overrule the recommendations of the teachers' planning group. For that, Josh relied more on intuition than analysis. Given time, Josh had faith that he could construct a well-reasoned justification for this decision—but since he had only a few minutes before the school board meeting, he had to trust his gut.

As he navigated through the labyrinthian array of problem attributes, Josh was influenced by his level and breadth of experience and his feelings of competence. These qualities led him to frame the problem elements around three fundamental heuristics: recognition, inference, and choice (Beach 1997). The recognition heuristic allowed Josh to arrive at a quick solution when an element of the problem was identical or similar to an old one. Recognition greatly reduces or even eliminates the need for lengthy analysis since the decision maker immediately knows what to do based on the successful outcomes of similar situations and decision responses. The inference heuristic provided Josh with the ability to make an educated guess when a current problem situation was not identical to, but sufficiently similar to, prior experience. Finally, the choice heuristic prompted Josh to carefully review and consider outcome probabilities and options when a particular problem element was unique or unfamiliar.

The choice heuristic, however, is only as successful as the amount and quality of information available to the decision maker. With highly complex problems, information is frequently scarce, ambiguous, and evolving. When this occurs, highly experienced decision makers rely on their powers of limited rationality and intuition.

Most decisions unfold around two key dimensions: action and interest. The action dimension is actually a continuum of decision-maker perspectives that range from highly coherent and rational to highly chaotic and intuitive. The interest dimension is likewise represented by a continuum of motivations possessed by the decision maker. The continuum ranges from highly goal directed to highly political. The highly goal-directed decision maker is likely to be highly analytical, whereas the highly political decision maker is likely to be highly intuitive (Miller, Hickson, and Wilson 1999).

Typically, decisions in schools can be organized around three key types. First, there are policy decisions that involve principles for organizational conduct. Second, there are administrative decisions that translate policy into action. And third, there are executive ad hoc decisions made at the point of action (Harvey, Bearley, and Corkrum 1997). Most nonprogrammed decisions fall under the executive type. According to Harvey, Bearley, and Corkrum (1997), decision types such as these are facilitated, or operationalized, through four basic approaches.

The first approach, consultation, involves decisions that are made after consulting with others. The second, command, involves decisions that are made autocratically by the decision maker with little or no input from organizational stakeholders. The third, consensus, involves decisions that require group agreement. Finally, the fourth, convenience, refers to decisions that are made to avoid conflict, inconvenience, or protracted decision processes. A look at the decision dilemmas faced by our three principals reveals evidence of all four decision approaches at work, with some overlapping occurring between approaches. Such is the nature of complex decisions. They defeat simplistic descriptions or attempts to construct neat, linear, solution pathways. We should add, there is no evidence to suggest that the use of intuitive decision making is better suited to one approach or another.

Administrative decisions in schools can be characterized according to several themes and dimensions. When a decision involves the distribution of human and material resources, it is referred to as an allocation decision. Josh's bilingual problem was a good example of an allocation decision. When the physical or psychological safety of students or staff is at stake, a decision can be called a security decision. Marsha's angry parent and fighting boys situations involved security decisions. Boundary decisions include those where the decision maker has an interest in the control of information and material between domains within a school, or between a school and its surrounding community. Dan's efforts to manage the highly sensitive and confidential aspects of Darla's crisis involved boundary decisions. Judgments about individual or group performance are referred to as evaluation decisions, and decisions that pertain to the teaching and learning processes are called instructional decisions. Marsha's decision about how to handle at-risk probationary teacher Peter Allen was both an evaluation and an instructional decision (Hanson 1996).

As all three principals worked their way through their problem situations, they made decisions around two overarching purposes. They would make adoption decisions or progress decisions. Adoption decisions would be those that screened options and possible actions according to the goals and objectives of the decision maker or the organization. Dan's efforts to address Darla's poor behavior in Mr. Colt's class as well as her horrible experience at the hands of her father are good examples of adoption decisions. Progress decisions consist of efforts to determine if a particular action plan is making acceptable progress toward the goal or objective (Beach 1997). Josh's decision to overrule the teacher work group was a progress decision. Although he had yet to work out the details of an action plan, he was intuitively convinced that the group's progress toward resolving the bilingual program problem was not satisfactory.

Complex decisions are shaped and defined by situational contexts that contain the interaction between the decision maker, the organization, the problem, the external environment, the task requirements, controllable factors, uncontrollable factors, and possible decision outcomes (Arsham 1996). As we mentioned earlier, the salient traits of situational contexts are influenced by the intensity of the turbulence confronting an organization (force), the focus of the turbulence or discontentment (target), and the status, or importance, of the turbulence (source) (Greenberg and Baron 1997). Other factors include the levels of certainty or uncertainty about the problem attributes and possible decision outcomes, the level of risk (to the decision maker, the organization, other people), the competition for power and control within the organization or exerted upon the organization, and the structure of the organization itself (Razik and Swanson 2001; Bolman and Deal 1997).

There are almost infinite numbers of possible combinations, or interactions, between the contextual components of a decision (i.e., categories, dimensions, types, approaches, themes, and purposes), the task characteristics of a chosen solution, the situational and environmental characteristics, and the personal attributes of the decision maker. It is precisely because of such complexity that the field of decision research has struggled to find prescriptive decision-making models with universal applicability in the field (Hanson 1996; Miller, Hickson, and Wilson

Table 2.1. Contextual Components of a Decision

Category	Dimension	Type	Approach	Theme	Purpose
Programmed	Action	Policy	Consultative	Allocation	Adoption
Nonprogrammed	Interest	Administrative	Command	Security	Progress
		Executive	Consensus	Boundary	
			Convenience	Instructional	

1999; Pashiardis 1994). Table 2.1 shows the key contextual components of a decision.

The anatomy of a complex decision involves more than the contextual components alone. When any one of the decisions made by Marsha, Dan, and Josh are deconstructed, there are three fundamental forces in play that exert influence upon the decision maker: (a) forces within the decision maker, (b) forces within the environment, and (c) forces within the situation. Each of these factors contains several attributes or characteristics with the potential to interact in any number of combinations.

Forces within the decision maker consist of the knowledge, skills, dispositions, and other idiographic attributes that are unique to the individual making the decision. Forces within the environment contain those structures, demands, barriers, opportunities, and settings in play at the time of the decision. Forces within the situation contain factors and influences that arise as a result of the specific decision at hand. In table 2.2, we provide a look at how these three forces and their component parts constitute the anatomy of a decision.

When faced with a complex problem, decision makers align the three forces in ways that increase the chances of making an effective decision. Sometimes, the most effective decision is one that is carefully and thoroughly worked out. Sometimes, it is the one that is made quickly and efficiently; sometimes, it is one that meets the minimum threshold of an acceptable outcome. Given the unlikely possibility that all of the forces depicted in table 2.2 can be simultaneously and equitably controlled, most scholars in the field of complex decision making recognize that few decisions can be made according to the framework of prescriptive decision theory (Wagner 1991).

In the following section, we examine in greater depth the elements of modern (classical) and postmodern (naturalistic) decision theories. We begin the discussion with an overview of rational/analytical decision theory, followed by reviews of the theory of bounded (limited) rationality and naturalistic decision theory, of which intuition is a component part. Most scholars in the field of decision making recognize that decision making in complex organizations requires a constellation of skills that, depending upon the situation, can include elements of both modern and postmodern approaches. Nevertheless,

Table 2.2. The Anatomy of a Decision

Forces within the Decision Maker	*Forces within the Environment*	*Forces within the Situation*
Knowledge:	Available resources	Degree of risk
Content area experience	Competing interests	Immediacy
Related experiences	Demands to participate	Complexity
Direct experience	Motivations of others	Content domain
Level of training	Obstacles and barriers	Ambiguity/clarity
	Process demands	Decision type
Skills:	Competition	Volume of information
Component competence	Demands for quality	Accuracy of information
Holistic competence	Demands for control	Outcome predictability
Related competencies	Rewards and sanctions	Degree of novelty
Physical skill	Organization structure	Breadth and scope
Mental reasoning	Chain of command	Intensity/valence
Intuitive abilities	Receptivity to change	Intervening forces
	Working relationships	Symbolic forces
Dispositions:	Rules and procedures	Priorities, status issues
Personality traits	Physical setting	System efficiencies
Locus of control		Outcome possibilities
Motivation		Outcome clarity
Self-confidence		Contextual factors
Feelings of efficacy		
Feelings of empathy		
Need for affiliation		
Need for dominance		
Ambition/drive		
Sense of purpose		
Fears, doubts, regrets		
Moral/ethical qualities		
Mood		
Other/Idiographic Factors:		
IQ		
Ego strength		
Emotional intelligence		
Self-control		
Goals and objectives		
Physical health		
Semantic priming		
Age		
Gender		
Cultural attributes		
Language		
Ethnicity		

theories of rational/analytical decision making provide an idealized baseline from which the field of decision research and its various strands can be examined and compared.

THE ELEMENTS OF RATIONAL DECISION MAKING

Nearly one hundred years ago, the proponents of scientific rationalism advanced the belief that most complex problems could be solved given the right kind of logico-mathematical analysis. The roots of the Western analytic tradition rely heavily on the Pythagorean view of the world as an objective entity comprised of things bearing properties and entering into relations. From this perspective, it was believed that normative/prescriptive models could be created that would provide decision makers with foolproof pathways toward achieving optimal decision outcomes. Throughout much of the twentieth century, scholars in the field of decision making contrasted and compared the extent to which decision-maker behavior conformed with such models. A key goal of these scholars was to determine the ideal decision strategy to fit virtually any organizational problem (Arsham 1996; Beach 1997; Tenbrunsel et al. 1999).

Critical assumptions of classical rational/analytic theory are that all information related to the problem is known (or can be known); that the objective facts can be discerned; that all solution alternatives are known (or can be known); that all possible decision consequences or outcomes can be predicted with certainty; and that all preferences relevant to the selection of the optimal alternative are known, consistent, and stable (March 1994). Classical decision research frequently consisted of carefully controlled laboratory experiments often using well-structured problems and college students as subjects (Simon 1986).

Most formal efforts to study decision making in the early to mid-twentieth century were applied to the field of economics. Emphasis was placed on making decisions that could maximize the expected value of a course of action. The idea was to obtain the very best economic outcome possible while eliminating the risk of loss. Generally, outcomes were defined in terms of profits and losses (Beach 1997; Razik and Swanson 2001). The various strands of normative decision research also explored game theory, Bayesian statistics, probability inference, the theory of subjective expected utility, and other quantitative approaches to decision making. All of these approaches involved the notion that the solution of complex problems could be attained through sensible, logical, and carefully reasoned analysis. Through rational analysis, it was believed that managers and leaders could control the present and forecast the future (Peters and Waterman 1982). Although the proponents of classical decision theory often differ in their conceptions of the optimal decision-making model, they uniformly agree that analytic approaches to decision making are inherently superior to nonanalytical approaches such as image theory, heuristics, or intuition. Most of the classical decision theorists who acknowledge the role of intuition in decision making do so with a degree of skepticism. If and when intuition is used, they argue, it should only come into play after all rational/analytical approaches have been exhausted (Ubben and Hughes 1997).

Models of analytic decision making are quite prescriptive in laying out the sequence of steps to be taken in the process of making a decision. As we noted above, many variations exist among scholars. There are, however, a number of common elements found in most prominent models. We list these in table 2.3.

According to classical decision theory, all complex decisions, when subjected to the concrete, sequential steps outlined in table 2.3, can be resolved with not only satisfactory results but with optimal results. Classical decision making is a linear process with each step dependent upon

Table 2.3.   Common Components of Classical Decision Making

 1. Monitor the decision environment
 2. Identify the problem
 3. Diagnose the problem (e.g., decompose the problem into component parts)
 4. Define goals and objectives (e.g., decision maker and/or organizational)
 5. Make a predecision about how to approach the decision-making process
 6. Determine decision participants (e.g., preferences, skills, roles, influence, status)
 7. Collect data and information pertaining to the problem
 8. Generate possible solution alternatives
 9. Evaluate possible solution alternatives (e.g., predict consequences/outcomes)
10. Choose the best (optimal) alternative
11. Implement the best alternative
12. Monitor and evaluate solution

the completion of the step immediately before it. Skipping steps, or failing to fully address each step, results in a quantitatively flawed process that, in turn, increases the risk of a wrong, or less than optimal, solution (Daft 2001; Drake and Row 1999; Greenberg and Baron 1997; Pashiardis 1994).

Classical decision making requires several critical properties of analytic thinking. According to Kenneth et al. (1997, 148), these include: (a) a high level of cognitive control, (b) the slow and methodical processing of data, (c) a high level of conscious awareness, (d) low confidence in the answer to a given problem, and (e) high confidence in the analytic process in reaching a solution. There is little margin for error. If any one of the assumptions or data elements pertaining to the problem is wrong or incomplete, the ability of the decision maker to arrive at the correct solution is greatly diminished, even if she strictly adheres to the prescribed decision-making steps.

Classical decision models generally do a poor job of controlling for the intangible qualities of human decision making. Factors such as variations in individual temperament, conflicting preferences and values, and differences in individual experience and intelligence all conspire to foil even the most logically derived decision-making models.

Let us return to the simultaneously occurring dilemmas faced by principal Marsha Mahan. Marsha was confronted with an angry parent, two combatant students, and a critically important observation of an at-risk probationary teacher. Given the short time frame available to her and the emotional intensity of the situations confronting her, Marsha had little use for the classical twelve-step model of decision making. She couldn't possibly generate a complete list of possible alternatives for dealing with the angry parent in a reasonable period of time. To do so would require that Marsha explore all of the important facts and information pertaining to the parent's anger. Moreover, she would have to carefully consider and weigh all of the possible ways in which she could intervene, predict all of the possible consequences of all possible interventions, clearly identify all goals and objectives, and select not just a satisfactory but the very best solution. If Marsha were to strictly adhere to the classical model, she would have to repeat this process for all three dilemmas. Given enough time, perhaps Marsha could have made a pretty good stab at sorting through all of the steps and variables of each

dilemma. But, like most school principals, she had to move fast. Moreover, to arrive at the optimal decision for each problem would require
that she rapidly process a great deal of accurate and unambiguous information without error—a task that is nearly impossible to do given the
enormous complexities of human interaction.

So, just what kinds of problems faced by principals lend themselves
to the prescriptive models of classical decision making? In short, the
kinds that are routine, simple, quantitative, and unambiguous, and
where values and preferences are uniform and nonconflicting. We
can think of very few examples in areas of school administration that
really matter. In reality, principals rarely rely on classical decision
making in its purest form. Instead, they settle for vastly modified decision approaches.

During the past hundred years, it has become increasingly clear that
classical decision-making models represent the proverbial brass ring
that remains just out of reach for most leaders of complex human service organizations. The classical models are not without value, however.
They provide a template for decision behavior that even when partly followed can greatly improve decision efficiency and accuracy with certain
kinds of problems. Such models can provide a useful road map for decision makers who are at a loss as to how to grapple with the complexities of organizational problems and dilemmas. Most contemporary
scholars of organizational leadership agree, however, that the elements
of classical decision making play a limited role when leaders are faced
with complex problems that require the application of qualitative judgment. Moreover, such decision-making models fail to capture many features of intentional behavior (Harbort 1997; Miller, Hickson, and Wilson 1999; Owens 1995).

THE ELEMENTS OF DESCRIPTIVE/NATURALISTIC
DECISION MAKING

When decision making is studied in the field, the efficacy of prescriptive
models is greatly reduced. Real-world decision making requires holistic
thought and the ability to understand the complexities, interconnec-
tions, ambiguities, and uncertainties of organizational life. As a result,

scholars have turned toward descriptive forms of analysis. Such efforts have provided useful perspectives about decision making that have actually helped scholars to refine normative models (Owens 1005; Ton brunsel et al. 1000).

Naturalistic decision theory is less concerned with how decision makers ought to behave than with how they actually behave. The naturalistic decision-making approach is based on the premise that there is no single right way to make decisions when faced with complex problems (Bower 1998). In fact, there is considerable evidence that managers actually develop new strategies and tactics as they progress through the decision-making process. Of course, much of this depends on the demands of the tasks required to solve a particular problem (Payne, Bettman, and Johnson 1997). To complicate matters, it is often very difficult to determine just when a decision begins or ends (Miller, Hickson, and Wilson 1999). Although naturalistic decision making lacks the precision of the classical approaches, it builds on the strategies managers use in the field and focuses on situational awareness and decision contexts (Klein 1996a).

Below we discuss several models, or conceptions, of naturalistic decision making. Each contains unique as well as overlapping elements. The truth is that no single model adequately explains how all managers make decisions. Managers in human service organizations rely on an idiosyncratic mixture of these elements when solving complex problems. Nevertheless, a description of the most prominent naturalistic decision models helps us to appreciate how difficult it is to expect managers to adhere to a prescribed set of decision rules.

To begin, there are three primary sources of influence that act upon decision makers in the field. The first is defined as utilitarian and assumes that decision makers look for decisions that maximize the value, cost/benefit, and utility of a given course of action. These principles underlie classical decision theory. The second influence includes the myriad of social forces that can shape decision making. These include codes of behavior, cultural values and practices, and other socially derived external pressures. The third influence consists of the deontological forces at work within the decision maker. These consist of the various moral and ethical perspectives held by the decision maker. Understandably, the interaction of these three influences can result in infinite situational variations that are not effectively addressed by classical decision models (Beach 1997).

Theories of naturalistic decision making include a wide range of ideas about how leaders use flexible, efficient, and effective nonanalytical methods to make decisions on the job (Bergstrand 1998). Perhaps the most prominent of these is what Herbert Simon (1986) described in the years following World War II as bounded rationality. Of all decision-making theories, bounded rationality has most successfully withstood the scrutiny of scholars over the last fifty years and continues to provide a strong framework for understanding how leaders behave when making complex decisions (March 1994). However, bounded rationality is not without its own set of prescriptive rules. Not nearly as constrained as the classical models, bounded rationality assumes that decision makers have a limited capacity for rational analysis and, as such, must rely on a limited, but highly useful, set of heuristic judgments.

As we know, managers in human service organizations work in a world of swirling expectations and demands for immediate results. Time is limited; memories are limited; demands for attention are frequent; and differences in individual preferences, beliefs, and needs often lead to interpersonal conflicts and power plays. Information about any given problem is often incomplete, inaccurate, and nontransparent, and decisions are made on the basis of approximations and uncertain probabilities. Moreover, a manager's attitudes and desires often change over time, as do the elements of most complex problems. As a result, managers must rely on solutions that exceed a predefined target or criterion. Rather than striving to find an optimal solution, the focus is on finding a solution that is good enough. James March (1994) and Herbert Simon (1986) refer to this as *satisficing*.

Bounded rationality works by reducing the cognitive demands on the decision maker. By relying on heuristic rules of thumb, the manager saves time, reduces decision complexity, and attains a reasonably accurate solution. Managers may also edit problems in their search for solutions. To do this, they decompose complex problems into component parts and often frame problems narrowly to reduce complexity. In addition, managers may actually maximize one aspect of a problem and satisfice on others. In studies of decision making under conditions of uncertainty, ambiguity, and high risk, decisions made through bounded rationality actually led to better decision outcomes than highly analytical approaches (Johnston, Driskell, and Salas 1997; March 1994; Tenbrunsel et al. 1999).

Theories of naturalistic decision making include other descriptions about how managers make decisions on the job. One prominent model is commonly referred to as Recognition-Primed Decision Making (RPDM). With RPDM, the decision maker uses his experience to size up situations (i.e., recognize and understand), to evaluate potential problem-solving actions, and to mentally simulate possible solutions. The key to RPDM is the recognition of situations that are similar to past experiences and to draw upon the aspects of past decisions that worked well in constructing a solution to the current problem (Beach 1997).

Reason-Based Analysis is another model that is closely related to the principles of bounded rationality and RPDM. With Reason-Based Analysis, choices are often made from affective judgments that preclude thorough analysis. The decision maker considers such subjective factors as the relative advantage and disadvantage of a course of action, or the level of anticipated regret in the event that the decision outcome is unsatisfactory. The decision maker also considers dominance structures in the organization and how these might generate conflict and disagreement among decision stakeholders. Finally, with Reason-Based Analysis, values and preferences are frequently constructed as decision making unfolds, rather than as an antecedent component of the decision process (Shafir and Tversky 1997).

Naturalistic decision theory includes incremental models of decision making whereby the decision maker concentrates on making marginal or incremental adjustments in the pursuit of a problem resolution. With the incremental approach, sweeping change rarely occurs. Instead, the decision maker nibbles away at the problem until the first best solution is reached (i.e., satisficing). The solution to the problem is shaped less by what the decision maker wants to move toward than by what she wants to move away from (Beach 1997).

Beach also describes three Narrative-Based Decision Models designed to help clarify what managers actually think about when making complex decisions. The Scenario Model describes how decision makers generate plausible narratives to forecast multiple scenarios. Simply put, the decision maker relies upon a series of "if-then" propositions to construct mental schemas of possible solutions and their predicted outcomes. The Story Model describes how decision makers construct stories based on their interpretation of past events. These stories provide a context through which the decision maker frames an existing problem and develops a decision approach. Finally, the Argument-Driven Model describes how decision makers carefully consider the pros and cons of a possible decision. Through this process, arguments are created and used to help the decision maker reshape the decision to increase its match with the demands of the situation.

One of the most controversial yet interesting descriptions of organizational decision making is the Garbage Can Model developed by Cohen, March, and Olsen (1972). The model is predicated on the belief that many complex organizations operate more like organized anarchies than carefully controlled bureaucracies. In organized anarchies, goals, problems, alternatives, and solutions are often ill defined and ambiguous. In addition, establishing cause-and-effect relationships within organizational processes is difficult. Finally, the participation of organizational stakeholders is fluid and often temporary. As a result, decisions are rarely, if ever, the result of a logical sequence of steps beginning with a particular problem and ending in a solution. Instead, decisions are often the product of an unpredictable stream of interactions between choice opportunities (i.e., events that trigger the need for decision making), problems, potential solutions, and participants. Decisions are frequently made on the basis of the temporal proximity of these variables rather than on a carefully constructed means-ends analysis.

The garbage can metaphor represents a choice opportunity. Flowing into and out of the can are problems, solutions, and participants. Solutions may exist before a problem is identified; the preferences, motivations, needs, and interests of participants will ebb and flow; and the existence of a particular problem does not guarantee that an appropriate solution is (or will be) available. The occasional connection of these variables is viewed more as the product of chance than logical processes. In many cases, problems will exist without ever being fully solved or with only partial solutions. Although the model depicts organizational decision making as chaotic and imprecise, most complex organizations will still move in the direction of problem reduction (Daft 2001).

Image theory offers, perhaps, the most realistic view of how managers actually make complex decisions on the job. Instead of engaging in laborious analysis to find optimal solutions, most decision makers rely on heuristic or intuitive processes that minimize the need for cognitive processing. A key assumption with image theory is that the decision maker contains a vast store of knowledge and experience that is used as a perceptual baseline from which to examine new problems and derive appropriate solutions. In addition, decision makers are assumed to have certain images of the future (e.g., a conception of what the future would look like in the ideal). When a problem arises, the decision maker probes her memory of a similar past event and reflects on the outcome of the plan of action used to resolve the problem. If that action plan was successful and matches the decision maker's image of the future, then she will likely attempt to apply the same decision strategy to the current situation (Greenberg and Baron 1997).

Before settling on a particular course of action, the decision maker considers two key factors: compatibility and profitability. First, the proposed decision is examined according to its compatibility with three fundamental images held by the decision maker. The value image consists of the decision maker's values, morals, and ethics. The trajectory image consists of the decision maker's goals and objectives, and the strategic image consists of the decision maker's plans and tactics used to accomplish the goals. Second, the decision maker considers the profitability of a given course of action by estimating and evaluating the extent to which a possible course of action will best fit her values, goals, and plans. According to the theory, this thought process occurs very rapidly, and, for many people, is more intuitive than deliberative (Beach 1997).

On several occasions, we have referred to the term heuristics in describing decision-making processes in the real world. In the vernacular, heuristics refers to rules of thumb that help decision makers reduce the cognitive demands generated by complex problems. Given its prominence in contemporary decision research and its kinship with the kinds of mental processes that take place during intuitive thinking, we will provide a closer look at the characteristics, advantages, and drawbacks of heuristic decision making in the next section.

THE ROLE OF HEURISTIC THINKING IN REDUCING DECISION COMPLEXITY

Rules of thumb. We have all heard of them, and we all use them—often without being consciously aware that we are doing so. Consider Dan

Charles's dilemma of how to handle Darla Campbell's poor behavior in Mr. Colt's class. Dan's first impulse was to suspend Darla from school. He didn't have to deliberate long in order to reach that initial conclusion because, given Darla's poor behavioral record, the typical response would be to suspend her. No in-depth analysis needed. If Darla does this, then I will do that. That's what we always do in situations like this.

Another example. When developing the school district budget for the new school year, Josh Winters had to decide how much money to allocate to the various schools and district office departments. The answer was simple. Start by giving them the same proportion of the budget that they received during the prior school year and let the principals and department chairs negotiate changes later. No in-depth analysis needed here either. They will get what they always got. He will work out the wrinkles later.

Heuristic thinking allows us to cut problems down to size by chunking patterns of information into aggregate and easily managed pieces (Dreyfus and Dreyfus 1986; Simon 1986). According to Simon (1986, 3), "people solve problems by selective, heuristic search through large problem spaces and large data bases, using means-ends analysis as a principal technique for guiding the search." Gerd Gigerenzer and Peter Todd (1999) of the Max Planck Institute refer to this phenomenon as fast and frugal heuristics.

There is growing evidence that managers in complex human service organizations rely heavily on heuristic decision processes with most important decisions. Heuristic decision making, for example, is particularly useful when dealing with the kinds of complex, uncertain, and diffuse problems faced by Marsha Mahan and Josh Winters (Busenitz and Barney 1997; Hogarth and Kunreuther 1997).

The term *heuristic* is Greek in origin and refers to finding out or to discovering. It was first introduced into the English language in the early nineteenth century and describes the kinds of cognitive processes commonly used when solving problems that defy logic or probability theory (Gigerenzer and Todd 1999, 24). For much of the twentieth century, however, many social scientists came to view heuristic thinking as imprecise and inaccurate, at least when compared with the emerging normative models of decision making (Kahneman and Tversky 1982). Such skepticism may be due to the fact that the study of heuristic thinking is not based on a firm theoretical structure, nor does it relate to, follow from, or lead to any other major concepts in cognitive science (Beach 1997).

Today, heuristics has become the focus in an emerging wave of empirical inquiry into naturalistic forms of decision making. In fact, recent research has found that decision makers who use a diverse set of heuristics when solving complex problems can maintain high accuracy with minimal effort. Under conditions of extreme complexity, time demands, task novelty, and ambiguity, heuristic decision-making approaches often produce better results than highly logical and analytically crafted solutions. Ironically, the longer one consciously deliberates about one's preferences and judgments, the less accurate and predictive they become (Bargh and Chartrand 1999). Heuristics work best, however, when the decision maker is able to read environmental cues and change decision-making rules as contextual and task characteristics change (Payne, Bettman, and Johnson 1997).

Heuristic thinking is different from intuition in that heuristics depends on predetermined metarules that are category based and whole-pattern in structure (Hogarth and Kunreuther 1997). Intuition, on the other hand, is based on a broad constellation of past experiences, knowledge, skills, perceptions, and emotions. Intuition is not a formulated action plan predicated upon predetermined metarules, but rather is knowledge constructed whole-cloth in a sudden shift from the subconscious to conscious awareness. The intuitive mind often arrives at judgments or choices before consciously considering them (Bargh and Chartrand 1999). Heuristic and intuitive thinking, however, are similar in that both are ways in which decision makers can reach quick decisions in rapidly changing environments and in which complex situations can be managed with cognitive efficiency and dispatch (Krabuanrat and Phelps 1998).

Not surprisingly, heuristic decision making can be subject to a host of perceptual biases that can influence the quality and accuracy of decisions. The way in which such heuristics affects decision quality and accuracy, however, can vary from highly positive to highly negative. Much depends upon the quality and characteristics of a person's mental schemas, which give shape and meaning to prior experiences and which help one to understand and interpret new information. Three especially prominent heuristic biases described in the research include the availability heuristic, the representativeness heuristic, and the anchoring and adjustment heuristic. The availability heuristic prompts the decision maker to estimate the outcome probability of a potential decision when prior similar situations are readily available in memory. The ease by which past decision experiences can be brought to mind will influence the decision maker's approach to the current situation. When this happens, decision makers will default to the decision strategy used to solve a similar problem in the past (Gigerenzer and Todd 1999; Tenbrunsel et al. 1999).

The representativeness heuristic has less to do with ease of recollection than reacting in ways that approximate typical responses from the past. For example, Dan Charles's first impulse was to suspend Darla from school because suspension represented a typical response to similar situations in the past (e.g., "With this kind of behavior, we always respond in this way").

The anchoring and adjustment heuristic is the way in which decision makers establish an initial value, or baseline, from which to compare, assess, and select decision options. For example, in Dan's case, profanity in the classroom was first and foremost a suspendable offense. According to school policy, for the first offense, a one-day suspension was the minimum penalty. Thus, Dan had an anchor point from which to construct his final decision (e.g., "If I suspend Darla, my possible decision options begin with a one-day suspension and I can adjust from there").

Tenbrunsel et al. (1999, 70) provide a useful list of several other common biases that can influence the quality and accuracy of a heuristically derived decision.

1. Presumed associations: The overestimation of the probability that two events will co-occur (e.g., "If this happens, then that is sure to happen as well"). Most school administrators believe that if an exception is made in the application of a particular disciplinary rule, then a dangerous precedent will be set that will result in a wave of future challenges by students and parents if the rule is once again applied in subsequent situations. As a result, it is not uncommon to find rule-driven administrators who fail to see the nuances and unique situational factors that can influence student behavior. This kind of blind adherence to the rule relieves the administrator from the burdensome task of conducting thorough investigations at the expense of student welfare and due process.

2. Insensitivity to base rates: Often managers have a tendency to ignore base rates in assessing the likelihood of an event. For example, later in the day, when Marsha Mahan was describing her experience with the angry parent to a small group of colleagues at a district office principals' meeting, she was lamenting the fact that "It seems like every day I'm dealing with disgruntled parents." The reality was, however, that the frequency of conflicts with angry parents was far less frequent, but given the intense emotional toll extracted from such incidents, it seemed to Marsha that the base rate was much higher than it actually was.

3. Insensitivity to sample size: Managers often fail to appreciate the role of sample size when assessing the reliability of information. In addition, they often make generalizations about someone or a situation based on limited observations or attributes. This happens frequently in schools when generalized assumptions about such issues as student behavior, curriculum, or testing results are made on the basis on small numbers of events, cases, or participants.

4. Misconceptions of chance: Managers often overestimate statistical significance and underestimate the probability of randomness. Again, in schools, it is not uncommon for administrators to make causal inferences about certain events or behaviors that are only loosely or indirectly linked to the phenomenon at hand. For example, the failure of a highly touted reading curriculum to boost reading competency for disadvantaged students may have less to do with the curriculum itself than factors such as instructional methods, teacher expectations, teacher biases, or lack of support or resources at home.

5. Regression to the mean: Managers frequently fail to recognize that extreme events tend to regress to the mean. For example, in schools, administrators and parents often place far too much emphasis on trying to remedy one or two years of declining student test scores, when over a period of several years the school has shown an average annual increase. We are reminded of investor angst when the stock market takes a turn for the worse. When considered over a ten- to fifteen-year period, the market has made considerable growth.

6. Confirmation trap: It is not uncommon for managers to seek out, or give greater weight to, information that confirms long-established beliefs. Over time, Dan had had several run-ins with Darla Campbell. As a result, when Mr. Colt sent her to Dan's office following her defiant use of profanity, the situation initially confirmed Dan's growing belief that Darla was simply a trouble-maker who deserved punishment. Fortunately for Darla, Dan's intuition led him to make a phone call to the juvenile probation officer first, thus uncovering a far more serious problem and altering Dan's perception about Darla.

7. Hindsight: We all do this at one time or another when we overestimate the degree to which we would have predicted a correct outcome if given the chance. Of course, the reality often is that when managers are in the throes of complex decision making what may, in hindsight, seem self-evident was anything but that at the time the decision was being made.

8. Overconfidence: Again, it is not unusual for managers to overestimate the infallibility of their judgments or their abilities. Oftentimes, it is more important to know what questions to ask than what answers to provide.

Despite concerns about biases like those described above, there is growing empirical evidence that heuristics can be a useful cognitive tool for making reasonable decisions in complex situations where optimal logical/analytical strategies are not available, or are of limited usefulness (Gigerenzer and Todd 1999). It is important to note that the value of heuristic decision making is not in its ability to provide highly precise or accurate solutions, but in its ability to offer reasonable approximations or solutions with a minimum of effort or time. We still have much to learn in this area. For example, little is known about how school leaders use heuristic thinking when faced with varying conditions of emotional stress or task complexity. There is also little known about the comparative effectiveness of heuristic and normative decision approaches when levels of stress and task complexity change during decision making.

The next conceptual step in the review of naturalistic decision approaches would be a discussion of intuition. However, because the subject of intuition is so central to the organizing thesis of this book, we have devoted an entire chapter to its description and empirical bases. Before we turn our discussion to intuition, we take a closer look at various factors that can influence decision-making behavior in real-world settings.

THE EXPERT DECISION MAKER

The level of an individual's expertise in a given domain clearly influences decision-making approaches and decision quality. In general, experts use their experience to frame situations rapidly and accurately. They are particularly adept at predicting situational variables, remembering solutions that worked in the past, and adapting past solutions to meet the demands of the present situation (Beach 1997). Oftentimes, judgments are made based on prior concrete experiences that defy explanation. In fact, experts can't always articulate what it is they know. In addition, they prefer quick generalized responses versus detailed analysis. In crisis situations, their decision-making skills are so refined and efficient that their actions are almost automatic. They act in order to think (Bower 1998; Cuban 2001; Dreyfus and Dreyfus 1986). Neuropsychologists have determined that mental processes recede from consciousness with repeated use, or as they are no longer needed. Such processes become deeply embedded in the subcortical long-term memory structures of the brain, thus freeing up the neocortex to tackle new learning skills. However, when needed, these deeply embedded memories can spring into consciousness instantaneously (Bargh and Chartrand 1999).

Highly trained athletes are good examples of the act-think phenomenon. When Michael Jordan grabs a quickly thrown pass from behind the back of a teammate, deftly dodges one defender, and gyrates past another to sink an other-worldly, over-the-head slam dunk, there isn't a lot of analytical thinking going on. He just does what he does. According to Dreyfus and Dreyfus (1986), this type of Jordanesque thinking is neither rational nor irrational, but arational.

The arational thinker's performance is ongoing and nonreflective. Knowing what to do is based on mature and practical understandings without laborious logical/analytical thought processes. Moreover, the arational thinker heuristically chunks patterns of information into aggregate and manageable pieces. This allows him or her to see both the forest and the trees while developing deep situational understandings. Subsequent actions and behaviors are seen as fluid, highly responsive, and based on a deep repertoire of reasonably accurate schemas (Dreyfus and Dreyfus 1986; Lipshitz and Ben Shaul 1997).

Not surprisingly, studies reveal that expert decision makers tend to behave in ways that are different from the tightly prescribed steps of normative decision making. First, most experts tend to be highly action oriented early on in the problem-solving process. Second, they often conduct only cursory analyses of complex problems and rely on intuitive hunches in reaching solutions. Third, they frequently handle several problems simultaneously, each in various stages of completion (Wagner 1991). According to Dreyfus and Dreyfus (1986, 177), "Analytical decision making requires decomposed and decontextualized information that concerns beginners, not experts. For experts to engage in such rational processes, they must regress to seeing the world like an advanced beginner or even a novice."

Interestingly, it is the expert who is least likely to rely on deeply analytical decision-making processes. Novices, on the other hand, lack the deep contextual experiences and perspectives of the expert. Their repertoire of schemas, heuristic solutions, and intuitions are far less developed than those of the expert. As a result, novices must rely on deep deliberative and analytical thought processes when solving complex problems. The downside, of course, is that novice decisions are often less accurate and less efficient than those made by an expert.

Obviously, expertise alone doesn't explain the various factors that can influence a decision maker's behavior. Other factors such as biases, personality style, and orientation toward autocratic or participative decision making play a major role in how decisions are made and in the quality of their outcomes.

THE BIASED DECISION MAKER

The lack of precision, objectivity, and systematic approach during decision making is a recurring and disturbing theme throughout the literature. As we discussed earlier, when faced with complex problems, decision makers often don't know how to decide. According to Wagner

(1991, 164), "they tend to grope along with vague impressions about the nature of the problem, and with little idea about what the best possible solution would be until they find it." As a result, they frequently use heuristic approaches to simplify and speed up decision making (Harvey, Bearley, and Corkrum 1997). The danger with heuristic decision making is its lack of precision and tendency to manifest itself through the idiosyncratic biases of the decision maker. Of course, this is not altogether surprising since most decisions are the product of the interaction between the decision maker's perceptions and interpretations of problems and situations, and his values, goals, personality traits, needs, interests, and cognitive skills. When faced with a problem stimulus, these elements synthesize to form cognitive schemas or maps that help the decision maker make sense of things and reduce uncertainty (Harvey, Bearley, and Corkrum 1997; Pashiardis 1994; Tenbrunsel et al. 1999).

The decision-intelligent manager is one who can correctly identify the core issues of a problem and assign the proper weight to each problem element, while minimizing the influence of personal biases. However, this appears to be easier said than done. First, decision knowledge is rarely innocent. Rather, it is highly political and tainted in the way it is generated and by the context in which it is presented. Second, decision makers are best at reflecting upon past events, not at predicting or anticipating the future; when problems arise, they often find themselves in the position of having to act before they can think (March 1994).

In our review of the literature, we came across a number of other common decision-making biases beyond the heuristic biases described by Tenbrunsel et al. (1999). Some of these are heuristic and some are not. We were able to distill them into the following list of twenty-seven common biases (Beach 1997; Busenitz and Barney 1997; Hogarth and Kunreuther 1997; Kahneman and Tversky 1982; March 1994; Pashiardis 1994; Simon 1986; Tenbrunsel et al. 1999; Wagner 1991):

1. Decision makers tend to fixate on numerical representations of reality and attempt to stabilize numbers while developing a shared confidence in them.
2. Decision makers seek solutions that satisfice, rather than optimize, outcomes. As such, they will frequently choose alternatives that differ only incrementally from existing conditions.

3. Decision makers often attempt to maximize one aspect of a problem and satisfice on other aspects.

4. Decision makers often deliberately reduce organizational performance in order to manage their own expectations of the future and to avoid overachieving a targeted level of performance.

5. Decision makers frequently exaggerate their perceptions of control over the environment and of the influence of their actions.

6. Decision makers often discover what they expect to discover.

7. Decision makers often overestimate the probability of events that they have actually experienced, and underestimate the probability of events that might have occurred.

8. Decision makers typically possess an anthropocentric focus; that is, they tend to attribute events to the actions and intentional behavior of people and not to chance.

9. Decision makers tend to take action as the problem-solving process unfolds. They then use incremental assessments of these microactions.

10. Decision makers overestimate the frequency of highly publicized events and visa versa.

11. Decision makers place a disproportionate amount of attention and weight on information acquired early in the problem-solving process.

12. Decision makers often have a difficult time conceptualizing problems in ways that transcend their own experience.

13. Decision makers frequently give greater weight to the total number of successes than to the ratio of success to failure.

14. Decision makers tend to apply evaluation criteria inconsistently across different decisions.

15. Decision makers are unlikely to change a formed opinion.

16. Decision makers have trouble estimating the outcomes of nonlinear relationships.

17. Decision makers often continue to rely on obsolete solutions that worked before.

18. Decision makers are prone to wishful thinking.

19. Decision makers tend to be especially action oriented early on in the decision process.

20. Decision makers attempt to identify and understand the causal forces at work in a situation. As a result, blame and praise are often narrowly and incorrectly distributed.
21. Decision makers are often swayed by simple arguments that serve to resolve conflicts of choice. Similarly, they often rely on singular data, even if the data is scanty and unreliable.
22. Decision makers often make extreme predictions on the basis of information of relatively low reliability or validity. Similarly, they often frame problems on the basis of irrelevant information.
23. Different decision makers often construct different probability estimates for the same event.
24. Decision makers tend to place undue confidence in early trends.
25. Decision makers often overestimate the significance of decision outcomes.
26. Decision makers take greater risks in response to threats than to opportunities.
27. Decision makers often make a decision early on in the process and work to convince themselves that they are right.

There are undoubtedly many more biases that can contaminate decision accuracy and effectiveness. The sobering message is one that we have noted several times in this book: that decision making in complex organizations rarely conforms to rational expectations and analytical designs. Intangible human factors can simultaneously frustrate logic and analytical processing and stimulate creative thinking and novel approaches to complex problems.

DECISION STYLES AND BEHAVIORS

The ways in which decision makers decide have been described by Greenberg and Baron (1997) as falling within four preferred styles: directive, analytical, conceptual, and behavioral. These four categories are really derivatives of the kinds of personality style orientations first described by Carl Jung in the 1920s and later by Isabel Briggs-Myers and Katherine Cook Briggs. The directive decision maker is one who prefers simple, clear solutions that are rapidly made and based on established rules and procedures. Attending to interpersonal relationships, subtleties, and nuances in behavior are less important than getting the job done quickly, accurately, and impersonally. Although the directive decision maker may, from time to time, delegate responsibilities and decision tasks to other individuals or groups, he prefers to make most important decisions alone. When he does delegate, it is done with clear mandates and tight parameters.

The analytical decision maker thrives on deep, data-driven explorations of a complex problem. Decision making is a carefully crafted process based upon a thorough examination of all relevant information. Propositional thinking drives the analyst's quest to leave no stone unturned and no possibility left fallow. In a recent article in *Fortune* magazine on the dot-com sensation eBay, Eryn Brown (2002, 80) described how the vice president of marketing and merchandizing typically arrives at meetings carrying "piles of printouts and spreadsheets filled with pie charts and line graphs and tables detailing exactly how many people visited eBay in the past week, which items they looked at, which they bid on, which they bought, and which special promotions they seemed to like." That's an apt description of the quintessential analyst.

The conceptual decision maker is the visionary, the artist, and the humanist. Decisions are the product of creative and intuitive thinking situated within an orientation toward social awareness and concerns. Breaking rules, taking risks, and exploring uncharted territory are signature behaviors of the conceptual decision maker. Although conceptual thinking can be a highly effective approach to initiating bold-stroke organizational change, it can, without the checks and balances provided by the analyst, drive the organization into making high-risk and speculative decisions.

The behavioral decision maker's primary orientation is toward meeting the needs of coworkers. In doing so, the decision maker seeks ways to motivate individuals and groups and to enhance their feelings of empowerment. The behavioralist also understands the nature and role of conflict in complex organizations and the political machinations that often accompany complex or sensitive decisions.

Nearly forty-five years ago, Tannenbaum and Schmidt (1958) developed a popular taxonomy of decision-making styles that described a leader's behavior along a continuum that ranged from highly autocratic to highly participative. Unlike the four decision-making style orientations described by Greenberg and Baron, Tannenbaum and Schmidt's taxonomy describes the kinds of behaviors used by decision makers at various points along the continuum.

At one end of the continuum is the highly autocratic decision maker characterized as a person who unilaterally makes a decision and announces it. On the second step of the continuum is the leader who makes a decision but attempts to sell it to subordinates before implementing it. Next comes the leader who presents her ideas about a possible decision and then invites questions before settling on a final course of action. In the middle of the continuum is the leader who presents a tentative decision, but is open to changing or modifying it pending feedback from subordinates. Moving toward the participative end of the continuum is the leader who presents a problem to subordinates, gets suggestions, and then makes a decision. Next comes the leader who defines limits and decision parameters and requests that a group (of subordinates) make the decision. Finally, on the opposite end of the continuum, is the leader who permits group decision making within prescribed limits. We would suggest an eighth step, and that is the leader who delegates the task of problem identification and decision making to subordinate groups within general guidelines.

In reality, few decision makers possess only one style or operate from only one point along the continuum. Effective leaders possess qualities of each style and work their way back and forth along the continuum as the situation requires. Regardless of style orientation or decision behavior, leaders of complex organizations are generally influenced in their decision making by utilitarian (e.g., cost/benefit, expected utility), social (e.g., codes of behavior, external pressures, cultural values), or deontological (e.g., moral and ethical perspective) concerns (Beach 1997).

BARRIERS AND CONSTRAINTS

There is no universal sequence of events or strategies that leads to perfect decisions. In fact, determining the level of decision effectiveness is often a hotly contested issue in complex human service organizations and is complicated by differing frames of reference and differing perspectives about problems, solutions, and probable outcomes (Beach 1997; Pashiardis 1994).

When Josh Winters decided to override the recommendation of the teacher task force on how to best address the needs of the limited- and non-English speaking students, his decision was hailed as a great victory for Hispanic parents in the community. Conversely, it was highly criticized by teachers as a sign of his lack of respect and trust in their professional judgment. Was it a good decision or a bad decision? It all depends on one's perspective. Even three years down the road when the data substantiated the wisdom of Josh's bilingual program, there were still naysayers and critics who claimed that better results could have been achieved through the teachers' proposed plan.

This leads us to a number of conclusions about why trying to determine decision effectiveness is such a difficult task. First, decision outcomes are often delayed and not easily attributed to particular actions or choices made by the decision maker. For example, in the first year after Josh's bilingual program went into effect, there was a considerable level of concern about its effectiveness. Teacher commitment to the program was questionable; non-English speaking students still lagged far behind their English-fluent peers in all academic areas, and the new program cost the district over $250,000 in general fund revenue—money that many parents felt would have been better allocated to other programs and educational materials. After twelve months, even Josh began to have second thoughts about the wisdom of his decision. But three years later, Hispanic student test scores were up, teacher morale and commitment to the program had improved, and the start-up costs of the program had been assimilated into the ongoing expenditure budget of the district.

Second, variability in the environment can degrade the reliability of feedback about the decision. Once again, differing frames of reference and perspectives influence how decision makers receive and interpret feedback from organizational stakeholders. What information is factually accurate and objective? Whose perspective is to be trusted?

Third, there is no way to know for sure what the outcome would have been if another decision had been made. Thus, there is no accurate way to compare the relative effectiveness of the decision to other feasible alternatives. Even if the outcomes were positive, were they the best possible outcomes? Of course, hindsight is always 20/20.

Fourth, important decisions are often unique and provide little op-portunity for learning. For example, how many times will Josh have to confront the decision of whether to adopt, or not adopt, a teacher task force recommendation on the implementation of a program to meet the learning needs of non-English speaking students? Most likely only once. So what did he learn from the experience that will guide future impor-tant decisions? Probably very little that he could apply directly toward the solution of future problems. What he did learn was more likely re-lated to the subtle behaviors, personality styles, and power relationships among parents and teachers. He may have also learned the importance of setting parameters when asking employees to participate in group de-cision making. Such information might be useful in the future—but then again, it might not. It all depends upon the situation and the par-ticipants (Tenbrunsel et al. 1999).

We know that a number of factors such as time constraints, political pressures, quality of information, contextual or environmental attributes, leader-member relationships, power plays, task structure, and constituent needs, values, and preferences can influence and impede decision making (East 1997; Greenberg and Baron 1997). Other variables such as the de-cision maker's fear of making mistakes, avoidance of conflict, ethical or moral dilemmas, or the need to exert a high level of cognitive effort can likewise impede decision making (Payne, Bettman, and Johnson 1997).

The degree of organizational slack and resistance to change can also create barriers to decision making. Slack refers to the excess of resources available to an organization. Such resources could be fiscal, human, in-formational, or physical. Excess resources often decrease a diligent search for problem solutions and decision-making processes. Under slack conditions, organizations and their leaders can become overconfident and sluggish in response to problems or opportunities (Pashiardis 1994).

Vroom and Jago's (1978) model of participative decision making has been a popular method of tracing the relationship between certain con-textual variables and the need to involve others in decision processes. The model contains eight important factors that can constrain a leader's ability to make autocratic decisions. The leader's incremental analysis of each of the eight factors produces a decision path that leads to a contin-uum of decision-making approaches from highly autocratic to highly collaborative. Under the model, the type of decision process used by a leader is mediated by the quality requirement of the decision, the level of subordinate acceptance required, the amount and quality of information possessed by the leader, the structure of the problem, the alignment of subordinate and organizational goals, the likelihood of subordinate conflict over the decision, and the amount of information possessed by subordinates.

We turn next to the examination of intuition and its role in organizational decision making. We have included in our discussion a review of important literature in the field of intuition and the results of our research with public school principals on how they use intuition to solve complex problems.

SUMMARY

We have discussed several important factors related to problem solving and decision making. Formal research in the fields of organizational problem solving and decision making emerged during the last half of the twentieth century. Early efforts to understand and predict certain economic variables and decisions evolved into more recent efforts to understand decision making at all levels of organizational leadership and in multiple environmental contexts.

Understanding and framing problems is a highly subjective process and can vary considerably among leaders and experts in a given field or occupation. In human service organizations like schools, problems are often highly complex, ambiguous, novel, dynamic, and nontransparent. Most complex problems defy efforts to apply highly analytical or rational decision-making approaches. As a result, leaders often rely on heuristic shortcuts in order to manage both the complexity and steady stream of problems confronted during a typical workday.

Early research in decision making focused largely on efforts to develop normative models that could be broadly applied to managers and leaders in all types of organizations. Although the sophistication of normative models progressed throughout the last quarter of the twentieth century, efforts to develop a uniform theory or paradigm of rational decision making have been unsuccessful. Instead, researchers have refocused their efforts toward better understanding the situational and contextual variables that can influence decision making in complex organizations. Over the past twenty years, a subtle shift occurred toward conducting research that describes how decisions are actually made rather than how decisions should be made. This new form of naturalistic decision research has spawned a great deal of interest in studying qualitative aspects of decision making, including limited rationality, heuristics, and intuition.

Finally, the quality and effectiveness of decisions can be greatly influenced by various decision-maker biases, levels of expertise, decision styles, and environmental/contextual barriers or constraints. Such factors underscore the fact that leaders of complex human service organizations like schools must rely on subtle, efficient, and idiosyncratic decision-making approaches. The use of intuition is one such approach that has gained interest among researchers in the field of organizational decision making.

3

UNDERSTANDING INTUITION

It should be noted that the seeds of wisdom that are to bear fruit in
the intellect are sown less by critical studies and learned mono-
graphs than by insights, broad impressions, and flashes of intuitions.

—Carl von Clauswitz

DEFINITIONS AND DESCRIPTIONS

Just what is this phenomenon we call intuition? In our varied conversations
with school principals there seemed to be a common, if not vague, sense
that it had to do with feeling and knowing. Some used the term intuition
and instinct interchangeably; some framed it as a kind of common sense;
some described it as a spiritual experience, and others equated it with a
hunch. Some principals believed that their intuitions provided highly reliable "truths," some saw it as one of several decision-making tools, and a few
argued that it was unscientific and fallible. In this section, we discuss the
meaning of intuition and the characteristics of the intuitive experience.

Derived from the Latin term *intueri* (to look at, look toward, to contemplate), the precise meaning of the term intuition continues to be the

subject of wide interpretation (Brown 1990; Mishlove 2001). Although intuition is often a very unique experience, we offer some common themes among its many definitions. To begin, intuition is a phenomenon hidden in the subconscious. It is a product of both factual and feeling cues and a form of associative thinking that "integrates knowledge, experience, intelligence, and respect for the unknown into responsive and productive decision making" (Agor 1986; Glaser 1995, 43). Intuition is also a perceptual phenomenon, rather than an interpretive or evaluative one. It resides primarily in the repository of implicit memories that are maintained and governed by various structures of the primitive brain (e.g., limbic system). Intuitive decisions and judgments are not made on the basis of an explicit conscious reasoning process and are, instead, automatic responses that have bypassed the brain pathways and networks responsible for conscious thought (Gopnick and Schwitzgebel 1998; Hogarth 2001; Landry 1991).

For the purposes of our research, we defined intuition as an immediate, novel, and striking synthesis of what was previously unrelated or loosely related that springs into conscious awareness without the mediation of logic or rational thought processes (Arvidson 1997, 43; Boucouvales 1997, 7; Laughlin 1997, 11). Or, as Mishlove (2001, 1) states "Knowing without knowing how you know."

Intuition is not an instinct, an insight, or an educated guess. Residing just below the conscious level, it is a stratum of awareness consisting of a mix of psychological constructs like imagery and narrative formation, grounded in experience. Whereas an instinct is a primitive, automatic, and unconscious life-sustaining impulse (e.g., fight-or-flight response, sexual drive), intuition is a thought-generating process that springs into consciousness without the activation of logic or rational thinking (Boucouvales 1997; Harbort 1997; Landry 1991; Laughlin 1997; Rowan 1986). Insight, on the other hand, is similar to intuition in that it comes quickly to mind. However, insight, unlike most intuitions, is the result of a conscious effort to analyze, assess, or evaluate information already known. It is the end product of a conscious attempt to resolve a problem. Its result may be highly accurate and precise. Intuitions, on the other hand, are most often approximate and often arrive in the haze of problems cloaked in ambiguity and uncertainty (Hogarth 2001).

Intuition provides a number of important functions in our lives. First, it can reveal an answer to a perplexing problem. It can also provide a sense of creativity through the emergence of a new idea or novel solution. In some cases, intuition offers an evaluative perspective that a particular approach or solution is good or bad (i.e., has met certain quality criteria). In other cases, intuition may act as a predictor of future events or decision outcomes. There may be an operational function to intuition in which a sense of direction is revealed. Finally, intuition may provide a sense of illumination, or self-realization, that raises one's level of awareness. It is important to note that these are not mutually exclusive functions. A single intuition may cross over one or many functions (Morris 1990).

Daniel Cappon (1994, 178) lists several attributes that are commonly found among especially intuitive people. These are highly interrelated and may overlap or represent particular intuitions at particular times. Individual attributes will vary in frequency and intensity among different people and in relation to certain problem or task characteristics. We have identified them as "abilities." As such, they may include elements that are trained (or learned skills), associated with one or more forms of intelligence, or innate (e.g., genetically endowed).

1. Perceptual synthesis—The ability to put disparate ideas, images, objects, or experiences together in ways that reveal new understandings or insights.
2. Recognition—The ability to match memories of an experience, event, or thought to a current (or predicted) image, experience, or event. In other words, to recognize similarities and differences.
3. Finding things—The ability to discriminate between the important and unimportant and/or the ability to sort through complex and shifting perceptual fields to identify a particular object, image, or memory.
4. Estimation of time—The ability to know when to act or not act. A sense of timing that involves the ability to place planned events or behaviors within a temporal context that will maximize their chances of success.
5. Sense of the whole—The ability to see beyond the fine details of an object, event, or image and to see how the sum of its aggregate parts fits within or influences the environment.

6. Quick memory—The ability to retrieve memories of past events, to find associations between unrelated yet similar memories, and to synthesize memories, thoughts, and images into new understandings.
7. Passive and active imagination—The ability to construct creative or novel ideas, images, or solutions through conscious and unconscious cognition. This includes the capacity for playful thinking and the ability to see through foreground images and into the subtle and nuanced background elements of an event, image, or idea.
8. Foresight and hindsight—The ability to "see" forward and backward in time in ways that either predict or assess the effects of a particular event, behavior, or decision outcome.
9. Knowing the unknown—The ability to construct meaning from objects, events, or images that may appear to be unrelated or whose meaning is unclear.
10. Knowing why—The ability to grasp the causal relationships between certain behaviors, events, objects, or images and the progenitive factors responsible for them.
11. Optimal solution—The ability to choose from among multiple options that which best resolves a given problem or dilemma. This requires the ability to sort and sift through the chaff and clutter that often accompany complex problems and decision-making efforts.
12. Optimal use or application of a discovery—The ability to use a new idea, image, or object in a practical way.
13. Optimal matching of things and people—The ability to recognize the symbiotic potential when certain objects, images, events, or individuals are combined or when a conjunctive effort among them is facilitated.
14. Knowing the meaning of things—The ability to interpret objects, events, or images into understandable representations of reality. This may include the ability to make logical connections or the ability to make inferences based on a noetic sense.
15. Quick eyes—The ability to read people, the surrounding environment, or situational contexts. Subtle cues and nuanced behaviors are quickly recognized and interpreted in ways that increase one's understandings of certain behaviors, decision outcomes, or environmental dynamics.

These fifteen attributes are not mutually exclusive, and they may or may not represent a particular intuitive experience. Although they may be products of a highly analytical mind, they best represent the kinds of abilities possessed by intuitive thinkers. Because these are cognitive qualities, there may be ways that one can nurture and develop them (Hogarth 2001). We will say more about that later.

Most intuitive experiences fall within one of two overarching characteristics: discovery and verification. The first, discovery, is a mental representation of a new or innovative approach, solution, or response to a complex problem. It often involves a feeling of synthesis, where the pieces of a problem suddenly take shape or fit together in a new way. Think back to our earlier example of Josh Winters and his struggle to develop a new bilingual program for his school. If we were to track Josh's intuitive experience, we would find that he actually experienced both forms. His first intuition was that the proposal offered by the teachers would be a bad choice for the school. With enough time and conscious reflection, he could eventually articulate the basis for his intuitive feeling, but given the immediacy of the upcoming school board meeting, he had to rely on his gut. Josh's first intuition was a form of verification. He didn't have a solution yet, but he suddenly "knew" that what the teachers had proposed wouldn't fly.

Josh's second intuition, however, came later. Following a long and tortuous path through an exploration of the theories and models of effective bilingual programs, Josh found himself nearly as confused about what to do as he did when he started. He had a head full of ideas, propositions, and models, but they were simply a collection of facts and perceptions that were hopelessly tangled in his mind. Just before the school board meeting, Josh took a walk to clear his head. For Josh, removing himself from the physical, as well as emotional, context of the district office helped him to relax and to settle his mind. For some reason, walking in and of itself seemed to help him think better. About half way through his walk, Josh's mind began to wander. As it did, various memories, images, and thoughts emerged. Some seemed to spring out of nowhere, triggered by the smell of freshly cut grass or the sound of the breeze blowing through the trees. One thought seemed to tumble into another. Some took him back in time to when he was a boy, others to various attitudes and perspectives that he held strongly as a professional educator. Oddly, he was remembering the stunning view of the red rock cliffs behind his parents' Sedona, Arizona, home when he suddenly discovered the right way to go. It simply came to him out of nowhere. He didn't have all of the specific details worked out yet (remember, intuitions are largely approximate), but he had a sense of certainty about the shape of a program that would best meet student needs. Josh felt excited and energized. His thoughts now began to consciously sort through the details and creatively construct new mental images.

As with Josh, it is common for people to experience a creative aspect to the intuitive impulse that produces a mental image, idea, emotional feeling, or physical sensation (Agor 1986; Cappon 1994; Laughlin 1997). The intuitive experience can also produce a noetic awareness described by Mishlove (2001, 1) as, "Knowing without knowing how you know." Like Josh, most people describe the intuitive experience as a sudden flash or an instant of inspiration. For some, however, intuitions can come in staccato bursts as their thought processes move from analytical to intuitive modes and back again. Some people find that their intuitions are generally most helpful at the tail end of a conscious problem-solving effort. It is also quite common for people to actually "see" a mental image of the intuitive solution (e.g., a mind's-eye picture of what the outcome of a certain decision would look like). In fact, because visualization correlates so strongly with intuition, it is believed that conscious efforts to visualize problem solutions and contextual scenarios actually enhance intuitive ability (Hogarth 2001). We will say more about this later.

Although the experience of intuition is highly subjective and may vary widely between individuals, it has generally been divided into four categories: physical, emotional, mental, and spiritual. The first category, physical, is characterized by various bodily sensations such as elevated heart rate, sweating, warmth, tingling sensation, visceral gut feeling, high energy, etc. The emotional may be experienced as feelings of certainty, calmness, joy, anxiety, anticipation, etc. The mental may be represented by certain images or ideas, patterns of perceptions, or the formulation of new theories and hypotheses. And the fourth, spiritual, is often represented in the form of revelations, illuminations, and transpersonal experiences (Agor 1986; Boucouvales 1997; Landry 1991). Such experiences may overlap and may vary from one intuitive event to another or from one person to another.

No matter how an intuition is experienced, it is almost always driven by an automatic emotional response to some internal or external stimuli and is shaped by the conscious feeling produced by the emotion. The role of emotions in the intuitive experience is critical primarily because of their ability to generate autonomic responses without corresponding awareness (Dickmann and Stanford-Blair 2002; Damasio 1999). According to Hogarth (2001, 61), "feelings when not connected consciously to a particular emotion or affect, are often experienced as intuitions." As we will discuss further in chapter 4, neural circuitry in the brain triggers autonomic responses to emotional stimuli before the conscious brain-mind has had an opportunity to evaluate and modify its effect.

There is little question that intuition represents a shift in consciousness. One way to conceptualize the conscious effect of an intuition is to examine it through the Field Theory of Consciousness (Arvidson 1997). The field theory describes three dimensions of consciousness that shift dialectically as stimuli from external and internal (e.g., outside and within the body) environments change. The first dimension is called the theme, or the focus of attention at any given time. The second dimension is the thematic field, or the relevant context within which the theme exists. The third dimensions is called the margin, or the collection of stimuli that are copresented within the theme and thematic field, but are largely irrelevant to the theme itself. When attention shifts, the theme and thematic fields reverse themselves. Prominent parts of the thematic field bind together in a coherent synthesis—a sort of "zooming out" process that reveals a new sense of the whole.

For example, as I type this manuscript, my attention is riveted on the computer screen and notes before me. These represent, for the moment, the thematic dimension of my consciousness. My computer sits on a very large desk that is covered with a variety of objects (e.g., printer, plant, Coke bottle, books, lamp). I am aware of the fact that I am sitting in a fairly large and somewhat warm room. The warmth is just about at the edge of my comfort zone, and I'm thinking about turning on the fan. Since my window is slightly open, I am subtly aware of the wind blowing through the tall grass of the field next to my home. Birds chirp and the sound of an airplane drones in the distance. There is the sensation of sunlight and of open space somewhere beyond the proximal presence of my computer. Although these objects are not focal to the tasks of typing and note reading, they are part of the thematic field that surrounds me and to one degree or another exert subtle effects on what I do and how well.

Suddenly, I'm aware of a cow mooing on the hill behind the house. My attention shifts as I gaze out the window in response. In an instant, what was once a part of my thematic field has become the focus of my attention, and the computer is now part of the background images that surround me. The stimulus for this shift in consciousness was external and concrete. I heard a sound, recognized it as cowlike, and turned my head in a conscious effort to confirm its proper identification.

An intuition also reflects a shift in the field of consciousness. It does so not through conscious effort, as in responding to a mooing cow, but through the unconscious synthesis of external and internal stimuli at the moment of solution. That is, at the moment upon which an intuitive thought shifts from the subconscious to the conscious, a parallel shift in the field of consciousness occurs. That which was but a moment ago part of the mind's background thematic field has moved into the foreground of consciousness as the subconscious cognitive processes completes the synthesis of multiple internal and external stimuli.

Intuitions are shaped primarily by our environmental and cultural experiences. This process begins in infancy and continues throughout our lives. Although researchers admit that genetic factors contribute in important and idiosyncratic ways to our cognitive orientations and abilities, the degree to which they influence our intuitions is unknown. Genetic and environmental factors notwithstanding, our capacity to develop, modify, and make use of our intuitions lasts a lifetime.

Our intuitions, however, tend to be domain specific. That is to say, each of us experiences intuitive thoughts, but they are most frequent and reliable in areas with which we have a great deal of experience or expertise. Over time, patterns of experiences reinforce and strengthen the neural circuitry of the brain so that less and less conscious effort is needed to process and remember the elements of an experience or the tasks necessary to perform a particular skill. In fact, we are generally not aware that we have developed a domain specific intuition until it actually occurs. As a result, certain behaviors become automatic, or nearly so. Driving a car is a good example of this. Experienced drivers can carry on cell phone conversations or daydream about the family vacation to Hawaii and yet still manage to steer the car, accelerate or decelerate as needed, and scan for danger. They seem to be controlling the vehicle without much conscious effort. In fact, the skills needed to drive have become so deeply ingrained in memory that the brain-mind-body has learned to react to subtle environmental cues and stimuli without the need to consciously reason through each movement or each new piece of environmental information (Hogarth 2001).

As we become expert at a physical or cognitive task, we become less dependent on analytical forms of problem solving and decision making. Experts tend to process information by chunking information into large patterns. They often construct solutions to complex problems by inductively (and often intuitively) piecing together patterns of data and applying responses appropriate to their emerging interpretations of the problem's structure and context. Experts also have a vast reservoir of mental images, schemas, and emotions pertaining to particular skills, particular problems, and solutions to past problems; the larger the reservoir, the greater the possibility of combining and retrieving mental images, and applying them to existing problems and dilemmas. For the expert, much of this work is done subconsciously. In fact, most of the brain's work is performed subconsciously. As we will discuss in chapter 4, the subconscious mind is a highly dynamic and continuously active mechanism that works to filter external and internal stimuli, to activate certain somatic responses, and to ensure that subsequent behaviors are aligned with the contextual demands of the environment (Damasio 1994, 1999; Hogarth 2001; Dreyfus and Dreyfus 1986).

For the expert, domain specific intuitions come more easily than for novices. The novice, in contrast, must subject the vast neural circuitry of the brain to repeated and patterned behaviors. In the early stages of skill development, this takes a great deal of cognitive energy and analytical thought. Unlike experts, novices often solve problems deductively by identifying a specific goal (or desired outcome) and then working backward through the details of the problem to construct a solution.

Interestingly, there are neurophysiological markers that reveal how expertise in a particular domain influences brain activity. Brain scan imagery has shown that certain areas of the brain's neocortex (i.e., the outer brain's executive/rational processing center) are highly activated when new skills are being acquired. The brain region that is engaged in the conscious effort to learn the new task actually lights up on the monitor. However, over time, as the task becomes increasingly automatic, the same regions of the brain grow dimmer. The mental images required to perform the task are driven deep into the limbic structures of the brain such as the amygdala, hippocampus, anterior cingulate gyrus, and the cerebellum, thus freeing up the outer cortex to learn new tasks and skills. It is believed by neurophysiologists and neuropsychologists that intuition is an experientially based and subconscious neurobiological phenomenon that is the product of a long evolutionary process to enhance human problem solving and decision making. As such, a highly experienced or expert principal has at his fingertips a highly evolved response system that allows for quick, efficient, and reasonably accurate decision making (Damasio 1994; Ratey 2001).

For years, there has been a long-standing debate over the role of gender and intuitive ability. Most of us are aware of the old saying "woman's intuition." Is it true? Are women innately more intuitive than men? Although we will address this question in more depth in chapter 5, Agor (1986) and Hogarth (2001) suggest that this may be true. For example, women tend to be more responsive than men in expressing emotions and feelings. They also seem to do better at decoding nonverbal signals and cues from other people. As problem solvers, they tend to rely on more comprehensive strategies for processing information that involve looking for details, nuances, subtleties, and deeper meaning. Men, in contrast, are less expressive emotionally, seek quick and efficient solutions to problems, and focus more on limited and highly focused information. Because women seem to be more attuned to emotional and nonverbal cues, it follows that their intuitions are more frequent and accurate with problems that contain such elements. There is also evidence that intuitions come more readily when the mind is open to unexplored possibilities and spontaneous opportunities. Are men more closed minded than women? We are not prepared to say with certainty, but we suspect that in general, women may be more comfortable than men in the use of intuitive thinking.

According to Hogarth (2001), two fundamental kinds of knowledge domains underlie human cognition: deliberate and tacit. The deliberate system is that aspect of conscious thought that carefully analyzes, interprets, and manages information and plans subsequent responses. The tacit system is nondeliberative, subconscious, quick, efficient, and is constructed upon acquired knowledge and experience. Intuition falls within this system. It is important to note that tacit and deliberate systems operate on a broad continuum. Rarely do people think or resolve problems while operating solely from one end of the continuum. These systems weave in and out of our thought processes with differing frequencies and levels of intensity.

The use of deliberate or tacit systems by themselves cannot determine whether a decision or problem-solving effort will turn out well. It all depends on the nature of the learning structure. In other words, how good was the information used in forming the acquired skill or experience? It also depends upon the type of problem. Problems that are highly structured, routine, and subject to a small set of decision rules lend themselves best to analytical approaches. Novel, complex, and ambiguous problems exemplify the domain of intuitive thinking. Finally, the effectiveness of an intuitive decision also depends upon the assessment of the decision as it compares to some normative or baseline standard. For a decision to be judged as good requires a threshold standard of quality. With the kind of complex and ill-defined problems encountered in most human service organizations, such thresholds can be highly subjective, if they exist at all. Ironically, if the criteria upon which a good decision can be made are framed around analytic/deliberate models, the quality of an intuitive decision can only be as good as that produced through analysis (Hogarth 2001). In assessing the quality of an intuitive decision, one must also consider the risks and costs of error, time constraints, and the need for precision. As most of us who have occupied leadership positions in schools know, a good decision is rarely a perfect one.

Hogarth (2001) refers to learning structures as "wicked" or "kind" (89). Wicked learning structures are, as it might sound, constructed upon biased, faulty, inaccurate, irrelevant, or incomplete information. Kind learning structures are constructed upon accurate, clear, relevant, or complete information. Predictably, intuitive decisions that are based upon wicked learning structures most often turn out poorly. Even experts occasionally exhibit behaviors unintentionally shaped by the wicked/kind dilemma. Take, for example, a teacher who, at the start of each school year, routinely groups certain minority students into peer support teams in order to facilitate feelings of cultural identity and the implementation of targeted reading strategies. The teacher's intentions may be honorable, but the grouping strategy is based on the faulty assumption that all minority students are in need of social adjustment and specialized reading assistance.

In another example, a highly experienced and analytical science teacher whose knowledge of human genetics is based on forty-year-old college course work has framed her expertise around a "wicked learning structure." Even though the information she conveys to students is seriously outdated, students and administrators may highly rate her performance in the classroom. To the uninformed, she may be considered an expert in the field.

Time itself can introduce wickedness into learning structures that once were kind. For example, the perceptions and memories of even the most accomplished surgeon, teacher, or engineer can be modified over time in ways barely perceptible. The lack of practice in a particular aspect of one's craft can slowly diminish the neural pathways that form the mental image and somatic representation of that skill. The reconstruction of a little-used skill that has been stored away in the recesses of one's long-term memory can contain errors, distortions, omissions, or unsubstantiated additions. Hindsight and retrospect can be powerful modifiers of our deeply held memories as we inject new emotions or fresh perspectives into our thinking. Over time, elements of our professional experience and areas of expertise can also be colored by subtle (or overt) biases and stereotypes that we have developed over the years (Dreyfus and Dreyfus 1986; Kahneman and Tversky 1982). Our continuous interaction with the world produces new mental images, new thoughts, and new neural pathways. We are reminded of the old saying that "practice doesn't make perfect, practice makes permanent." In other words, bad habits and wicked learning structures can contaminate both conscious rational thought and intuitive thinking.

The quality of a learning structure also includes ethical behaviors and personal motivations. Good information put to bad ends is a problem that has not been extensively addressed in the empirical literature on decision making. Even though one may be highly expert in a particular domain, highly intuitive, and a highly effective decision maker, a decision made with unethical intentions and selfish motives is based upon a wicked learning structure. Some popular authors on the subject of intuition have argued that by its very nature intuition is inherently good. Other authors, however, maintain that an intuition should be judged by what it is applied to rather that by what it is in itself (Cappon 1994). History reminds us that men like Adolf Hitler and Joseph Stalin were, at times, perversely effective decision makers who based their judgments and personal intuitions on extremely wicked learning structures.

Thinking about intuition, its origins, its effects, and its effectiveness is not a recent phenomenon. In fact, people have discussed and debated the meaning of intuition for centuries. In the following section, we provide a brief history of intuition in an effort to provide a framework for understanding how it has evolved as a concept, as a cognitive phenomenon, and as a subject of interest to modern-day scholars.

INTUITION THROUGH THE AGES: A BRIEF HISTORY

As a subject of serious research, intuition continues to contend with a long tradition of Western skepticism about nonrational forms of cognition (Owens 1995). Nevertheless, scholarly debates about the meaning, experience, and usefulness of intuitive thinking extend many centuries back in time. Its literary and conceptual foundations are broad and can be found in the writings of Plato, Socrates, Descartes, Spinoza, Kant, Croce, Jung, the New Testament, the Talmud, the Torah, and in the principles of Confucianism, Buddhism, Hinduism, Taoism, and Zen (Brown 1990; Mishlove 2001; Morris 1990).

For centuries, much of the thinking about intuition centered on notions of divine inspiration. Intuitions were viewed as "prophetic endowments from God" and were considered to be beyond the capacities of the common person (Green 2001, 1). In ancient times, Pythagoreans and Neoplatonists attempted to draw comparisons between mathematical intuitions and intuitions held by mystics and visionaries. However, efforts to link intuitive thinking to mathematical principals were largely lost during the Middle Ages. Until the dawn of the Age of Enlightenment in the early seventeenth century, intuition was widely believed to be a godlike property that could be ascribed to only a select few divinely inspired individuals.

The Age of Enlightenment spawned new and fresh debates about man and his place in the larger scheme of things. Rationalist philosophers such as René Descartes and Benedict Spinoza, British empiricists such as John Locke and Francis Bacon, and reformed rationalists such as Immanuel Kant began to peel away the veil of religious dogma from conceptions about truth and knowledge. The Cartesian rationalists of Descartes's era argued that man was a rational being who could discern truth through reason, certain mathematical principles, and deductive thinking. Although some knowledge could be acquired through the senses, ultimate truth could only be determined a priori (i.e., innately and intuitively reasoned). The empiricists, in contrast, argued that all ideas could be traced back to one's experiences, sense perceptions, and emotions and that truth was best revealed through the process of inductive thinking. Importantly, these conceptions of knowledge and truth provided the foundations of modern philosophical inquiry. Such debates also began to identify and clarify the multiple dimensions of human thought and knowledge construction.

Among the most notable contributions of the period was the sense that intuition represented a higher dimensional space of the human experience (rather than metaphysical) and a notion that intuitions could be traced to experiences, sensory perceptions, and emotions. The Kantian perspective was that "through intuition we construct and maintain our sense of space and time, of personal identity, of the truth of things, and of beauty and goodness" (Mishlove 2001, 1).

However, conceptions of intuition as a noetic property distinct from scientific rationalism and religious connotation didn't begin to take hold until the late nineteenth-century theories of philosopher/psychologist William James. James conjectured that intuitions were really rooted in the human nervous system and as part of a complex tapestry of neural responses to life experiences and subconsciously formed mental images. James's views were not widely endorsed by his peers, nor were they honed against the more robust twentieth-century conceptions of the human brain-mind. However, they paved the way for a new way of thinking about intuition as a neuropsychological construct and a foundational component of human cognition (Wozniak 2001).

In keeping with the popular Darwinian ideas of the time, James's theory framed intuition as an evolutionary adaptation to thousands of years of human development and environmental demands. The essence of the argument was that man, like most surviving species, relied on certain genetically endowed subconscious instincts to survive (e.g., hunger, flight/fright response, sexual drive, social grouping). As we know, man's primitive instinctual brain continued to evolve into a complex organ that could independently reason, problem solve, contemplate, infer, and predict. Intuition emerged as a uniquely human synthesis of the subconscious and rational mind and was designed to both facilitate problem solving (hence survival) and to enhance the acquisition of knowledge when confronted with ambiguous, novel, or stressful environments (Damasio 1994; Green 2001).

The twentieth century saw a growing interest in the role of intuitive knowledge as a problem-solving process, as a subconscious element of human cognition, and as a neuropsychological function of the brain-mind. In the early 1900s, psychologist Carl Jung gave respectability to the concept of intuition and maintained that it was a distinctive element of human psychological types. Other contemporary researchers and scholars such as Weston Agor, Jerome Bruner, Daniel Cappon, Stewart Dreyfus, Daniel Goleman, Robin Hogarth, and Jonathan Schooler have come to accept intuition as an important component of human cognition, decision making, and constructivist learning theory. Although our notions of intuition have progressed dramatically in recent years, vestiges of anachronistic thinking about intuition remain. It is probably accurate to say, however, that for serious researchers and scholars, intuition has begun to take its rightful place among the varied and immutable dimensions of human cognition. We will talk more about twentieth-century developments in intuition later in the chapter.

Next, however, we turn to three important questions. Why is intuition so important? Who needs it? How has it become such an important part of research on complex decision making?

THE NEED FOR INTUITIVE DECISION MAKING

Intuition is an extraordinary cognitive attribute. All of us have it and all of us use it, yet it remains a mysterious and little understood phenomenon. Its role in the study of executive decision making has only recently become a topic of serious inquiry by researchers. The need for intuitive thinking among leaders and managers is underscored by the increasing complexity of organizational life, turbulent and ever-changing workplace environments, demands for leadership responsiveness and decisiveness, and the proliferation of instantaneous and virtually unlimited sources of information (Cappon 1994; Landry 1991; Owens 1995).

Today, a diminishing number of complex human service organizations in America operate according to the tightly structured and closed-system principles endorsed by scientific rationalists of the early twentieth century. Increasingly, complex human service organizations like schools are becoming organic and dynamic entities best characterized by open-system relationships with the outside world, fluid and flexible responses to problems and demands, and flatter hierarchies in which bottom-up input from empowered employees provides a reciprocal exchange of critical information, creative ideas, and skills (Agor 1986).

These ideas are not new. Nearly fifty years ago, Edwards Demming's notions about workplace cooperation, employee empowerment, flattened hierarchies, shared vision, and transformational leadership helped to propel Japanese industries to the forefront of product innovation and quality. Ironically, it wasn't until the 1980s that American managers and business gurus came to fully appreciate the power of such enlightened approaches in the shaping of organizational structures, in managing environmental influences, in enhancing workforce productivity and satisfaction, and in helping us think about how such approaches influence managerial decision making in complex open systems (Owens 1995).

A former superintendent of one of California's largest public school districts once told us that modern-day complex organizations do one of two things: they move forward or they fall behind. As soon as an organization believes that it has reached the pinnacle of success, it becomes complacent and is quickly surpassed by other, more highly motivated competitors. As a result, proactive leaders have become increasingly action oriented and concerned with keeping pace with marketplace demands and technological innovations. Such preoccupations require new, more agile ways of thinking and problem solving. Organizational systems once dependent upon ponderous analytical approaches to decision making and change have had to adapt to a pervasive culture of short-term demands for increased corporate profits, product quality, and decisions that are made quickly and efficiently.

Author and leadership expert Warren Bennis (1989) notes that in the modern era listening to one's inner voice has become a critically important, yet often overlooked, aspect of leadership. He states, "Our culture needs more right-brained qualities, needs to be more intuitive, conceptual, synthesizing, and artistic. CEOs must have both administrative and imaginative gifts" (102). Bennis's imperative underlies a much broader dimension of intuition and its contribution to humankind. Intuition has been the catalyst of "an enormous number of sensory and dialectic discoveries and inventions in all the creative fields of culture, science, mathematics, technology, social and humanistic disciplines, philosophy, art, religion, and ethics" (Sorokin 2001, 2). Testaments to the influence of intuitive thinking on the shaping of new technologies, the arts, and other domains of knowledge can be found in statements by many prominent twentieth-century pioneers such as Albert Einstein, Jonas Salk, Carl Jung, Paul Dirac, and Bill Gates. For example, Nobel prize-winning physicist Paul Dirac was motivated less by the structural science of mathematics than by its beauty and elegance. Albert Einstein firmly believed that his intuitions were largely responsible for his ability to make important conceptual leaps that allowed him to develop the theories that led the world into the nuclear age. Medical pioneer Jonas Salk once said, "It is always with excitement that I wake up in the morning wondering what my intuition will toss up to me like gifts from the sea." Perhaps Nobel prize-winning physicist Max Planck (2001) best summarized the point. He said, "Scientists must have a vivid intuitive imagination, for new ideas are not generated by deduction, but by artistically creative imagination."

According to twentieth-century sociologist Sorokin (2001, 2), intuition also provides the basis for "truth of reason and sensory experience." At the heart of Sorokin's argument is the reality that neither truth of reason nor sensory experience is easily measured or indexed according to some fixed or quantifiable standard. Even in the aftermath of rigidly applied rules of calculative analysis, the ultimate test of decision quality uses as its template human judgment and idiosyncratic perceptions and beliefs about what is good and what is not. Extending this proposition, it can also be said that good decisions do not always result in good outcomes (Baron 2000). When a decision maker adheres closely to normative models of decision making, it can be said that he has made a good decision. The quality of that decision, however, is subject to the subjective scrutiny of the individuals who are influenced by it. And, as we all know, human judgment is rarely pure. Rather, it is strongly influenced by a complex ensemble of the personality traits, beliefs, values, cultural patterns, perceptions, emotions, moods, needs, intelligence, experiences, and skills of the beholder.

There is a neuropsychological argument that can be made for intuitive thinking. This argument is framed around two important ideas described by neurologist Antonio Damasio (1994). First, the cognitive framework by which humans make decisions is structured around a long unfolding evolutionary process that, at its core, seeks to enhance adaptability to changing environmental conditions and, as such, increase the prospects for species survival. Decision making, at all levels of complexity, is a fundamental cognitive process that has evolved over time as human mental capacity extended beyond mere autonomic responses to external environments and into the domains of reason (e.g., sense making, creating, and inferential and predictive thinking).

Second, human decision making is shaped by two broad cognitive domains: practical reason and high reason. Practical reason is limited reason. It is concerned primarily with decision efficiency and with ensuring that fundamentally important stimuli from internal and external environments are quickly identified and used to focus attention. For example, when confronted with a problem situation, the mind instantly and simultaneously goes to work to recognize the essence and context of the problem and to situate the problem relative to the mind's nearly infinite array of mental images and schemas that have been carefully logged away among a vast reservoir of prior experiences, perceptions, and emotions. In fractions of a second, the subconscious mind sends positive or negative signals (as the case may be) that alert the decision maker and allow her to narrow the range of choice options to those that best align with preexisting option scenarios. This is both an efficiency and survival mechanism. Without conscious or rational analysis, the brain primes and orients the decision maker in ways designed to avoid catastrophe and to engender a successful outcome. We will discuss the neurobiology of intuition in more depth later.

As it relates to intuition, the properties of practical reason include low cognitive control, rapid data processing, low conscious awareness, high confidence in the selected answer (i.e., the margin for error is high), and low confidence in the method used to arrive at a solution (Kenneth et al. 1997).

As we discussed in chapter 2, high reason, on the other hand, involves deeply analytical and precise thinking. It is a highly deliberative process that draws upon both working and long-term memory and applies to them elements of logic and calculative analysis. High reason is characterized by high cognitive control, slow data processing, high conscious awareness, low confidence in the selected answer (i.e., the room for error is small), and high confidence in the method used to arrive at a solution (Kenneth et al. 1997).

The problem, as Damasio explains it, is that the human mind is limited in its capacity to retain working memory and attention long enough to work its way through the myriad of analytical pathways required to reach the best solution for many complex problems. Conscious awareness changes moment to moment and is subtly influenced by our fluctuating moods, body states, external environmental stimuli, and levels of attention. These influences, coupled with the fact that the mind processes only small amounts of information at any given time, can produce changes in our perceptions, judgments, and decision accuracy (Hogarth 2001). Thus, with particularly complex dilemmas, people take mental shortcuts. It is inevitable and unavoidable that we do so.

Not surprisingly, the utility of high reason in the process of day-to-day, moment-to-moment decision making is relatively low. One can only imagine the implications on a person's time, effort, efficiency, and life management if each decision made in the course of a typical day was forced to undergo a rigid and methodical exploration of all possible outcomes, the probability estimates of success for each, and the elimination of those options judged unlikely to produce the best outcome possible. Now imagine the implications if each of the dozens of administrative decisions made each day by a typical principal were subject to the same measure of analysis.

Let us summarize the task properties that either induce intuitive decision making or provide the context where intuition can most effectively be used. First, throughout the book, we make numerous references to problem or decision complexity, especially with classes of problems most commonly found in human service organizations like schools. As such, intuition seems to work best with highly complex problems. These are problems with a number of possible elements such as multiple or unclear goals, unclear or ambiguous data, poor predictive properties, value-driven properties, multiple solutions, and multiple assessment possibilities. Second, intuition seems to emerge under problem contexts where there are few precedents, where the assessment of problem attributes are largely perceptual and subjective, where there is limited time and a high element of risk to the decision maker or the organization, where there is a high degree of pressure for a successful outcome, where task certainty is low, where there is a high potential for latent effects, where displays of problem attributes are often simultaneous rather than sequential, and where analytical data are of limited use. Among school leaders, intuition is most often used to solve problems, to forecast and project, to manage human crises and conflicts, to build teams, or to design and conceptualize programs and management processes (Agor 1986; Cappon 1994; Kenneth et al. 1997).

As we have shown, there are strong organizational and neuroscientific arguments in support of intuitive thinking and decision making. This brings us back to the fundamental questions of which is better: intuition or rational/analytical decision making? Under what conditions would one make the best use of each approach?

INTUITION AND RATIONALITY

In chapter 2, we discussed the attributes and characteristics of rational/classical decision making and of naturalistic and heuristic decision making. We maintained that in human service organizations like schools, the utility of rational/classical decision-making approaches was of limited value for most complex problems. Most managers and school administrators rely on quasi-rational approaches as described in Simon's conception of bounded rationality or on various heuristics and intuitions. However, we left a number of important questions unanswered. For example, just how do rational and intuitive decision making relate to one another? Are they mutually exclusive? Can one exist without the other? Which is most effective? It is to these questions that we now turn.

Jonathan Baron (2000) maintains that intuitive forms of decision making should not necessarily be excluded from the realm of rational thinking. According to Baron (2000, 5, 33), rational thinking is "the kind of thinking we would all want to do, if we were aware of our own best interests, in order to achieve our goals. For most practical purposes, people can do better by using some simple heuristics or rules of thumb than by making calculations about outcome probabilities." What Baron proposes here, is the idea that rationality is context dependent rather than a phenomenon that is tightly connected to a set of universal principles and normative structures. So from this perspective, under conditions of high task complexity, ambiguity, and novelty, an intuitive decision could be a perfectly rational way to resolve a problem.

Rational thinking is not always the same as accurate thinking, although by its very nature it is implied that rational thinking will indeed produce more precise outcomes. The rationale for this seemingly contradictory statement is based on the following logic. Analytic errors are often exaggerated because judgments and decisions tend to be made on a small number of explicit rules. If any one of the rules is incorrectly addressed, the resulting analysis may be seriously flawed and may lead to disastrous consequences. Consider, for example, the 1999 loss of the multimillion-dollar Mars Climate Orbiter space probe. The technical design and operational implementation of the project were nearly flawless, except for one small break in the rules: the probe's builder used American measurements (e.g., feet and inches) while NASA scientists and technicians relied upon metric measurements. As a result, navigation software failed to properly guide the spacecraft along the correct trajectory and it was destroyed upon entering the Martian atmosphere. Amid the myriad of calculations and analytical procedures used successfully to construct and implement this highly sophisticated machine, one amazingly simple rule violation derailed the entire project.

On a more pedestrian note, how many of us have inadvertently inserted an extra zero in the calculation of our bank accounts or in the preparation of an income tax form? Clearly, simple analytic errors can produce enormous consequences.

Intuitive errors, however, are generally far less severe. In contrast to the rule-specific requirements of traditional forms of analytic decision making, the intuitive decision maker relies on multiple, imperfect cues, and schemas. The intuitive thought is constructed upon broadly integrated images of past events and experiences and tempered by an individual's emotional state, drives, level of attention, personality traits, biases and stereotypes, body state, and by the natural distortions that occur in human memories over time. As a result, small mental errors are rarely potent enough to fatally damage the holistic properties of an intuitive decision. In essence, intuitive decisions are, at best, approximately right, and rarely exactly right. Of course, at worst, they can be dead wrong (Hogarth 2001; Kenneth et al. 1997).

It is also true that the quality of rational thinking is relative to each decision maker at a given point in time, and, like intuition, is highly dependent upon the decision maker's beliefs, dispositions, and goals. Baron (2000) explains further that contrary to the beliefs of many twentieth-century rationalists, the idiosyncratic effects of emotions cannot be separated from rational thought. Neither can intuition. In fact, even the most rational thinkers apply the principles of scientific analysis in moderation. That is, they think in amounts and in ways that are appropriate to the demands of the particular situation. Emotions are simply too pervasive in the construction of one's dispositions and moods and cannot be put on hold while one goes about the business of grappling with complex problems.

There is some evidence that the longer one rationally deliberates about possible options or solutions, the less accurate and predictive they become (Bargh and Chartrand 1999). Most of us are aware of the saying that one's first impressions are usually the best. There is an important rationale for this. When confronted with a complex problem, the subconscious mind goes into action immediately, drawing upon deeply seated autobiographical and implicit memories of past events, feelings, contexts, and outcomes. It does this automatically, even before the neocortex has had a chance to thoroughly assess and evaluate the information. These initial impressions can be quite accurate. Remember, evolution has equipped humans with the innate ability to recognize and assess both internal and external stimuli very rapidly. We are especially adept at responding to social cues, facial expressions, and tone of voice. With especially complex or novel problems, once the conscious mind takes over, it searches for explicit memories. The chances are that memories of identical situations and of successful responses to them simply don't exist, so in an effort to resolve the problem, the mind looks for similarities and approximations among past experiences and simultaneously begins to cobble together associations between memories of past events, experiences, and emotions. The capacity to do this is infinite. However, this can be both a blessing and a curse. On the one hand, the associative and reflective powers of the human mind can lead to wonderfully creative and novel ideas and artistic expressions. On the other hand, they can overload the mind, slow down thought processes, and contaminate decision-making processes with irrelevant or inaccurate information. Finally, intuitive ability is constrained by time-consuming logical and analytical thinking as a highly activated level of consciousness can block access to the subconscious and automatic elements of the mind (Damasio 1994, 1999).

Some scholars are critical of efforts to compare rational/analytical and intuitive decision making. A major problem is that analytical models rarely fit what it is decision makers actually do. We have talked about this principle before. Real-world decision making operates along a constantly shifting continuum of rational, quasi-rational, heuristic, and intuitive properties. With complex problems, decision makers move freely back and forth along this continuum. Decision making rarely follows a linear trajectory. Instead, it unfolds in fits and starts. It may lumber over particular problem elements as rational/analytic processes are used and then engage in huge conceptual leaps as heuristic or intuitive thinking are used. Analytically derived pieces of a decision may be compared against the decision maker's intuitive senses before a next step is taken. Conversely, an intuitively derived decision element may be subjected to a more analytical review before moving forward. The point is, most complex decisions are made using uneven processes that integrate elements of rational/analytic and intuitive decision making along a broad continuum of decision approaches (Agor 1986; Cappon 1994; Kenneth et al. 1997; Pondy 1983).

In summary, most scholars in the field of decision making appreciate the dual and integrative roles played by the analytical and intuitive dimensions of the mind. According to Dunne (1997, 122), "although the exclusion of intuition and subjectivity in scientific practice can often result in pointless and unproductive lines of investigation, intuition untempered by critical analysis can just as easily lead to unsubstantiated conclusions, misinterpretation of data, and self-delusion." It is a delicate dance indeed.

In the following section, we address the question of what is really known about intuition. Is it simply an amorphous, intangible, and elusive concept used to describe an unsubstantiated feeling, or is it something more? Research over the past twenty-five years has not completely answered these questions, but it has shed some valuable light on the scientific bases of the intuitive phenomenon.

EMPIRICAL RESEARCH ON INTUITION

Just what do we know about intuition? More specifically, how have the principles of empirical inquiry been applied to the study of intuition? In a nutshell, the answer is that we really know very little about intuition as a form of cognition, as a decision-making tool, or as a neurobiological function of the brain-mind. For much of the early twentieth century, research on human cognition focused on mechanistic, stimulus-response perspectives of human behavior. It wasn't until the 1950s that the study of human cognition turned to more sophisticated forms of analysis. According to Hogarth (2001, 36), the 1950s witnessed the emergence of a "cognitive revolution" whereupon researchers began to expand their inquiries to explorations of thinking about thinking. More specifically, investigators tackled complex questions about how humans think and process information and how these functions intersected with conceptions of working memory. By working memory, we mean "the ability to hold information in mind over a period of many seconds and to operate on it mentally" (Damasio1994, 41).

From the 1960s through the 1980s, many efforts were made to replicate human cognition through the design of sophisticated technologies such as computer software programs that modeled analytic decision making. By the 1970s, researchers also began to explore distinctions between deliberative human information processing and automatic information processing and their respective domains of application, thus recognizing that human cognition operates at many levels of consciousness and subconsciousness and in ways not previously understood. In recent years, major discoveries have been made in tracing the neuroanatomic and neurochemical processes of human cognition. Thanks to such technological tools as magnetic and functional magnetic resonance imaging (MRI and fMRI), positron emission tomography (PET), magnetoencephalographics (MEG), electroencephalographics (EEG), and chemical spectrometer analyses, aspects of brain function never before seen could be identified, detailed, and mapped (Dickmann and Stanford-Blair 2002).

Over the past century, cognitive scientists, psychologists, and neurologists showed little interest in the study of human intuition. For many, the topic was perceived as soft, quirky, and without scientific foundation. Intuition was seen as something more akin to metaphysics and paranormal mysticism than to serious scientific principles. Such perspectives were undoubtedly influenced by centuries of debate and philosophical musings over the nonsecular structures, roles, and importance of intuitive thought. They were also heavily influenced by the emergence of the scientific method during the late nineteenth century and its concomitant principles of analytical reasoning. Since intuition could not be seen, measured, or tested, most scientists viewed it as an unverifiable truncated logic, as weak and idiosyncratic, and of minimal utility in the serious business of problem solving and decision making. Moreover, in the absence of a strong and elegant theory, notions of intuition were subject to various myths and conceptual distortions (Agor 1986, 1989; Arsham 1996; Hogarth 2001; Kouzes and Posner 1987; Laughlin 1997; Rowan 1986).

Recent years have seen a growing number of serious attempts to study the properties, experiences, and practical applications of intuitive thinking and, more specifically, decision making, within such fields as organizational management, mathematics, military science, law enforcement, medicine, and science. Research has generally fallen within one of the following five strands (Hogarth 2001):

1. Psychological perspectives about the nature and experience of intuitively derived cognitions.
2. Philosophical discourse about the meaning and structure of intuitive knowledge.
3. Classifications of intuition as a cognitive process.
4. Examinations of how intuition works to shape human decision making.
5. Examinations of how intuition is developed or enhanced.

Qualitative methodological approaches dominate the research literature on intuition and are largely phenomenologies. Not surprisingly, much of the research consists of anecdotal accounts and partially formed conclusions about its origins, structure, content, and utility. In fact, the preferred method for examining intuition has been the use of phenomenological inquiry, a process that focuses on thick descriptions of an individual's experience with a particular phenomenon (Arvidson 1997; Brown 1990; Landry 1991; Moustakas 1994). According to Arvidson (1997), the phenomenological method, when conducted properly, can best articulate what is going on in consciousness. The method, when applied to the study of intuition, can be used to examine cognitive and affective components of the experience or to examine the processes leading to an intuition, such as environmental influences. A few studies, most notably by Weston Agor, have used survey instruments derived from elements of the Myers-Briggs Type Indicator to examine intuitive behaviors and aptitudes (Agor 1986; Boucouvales 1997; Gopnick and Schwitzgebel 1998; Morris 1990).

In the 1980s and early 1990s, Agor developed the Agor Intuitive Management Survey (AIM) based to a large degree upon descriptions and criteria contained in the intuitive classification from the Myers-Briggs type indicator. The two-part survey was given to over five thousand American managers and executives from a wide variety of public and private organizations. Public schools were not well represented in the sample. On a twelve-point scale, with twelve indicating highly intuitive, Agor found that the typical respondent scored between a six and a seven. He also found that the higher a manager climbed on the career ladder, the more he relied on intuition to guide his most important decisions.

A doctoral study by Landry (1991, 9) posed a series of key research questions that typify in one form or another the kinds of questions that have guided investigators in this field. First, "How does one access intuition? What are the conditions conducive to its emergence? What is the sensory experience of accessing intuition?" Second, "How is intuition confirmed? How does one know it is true? By what means does one check it out?" Third, "How does one act upon it or decide not to use it? What is the outcome?" Fourth, "What meaning is ascribed to the intuitive process? How does it affect world view, creation of meaning, and decision making?" Fifth, "How can one enhance and develop intuition?" The fifth question is the focus of a wonderfully descriptive and well-researched book on educating intuition by Robin Hogarth (2001). We make several references to Hogarth's groundbreaking work throughout our book.

Until recently, many efforts to empirically study intuitive decision making attempted to compare its processes and outcomes with various normative models through the use of various Bayesian and predictive statistical measures such as regression analysis. Not surprisingly, most of these studies showed that with certain classes of well-structured problems, analytical decision making generally exceeded intuitive processes in terms of decision accuracy. The problem with this type of analysis is that the analytical models used contained all of the information needed to carry out the calculation. In addition, most comparisons were based upon simulated laboratory representations and not on real-world events and environmental contexts. Of course, we know that human intuition is never so structured or so well endowed with reliable and stable data sets. Such research has really not told us much about the relative efficacy of intuitive versus analytical decision making in the real world, especially within the same person (Kenneth et al. 1997).

Research in the late 1990s by University of Pittsburgh psychologist Jonathan Schooler provided some important insights about how people use their intuitions. One important finding was that when people were asked to consciously deliberate on a task or on various options, they were more likely to reverse their decisions or to express later dissatisfaction with their decisions than were those who relied on their intuitive thinking. Schooler, Ohlsson, and Brooks (1993) also discovered that for certain complex and ambiguous problems it is better not to think too hard and to avoid verbalizing your thoughts. It appears that verbalizing interrupts and even impairs intuitive thinking.

As we forecast into the future, we believe that new breakthroughs in our understanding of intuition will be forthcoming, especially in the intersection of the fields of neuroscience and cognitive psychology. As we noted earlier, new technologies used to scan and image brain structures and functions have already given us fantastic insights into the complexities of the brain mind and how it is shaped by certain neuroanatomical and neurochemical processes. In the following chapter, we discuss a number of important concepts and discoveries about the human brain-mind and how this knowledge has increased our understanding of intuition.

SUMMARY

In this chapter, we discussed a number of important ideas and concepts about intuition and its emergence as a topic of interest to scholars and researchers in a wide variety of fields. In particular, intuitive approaches to executive decision making have gained respectability in recent years as our knowledge of complex organizations and the constraints they place on classical/analytical decision approaches has evolved.

Intuition is not a new concept. Its meaning and origins have been written about and debated since ancient times, and our conceptions about it have matured over the years. Intuition is now commonly conceived as a legitimate cognitive property that is evolutionary in origin, widely distributed, and highly effective under certain problem/situational contexts. Intuition is a form of knowing that is based largely on an individual's experiences, skills, dispositions, and beliefs. It is widely believed that intuitions are domain specific and come with greatest ease and accuracy to individuals who possess high levels of expertise in a particular skill.

Intuition can be a uniquely distinct experience. However, some attributes of the intuitive experience seem to appear with common frequency. For example, intuition is often described as a sense of knowing without knowing how one knows. It often appears as a sudden flash of insight. However, it may manifest itself at the beginning or end of a decision, or incrementally as the decision unfolds. Intuition is often accompanied by an emotional feeling such as certitude, excitement, or fear.

There is considerable debate over the relative effectiveness of intuitively or rationally derived decisions. Arguably, an intuitive decision can be quite rational if made within certain constraints or situational contexts. For most people, intuitive and rational/analytical processes work hand in hand. Good decisions are rarely made when only one approach or another is used.

Although empirical research on intuition and its utility in complex decision making is sparse, there is growing evidence that one's intuitive abilities can be nurtured and expanded. There is also growing interest in studying the neuroscience of intuition. Efforts to trace its origins in the brain and its biochemical properties are shedding new light on the scientific rationale for intuitive thinking and serving to dispel many of the myths about its legitimate role as a functional and important aspect of human cognition.

We believe that to fully understand intuition and appreciate it as an important resource for executive decision makers, one must also understand several fundamental concepts about the human brain-mind. In the following chapter, we explore some basic ideas about the neuroanatomical, neurochemical, and neurophysiological functions of the brain in an effort to root out and situate the scientific origins of intuitive thought.

4

UNDERSTANDING THE BRAIN-MIND

The mind exists in and for an integrated organism; our minds would not be the way they are if it were not for the interplay of body and brain during evolution, during individual development, and at the current moment.

—Antonio Damasio

Despite amazing advances in brain research, no one has yet traced the neurophysiological path of an intuitive thought. At best, researchers can make extrapolations about how intuitions are triggered and how they pass with effortless speed through the myriad of neural pathways in the brain to emerge as conscious thoughts and feelings. An investigation of brain research yields a number of important clues, however, as to how an intuition is likely to develop. In this chapter, we review some of the most recent findings about the brain and its complex structures, functions, and processes, and we present a framework for better understanding the neuroscientific bases of intuitive decision making.

We begin our examination of the brain-mind and its relationship to intuitive decision making with some general but important facts about the structure and function of the human brain. We then move through a series of discussions of the relationships between the brain, the mind, the body, the anatomy, and physiology of the brain, as well as consciousness, emotion, memory, theories of cognition, and intelligence. As educational administrators, we freely admit our limitations in these areas. However, as we pursued our investigation into the field of intuitive decision making, we found that a basic knowledge of how the brain works was fundamentally important in our efforts to fully understand and appreciate the attributes of intuitive thinking. We also found that a working knowledge of brain structures and functions led to some important hypotheses about how one might enhance the ability to access and use intuitive skills to become a more effective decision maker.

BRAIN BASICS

The human brain has been described as the most complex and sophisticated information processing machine on Earth. Its capacity for data collection, storage, analysis, and creative thought construction exceeds even the most advanced computers in the world (Dreyfus and Dreyfus 1986; Hogarth 2001). The brain has been described as a "collection of physiological structures that support electrochemical communications within neural networks—enabling consciousness and intelligence" (Dickmann and Stanford-Blair 2002, xvii). Comprised of literally billions of neurons (brain cells) and neural pathways, the brain is capable of an almost infinite array of neural connections. In fact, the number of electrochemical configurations (i.e., the processes responsible for brain activity at the cellular level) possible at any given point in time has been estimated at ten to the trillionth power! It is an organ that is always turned on, even during sleep, and conducts the vast majority of its business subconsciously. As a result of its enormous complexity and constantly shifting and evolving state, efforts to map certain brain activities have proven to be extremely difficult (Damasio 1999; Dickmann and Stanford-Blair 2002). However, as we noted in chapter 3, recent advances in brain-scanning technology have revealed much about how the brain works at the molecular level.

The brain is incredibly "plastic." That is, it changes its neural connections and circuitry continuously, both through conscious and unconscious processes. Its capacity to change is infinite and lasts a lifetime.

The brain acts as an exquisitely tuned command center that receives, deciphers, catalogues, and processes stimuli from the external environment and from the internal environment (e.g., thoughts, emotions, and physical senses). Each thought, each emotion, each incoming stimulus induces changes in the way the brain aligns and realigns its neural circuits and stimulates a host of neurochemical changes which facilitate various neural activities.

Since the way in which the brain links its vast array of nerve cells is responsible for how memories, cognitions, and emotions are formed, retained, and accessed, changes in these links produce changes in what we remember, how we feel, and how we behave. Sometimes these changes are subtle; at other times, they may be dramatic.

Overt and highly intense stimuli can have dramatic effects on neural circuitry. For example, most of us can remember with remarkable clarity certain childhood events that at the time of their occurrence made deep and lifelong imprints upon our emotional memories, our self-perceptions, or our dispositions. Other more incremental and subtle stimuli can also change the dynamics of the brain's neural circuitry. Taking a class of great interest and relevance to one's life or career can change the way we think. Sometimes the changes are immediate. Sometimes they occur over time as our life experiences and personal reflections draw upon relevant ideas once learned and now returned to the forefront of our conscious thought processes (Ratey 2001).

The brain responds to practice just as the body does. Lots of practice with particular mental activities (like reading) builds and strengthens the neural circuits responsible for that activity and for other related or parallel mental processes. Likewise, a lack of practice reduces neural connections as unused neurons either wither away or realign themselves with other more frequently activated circuits. The brain, then, is constantly active and constantly adjusting itself to meet new challenges and to process new information from continuously changing environments.

Each brain is unique. Although the basic anatomical structures of the normal human brain are similar, each individual possesses uniquely configured neural circuits and uniquely efficient (or inefficient, as the case may be) ways of processing information. The brain has also been described as a kind of ecosystem in which numerous regions and information processing centers act in concert with one another in a complex tapestry of mutual dependencies and benefits. There is, for example, no single brain center for vision, language, social behavior, emotion, or conscious memory. According to Ratey (2001, 161),

> We are also discovering that areas of the brain heavily associated with executing particular functions are actually just way stations in the neuronal transmission process, places where inputs converge from other brain areas, especially emotion, cognition, memory, and perception, before the brain determines which actions and behaviors it will order.

Although there are areas where such functions tend to be focused, on the whole, they cannot operate without a wide range of parallel processes and interrelated brain functions. For example, when we see an object in front of us, the image is processed via the visual cortices of the occipital lobe. However, sight involves other component dimensions such as shape, spatial orientation, texture, color, meaning, and emotional context. Each of these facets that compose "vision" draws upon multiple regions and resources within the brain and collaborates to produce the full and comprehensively presented image before us (Damasio 1994).

The human brain's defining characteristic is the cerebral cortex (also called the neocortex). This outer region of the brain distinguishes us from other creatures and produces the kinds of mental activities that make us uniquely human. The cerebral cortex is the most recently developed area of the human brain and is responsible for such activities as rational thinking, creative thinking, and self-awareness. Moreover, it connects with virtually all other (more primitive) areas of the brain to interpret various neural signals and to issue responses (both physical and mental) to them. The cortex is the culmination of the brain's evolutionary development from functioning as an "automatic regulator of internal physiological and biological mechanisms to the acquisition and assessment of environmental information" (Dickmann and Stanford-Blair 2002, 15).

There are four major functional theaters of the brain. Although we describe them individually, in reality they act closely together and in a circular fashion. The first is the theater of perception. It is through this mechanism that the brain recognizes and receives information from its internal and external environments. Actually, perception is a function of several mechanisms within the brain, including each of the sensory pathways (i.e., sight, sound, touch, smell). The second theater includes attention, consciousness, and cognition. It is through these brain functions that we become aware of ourselves and the world around us. It is also through these functions that we become aware of how we learn, interpret events, and represent the world to ourselves. The third theater includes those brain functions that control movement, memories, emotions, language, reasoning, and social behavior. The fourth theater represents brain identity and behavior. It is through this theater that brain outputs are constructed. In essence, the fourth theater includes the sum total of all neurological and psychological traits, a holistic representation of who we are and how we behave (Ratey 2001). We will discuss the anatomical structures and characteristics associated with each theater in the next section.

Throughout history, scholars have debated the distinctions between the brain, the mind, and the body. For centuries, it was widely believed that bodily functions and structures had little, if any, relationship to the brain-mind. Mental activities were understood as products of brain activity but were believed to be beyond the reach of scientific inquiry. Until recently, most brain research efforts have been directed at understanding the physical structures and functions of the brain (e.g., what does the brain do and where in the brain does it happen?). The concept of "mind" has been a subject of much controversy. Hard to define with precision or to measure empirically, the mind has long been relegated to the back pages of scientific research. However, with the advent of new technologies able to track and image various mental processes, a new interest has arisen in studying the mind as an integrated system of both the brain and body (Dickmann and Stanford-Blair 2002; Hogarth 2001). According to Harvard psychologist John Ratey (2001, 140), "The mind is an emergent property of the brain. It comes out when the brain runs."

The mind, in essence, is the symbolic representation of the active brain and is constructed around three parts: the conscious mind, the unconscious mind, and the nonconscious (or subconscious) mind. It is the nonconscious mind that is responsible for the generation of intuitive, automatic, and reflexive responses to various internal and external stimuli (Hobson 1999, 39). Hobson's description of the three-part mind encompasses virtually all of the information available in short- and long-term memory as well as working memory. The mind is not any one thing or any singular entity within the brain. Rather, it is constructed from a vast constellation of conscious and subconscious stimuli and neural processes. It functions in one mode when we are awake, another when we are asleep, and yet another when we are on the edge of wakefulness such as when we meditate.

Importantly, today, neuroscientists and psychologists conceptualize the brain, mind, and body as interdependent and integrated systems that automatically and deliberately monitor the environment and coordinate various mental and physical responses to it. Stimuli that affect one system also affect the other two systems.

In the following section, we outline several prominent features of the brain and their roles in facilitating and servicing human cognition. Understanding how the brain is constructed and what its component parts do sheds some light onto the mysteries of intuitive thought. As we stated above, no one has yet traced with precision the neurological pathways of an intuition. However, neuroscientists have come a long way toward developing a structural framework for explaining how the conscious and subconscious brain-mind works. There is little question that the phenomenon of intuition is indeed an immutable function of human cognition and is a product of a complex tapestry of neurobiological processes that tap into the vast resources of the mind.

ANATOMICAL BASICS: THE STRUCTURAL BRAIN

The brain is a complex and dynamic ecosystem comprised of several distinct yet interrelated structures. It has developed through 500 million years of progressive evolution and is constructed around three primary regions: the hindbrain, forebrain, and midbrain (see figure 4.1). Through its long evolutionary journey, it has retained many of the functional properties that emerged as the brain adapted to changing environments.

The hindbrain is the oldest, most primitive, region of the brain. Located just above the spinal cord, it contains a vertically stacked collection of neural processing structures that include the cerebellum, pons, and medulla. Together, they are referred to as the brain stem. Functionally, they communicate various somatosensory signals from

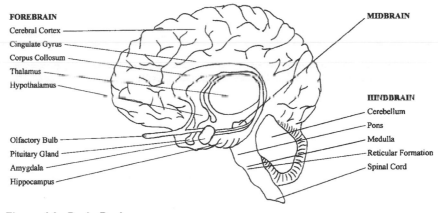

Figure 4.1. Brain Regions

the body to the brain and neural commands from the brain to the body. The brain stem also produces and regulates several important biochemical agents that activate the message-carrying capacity of the central nervous system.

Deep within the brain stem is a collection of brain cells called the reticular formation. Its primary duty is to regulate several involuntary body activities such as heart rate, respiration, blood pressure, and gastrointestinal function. Environmental signals (both internal and external) are received by various structures deep in the midbrain and are labeled, or tagged, with a degree of emotional valence. The signal then passes through the reticular formation, which triggers automatic physical responses. For example, when a frightening stimulus from the environment is received by the reticular formation, it passes that message along (through the release of various neurotransmitters) to the heart and lungs, which automatically and almost instantaneously respond by increasing their state of readiness, thus priming the body for a quick response to the perceived threat.

At the same time, connections from the reticular formation to other regions of the brain (i.e., the reticular activating system) activate conscious awareness levels and focus attention. As a result, one becomes more alert and sensitive to environmental cues that signify threats or provide opportunities for retreat. We commonly refer to this phenomenon as the fight-or-flight response. Importantly, it is this system that, when an intuition occurs, produces the "gut reaction," warmth, or tingling sensations so often described by those who have experienced intuition.

The cerebellum is a prominent component of the hindbrain, located posterior to the reticular formation and just below the occipital lobes of the cerebral cortex. Its primary function is to coordinate physical movement. However, recent investigations have revealed that it may also control the "movement" and sequencing of thoughts. This is of crucial importance to understanding not only intuition but also cognition in general. Movement, it seems, works hand in glove with thinking and behavior. According to Ratey (2001, 148), "Motor function is crucial to behavior, because behavior is the acting out of movements prescribed by cognition. If we can better understand movement, we can better understand thoughts, words, and deeds."

Ratey's statement has significant implications for understanding how intuitive thought processes might be activated and enhanced. The literature on intuition makes repeated references to physical movement as a mechanism for assembling and releasing (i.e., making conscious) creative thoughts. This makes sense since many of the same neural pathways dedicated to cognition are also responsible for signaling the body to move in certain ways. The tightness of these connections can be explained via the evolutionary development of mental and physical processes designed to respond to environmental threats quickly and effectively. It seems that many of our thoughts are, in fact, symbolically represented as movements. As we share in chapter 5, a number of school principals we talked to stated that their intuitions often came to them when they were walking, jogging, or exercising.

The cerebellum is also responsible for helping us to maintain posture, coordination, physical balance, and the maintenance of memories related to certain automatic physical processes that have been developed and refined through repeated practice and use. Take, for example, Tiger Woods's golf swing. Honed through years of practice, the neurological pathways that contain and communicate what is often referred to as "muscle memory" become, to a large degree, hardwired. They are so deeply engrained that they have become automatic. The cerebellum facilitates this process by communicating with regions of the cerebral cortex responsible for certain body movements. Again, we

point out that the functioning brain involves the systematic and interrelated actions of several distinct regions. Like the musicians in an orchestra, each region of the brain contains unique and indispensable attributes, but alone each cannot produce a symphony. Instead, each
depends upon the collective efforts of many other areas of the brain to
produce a comprehensive and coordinated action (Damasio 1999;
Ratey 2001). Although the exact role of the cerebellum in intuition is
unknown, it stands to reason that many of the automatic and physically
distinct responses experienced during an intuitive thought are mediated by the work of the cerebellum.

The midbrain represents the second evolutionary step in the development of the human brain. It is a comparatively small region that
sits atop the brain stem and in the center of the head. Its primary
functions are to coordinate head and eye movements and orient them
toward sounds. A midbrain structure called the superior colliculus receives input from the ears, eyes, and even skin (via touch) and assembles the input in ways that help to orient us to the surrounding
environment (Dickmann and Stanford-Blair 2002; Ratey 2001). As
with the cerebellum, the exact role of the midbrain in intuition is not
known. However, since intuitions are often triggered by some environmental stimulus (such as a sound or image), it is likely that the
midbrain plays at least an indirect role in the constellation of mental
processes that unfold as an intuition takes shape by helping one orient properly to relevant stimuli.

The third and most advanced region of the brain is the forebrain.
Among its many important structures is the cerebral cortex, the
crown jewel of the human brain. This is the thinking brain—the portion of the brain that receives signals from virtually all regions, that
analyzes and interprets the signals, and then constructs appropriate
responses that are sent to other areas of the brain and body. The cerebral cortex contains several structures that mediate memory formation and retrieval, rational thought, creative thought, problem solving, reflective thought, and consciousness itself. Nearly 80 percent of
the neurons in the brain (there are roughly 100 billion of them!) reside in the cerebral cortex and are arranged in parallel pathways that
allow for rapid and direct communication with various substructures
deep within the mid and hindbrain. The vast majority of neurons,

however, are not dedicated, or hardwired, for the operation of specific functional tasks. Instead, they are available on demand to respond immediately and creatively to stimuli from the environment or to other cognitive tasks (e.g., reflection, analysis) (Dickmann and Stanford-Blair 2002; Ratey 2001).

The cerebral cortex is a fist-shaped structure that contains numerous fissures and folds. These formations greatly increase the surface area of the cortex and thus enhance its operational capacities. The cortex is formed into two hemispheres that are joined deep in the midbrain region by a bundle of crossover neural pathways referred to as the corpus callosum. Although the hemispheres share many parallel structures and functions, each plays a distinctive role in the governance of motor activity, cognitive operations, and mental functioning. For example, it has been determined that the left hemisphere is responsible for rational/ analytical thought processes while the right hemisphere is responsible for creative thought. It is also believed that the left frontal lobe of the cortex is instrumental in the regulation of mood (Damasio 1999). Many authors have conjectured that activities that stimulate right-brained thinking are important to the development of intuition.

The cortex can be grouped into several functional areas. At the anterior or front of the cortex are the frontal and prefrontal lobes. In effect, the frontal lobes act as the brain's executive secretary. They command action, integrate attention with short- and long-term goals, deliberate, plan, and construct insights (i.e., the realization of a new thought or solution to an intractable problem). It is here that we process working memory. Working memory is the moment-to-moment memory that allows us to hold data, motivations, and thoughts long enough to activate longer-term memory functions deep in the hippocampus and in other areas of the cortex.

An interior region of the frontal cortex called the ventromedial cortex is responsible for reflecting upon and mediating emotional signals sent to it from the amygdala deep in the brain. Importantly, this region may also play a central role in the gut feelings experienced by people who have intuitive thoughts. It seems to be particularly important in shaping the emotions used during decision making relating to personal or social factors (Ratey 2001). Is the ventromedial cortex the seat of intuition? We don't know for sure, but it seems to play a vital role in the emotional experience of intuitive thoughts.

Behind the frontal lobes reside the motor and sensory cortices. The motor cortex controls voluntary motor actions on the opposite side of the body. For example, the right hemisphere controls movement on the left side of the body and vice versa. Just below this structure rests Broca's area, which is responsible for language production. The proximity of these two regions explains the interrelationship between motor learning and language development. For years, scientists have underscored the importance of developing motor skills in very young children as a mechanism for developing various cognitive functions, including language.

Just behind the frontal lobe resides the parietal lobe. It is here that the brain processes and mediates various sensory and somatosensory (i.e., pain, pressure, temperature, touch) signals from the opposite side of the body (just like the motor cortex). It is also here that the brain processes various spatial details of an observed object. Below the parietal lobe and just above the ear is the temporal lobe. It plays a critical role in processing hearing, facilitating memories and learning, and in recognizing colors, textures, and shapes. At the posterior of the cortex is the occipital lobe. There the brain records and processes visual information. Wernicke's area, which is located at the junction of the temporal, parietal, and occipital lobes, processes speech comprehension and the organization of words (Dickmann and Stanford-Blair 2002).

Deep within the forebrain are a number of vital structures that function as information way stations and coordinators. Lining the underside of the cerebral cortex and covering the dorsal surface of the corpus callosum is the cingulate gyrus. The anterior portion of the cingulate plays a particularly important role in coordinating the complex system of arousal, emotion, and motivations that influence what we pay attention to and how strongly. It sorts through pieces of sensory data and determines which will be forwarded to the frontal lobes for executive processing. It also determines how long these data bits will access the frontal lobes and with what degree of intensity.

Deeper within the brain lies a cluster of structures responsible for processing neuronal signals that are central to emotions, memory, pleasure, and learning. The first of these, called the thalamus, is a prominent structure that sits right in the middle of the brain and directly above the brain stem. Approximately the size of a walnut, it is the brain's Grand Central Station. Virtually all but olfactory stimuli are received by the thalamus, which redirects them to other, targeted locations in the brain for further processing.

Just below and slightly anterior to the thalamus is the hypothalamus. The hypothalamus receives signals from the body and passes them on to other areas of the brain. It also serves to regulate a number of automatic functions of the body such as heart rate, respiration, temperature, sex drive, hunger, bladder, etc. Working in concert with the pituitary gland, the hypothalamus is the hormone center of the brain. Together, these structures adjust the body's chemistry through the release of neuro-transmitters such as dopamine, serotonin, and norepinephrine, and pi-tuitary hormones. These substances work in various ways to activate the specific neural processes responsible for arousal, attention, stress, ag-gression, and pleasure. They also activate the body's endocrine system, which in turn generates automatic somatosensory responses.

Directly below the thalamus and hypothalamus sits the hippocampus. Shaped somewhat like a seahorse, the hippocampus is the brain's mem-ory center. It regulates, filters, and indexes sensory and cognitive stim-uli, compares the present with the past, distinguishes novel from ordi-nary stimuli, and thus enables the brain to form and retain memories. Not surprisingly, the hippocampus is instrumental for learning.

One of the most fascinating attributes of the human brain-mind is its capacity for passion. Passion exists on a broad continuum from feelings of extreme joy and excitement to murderous rage. It is passion that gives our lives significance and brings meaning to the myriad of events that shape our life experiences. In the extreme, passion can literally cause us to react spontaneously, without forethought, and in ways that defy rational/analytical thought. An intense intuition is, for most peo-ple, also a highly passionate experience. It generates strong emotions automatically without conscious reasoning or effort. We believe that deep within the brain a small almond-shaped structure called the amygdala plays a significant role in shaping the intuitive experience through feelings of passion.

In his best-selling book *Emotional Intelligence*, Daniel Goleman (1995) describes in detail the importance of the amygdala. Actually, there are two amygdala, one for each hemisphere of the brain. Nestled below the thalamus and next to the hippocampus, the amygdala has an enormous influence on human behavior. It is, in essence, the brain's emotional processing center where signals from the external and internal environments are interpreted for their emotional significance. To perform this function, the amygdala possesses a vast reservoir of emotional memories from which it compares incoming stimuli. Its proximity to the hippocampus and other brain arousal structures allows us to connect memories with emotional responses. It is constantly at work, sorting and interpreting incoming signals for emotional valence and routing those signals back to the cerebral cortex for additional processing. The amygdala receives its signals from two primary sources, the cerebral cortex via the thalamus and from the thalamus directly.

When an environmental stimulus is perceived as particularly important or intense, the amygdala springs into action. That portion of the signal that comes directly to it from the thalamus actually bypasses, or shortcuts, the conscious processing centers of the cerebral cortex and triggers automatic and nonconscious reactions. As Goleman (1995, 15) states, "the amygdala can take control over what we do even as the thinking brain, the neocortex, is still coming to a decision." All of us can recall episodes in our lives that generated sudden outbursts of joy, excitement, sadness, or anger. Often, those outbursts were accompanied by various physical reactions such as a shout, an explosion of laughter, hitting or punching, or recoiling. Regardless of the nature of the emotional response, the amygdala automatically signaled the arousal mechanisms of the brain and body, which activated and subsequently generated a physical response before we were consciously aware of what was going on. Granted, this process usually occurs only microseconds before the cortex kicks into gear and attempts to mediate the whole affair through the application of careful and measured reason. For most of us, however, when incoming stimuli are intense enough, our amygdala literally "hijacks" our emotional response system in ways that we may regret later once we have had the chance to apply more rational and refined thought processes (Goleman 1995, 16). The amygdala, then, serves to stimulate emotional reactions and memories without conscious mediation. In fact, a great deal of what we feel and remember emotionally occurs subconsciously.

The amygdala is also highly attuned to various social cues such as facial expressions, body language, tone of voice, etc. Its ability to identify and process ambiguous or abnormal social stimuli is due largely to its broad reach throughout the brain. Each of the amygdala's twelve neuronal clusters is linked to a vast range of brain regions such as the cerebral cortex, the hippocampus, the hypothalamus, and the brain stem. When each of these regions fires in response to a signal from the amygdala, a cascade of neurochemical and hormonal substrates floods the brain and body. Heart rate increases, muscles tense, the body heats up, adrenal glands activate, and the mind becomes hyperalert and focused. There are many more neural connections that flow directly from the amygdala to the cerebral cortex than vice versa, thus explaining why feelings of fear, anxiety, or anger can be very difficult to mediate consciously (Ratey 2001).

Especially intense emotional signals are imprinted by the amygdala into the brain's emotional memory banks. For example, a child who was once bitten and traumatized by an angry dog can carry that emotional memory for a lifetime. It can result in automatic and lifelong feelings of fear or discomfort when in the presence of dogs (angry or not). Memories of angry dogs don't have to be exact since the amygdala scans its reservoir of emotional memories for associations and similarities. The presence of a particularly playful dog that jumps up pawing at your pant leg can trigger the same feelings of fear and anxiety experienced years before when confronted with a far more threatening situation.

Interestingly, the olfactory system has a direct pipeline to the amygdala. Bypassing both the cerebral cortex and the thalamus, olfactory signals are processed by the brain without conscious mediation. Smells can trigger almost instantaneous reactions of pleasure or disgust. It is believed that the olfactory system was critically important to the development of the primitive brain and served as a primary source of information about the external environment. It still works in much the same way. Our sense of smell not only informs us and orients us toward feelings of pleasure or disgust, but it can trigger powerful memories of past events. The smell of freshly cut grass can resurrect memories of childhood experiences like softball practice after school or a family picnic at the local park. The aroma of perfume can bring back memories of past loves. As we know, intuition involves the activation of deeply seated memories and the construction of noetic sensations from an amalgam of experiential and cognitive processes. We also know that intuitions can be activated by various environmental cues, for example, the smell of cut grass, a visual image or object, or a sound. Smell, because of its unfet-tered access to the amygdala, can be a powerfully stimulating agent in the intuitive process.

As we noted above, the amygdala is sure to play a pivotal role in intu-ition as it provides both the emotional representation of the experience and the generation of an associative emotional memory that allows us to contextually frame the experience. The fact that the amygdala's work and the activation of an intuition are largely nonconscious is not coincidental.

Together, the amygdala, hippocampus, and the hypothalamus consti-tute the limbic system. Although each structure provides specialized func-tions in the processing of external and internal stimuli, they act in concert with one another. Thus, attempting to explain a particular brain-mind process, like intuition, by its affiliation with a single limbic, or cortical, structure would at best provide only a partial view into an enormously complex phenomenon. It is clear that the many forms of cognition are a function of a dynamic ecological system that works continuously to re-ceive and interpret various environmental signals, to provide mental and physical orientations and responses to them, and to self-regulate essential and autonomic life-sustaining processes.

A defining characteristic of intuition is its lack of a conscious founda-tion. It emerges from the subconscious mind in its entirety without de-liberative or rational thought. Thus, understanding the nature of con-sciousness is an important piece of the intuitive equation. Just what is consciousness and how does it influence how we think and solve prob-lems? How is consciousness related to intuition? In the next section, we attempt to provide some important insights into these and other ques-tions about what it means to be conscious.

CONSCIOUSNESS

Our opening statement on the topic of consciousness echoes other open-ing statements about the brain-mind: consciousness is very hard to de-fine and has endured years of debate and research into its precise mean-ing and function. Intuitively, it would seem reasonable to argue that when we are awake we are conscious and when we are asleep we are not. Clearly, wakefulness, sleep, and dreaming are key elements of the state of being conscious but there are other more subtle dimensions. Today, definitions of consciousness typically include the following ideas— awareness of the world, our bodies, and our selves. They also include the concept of the interconnectedness between the external world, the physical self, and the inner self (i.e., a holistic understanding of who we are, where we are, and how we interact with the environment that surrounds us). Consciousness can also be described as a "story without words" of our inner life and its responses and reactions to thoughts, objects, events, physical condition, and other people (Damasio 1999, 24).

According to Hobson (1999), there are two forms of consciousness: primary and secondary. These correlate closely with Damasio's (1999) description of core and extended consciousness. Primary consciousness is characterized by the perceptions, emotions, awareness of sensations, and sense of self that occur moment to moment. It also involves instinctual behaviors and the capacity for attention and arousal. The strength of primary consciousness influences our ability to solve problems, form long-term memories, plan for the future, and be creative. Secondary consciousness exists in an extended temporal framework. It involves the conscious activation of memories, thoughts, language, spatial/environmental orientation, and intentional behavior. It is within the state of secondary consciousness that our sense of self is elaborated and extended, that we link past experiences with anticipated future experiences, and that we maintain a full sense of our autobiographical selves (Damasio 1999).

Conscious awareness changes moment to moment as we encounter new and unexpected stimuli, thoughts, and images. Consciousness and attention "give rise to the mind" and can be profoundly influenced by such factors as fatigue, emotion, mood, motivation, hunger, or illness (Ratey 2001). Hobson (1999, 45) describes the "bumping" of conscious states from one form to another in response to the activation of various neural subsystems such as touch, taste, smell, sound, or sight.

Consciousness is selective and self-regulating. The wakeful brain-mind constantly scans external and internal environments, separates and filters the important from the unimportant information, and focuses attention sparingly. Imagine a world where all of the environmental stimuli around us cascaded upon our sensory systems in a flood of equally valent signals. We would be deluged with information. So much so, that our capacities for rational and deliberative thinking would be quickly overwhelmed.

Consciousness operates within a narrow range of brain activation levels. Even the sleeping brain has a high level of activation. The sleeping brain, however, demonstrates markedly different neuroelectrical patterns. When conscious, the brain emits electrical signals that are far more coordinated and patterned than it does when sleeping. The sleeping brain, in contrast, emits random and irregular signals. A popular analogy for comparing waking and sleeping forms of consciousness is the image of an orchestra and its conductor. When the conductor is not present, the orchestra still plays but with uneven and idiosyncratic noise. Sounds are not coordinated; rhythm and melody are fragmented and barely discernable. Once the conductor enters the stage and taps his wand on the podium, orchestra members immediately pay attention, and the independent noise settles down. The conductor then leads the group in a coordinated and finely integrated performance. The conductor represents the wakeful mind, and the disconnected noise of the conductorless orchestra represents sleep (Ratey 2001).

Wakeful consciousness operates at two levels, foreground and background. At the foreground are the various tasks at hand before us and our conscious intentions toward them (e.g., here's what I have to do, and here's how I plan on doing it). Such tasks include the simple and the sophisticated from walking down the street to composing a complicated symphony. Background consciousness includes our vast reservoirs of memories, emotions, and experiences. It also involves a constant hum of internal dialogues held beyond our conscious awareness as the brain-mind processes and regulates the flood of data before us. In combination, background and foreground consciousness connect the processes of inner life regulation with images (and ideas) that we construct from our real-world experiences and allow us to make deliberative adaptations to an ever-changing environment (Damasio 1999).

Wakefulness, however, should not be confused with productiveness. An enormous amount of cognitive work unfolds as we sleep. In fact, it is during sleep that we solidify our memories and reorganize mental stimuli of all kinds. The old maxim "I want to sleep on it" has a clear physiological basis. Dreaming, according to Hobson (1999) is our most creative conscious state. It is during dreams that our minds construct spontaneous and nearly infinite combinations of seemingly disparate and unconnected mental images and emotions. Moreover, because our dreams are unfettered by conscious deliberations or environmental interruptions, the mind easily produces novel configurations of thoughts, images, solutions, and insights. The fact that many people acquire their intuitions during sleep attests to the creative power of the unconscious mind.

Damasio (1999, 154) maintains that a sense of self is a central aspect of the conscious mind. The most primal aspect of self is the protoself, a preconscious state that "maps moment by moment the state of the physical structure of the organism in its many dimensions." The protoself does its work unconsciously through the various regulatory structures of the limbic system and brain stem. An important component of these structures is the reticular formation. It is there that the brain regulates sleep, wakefulness, homeostatic operations, attention, and consciousness. The reticular formation receives somatosensory information from the body and passes it along to higher regions of the brain. It also sends various neural commands from the brain back to the body. The protoself function of the brain-mind provides a scaffolding upon which the core self (i.e., here-and-now awareness) and autobiographical self (i.e., juxtaposition of self, experiences, and memories) are built and upon which we come to know things (i.e., the integration of neural regions and networks that produce a whole representation). It is the autobiographical self that provides the contextual domain for intuition.

Is there a level of consciousness that is especially conducive to intuitive decision making? We think so. As we will share in greater detail in chapter 5, our interviews with several intuitive school principals shed some light on this question. Intuitively derived decisions came to principals in two ways. First, for several principals, intuitions emerged during periods of high conscious arousal and when they were actively engaged in problem solving. Problems always involved conflict or an impending crisis of an interpersonal nature. Rarely, if ever, did a problem contain elements that were not subject to individual perceptual differences, that were not aligned with strongly held beliefs by stakeholders, or that could not be resolved in a variety of ways. Each problem also contained an element of risk to either the decision maker or the organization as a whole. Within such turbulent contexts, principals were highly motivated to find a solution. Their attention was focused and time was of the essence. There was little if any time for reflection. It was as

if their minds suddenly went into hyperdrive, rapidly scanning and di-
agnosing the situation while simultaneously searching for a solution.
Acting much like high-speed computer processors, they quickly sized up
their situations and almost automatically drew upon a vast reservoir of
past experiences and emotional memories. With little time to think,
their subconscious minds sorted through memories of similar events,
feelings about those events and their outcomes, and a series of if-then
propositions pertaining to the current situation. While this was happening, their heightened state of consciousness fed important environmental information to them through various sensory pathways. For example,
they unconsciously picked up subtle (and not so subtle) social cues, facial expressions, body language, tone of voice, and other contextual images. These were rapidly processed by the amygdala and other limbic
structures and routed back to the cerebral cortex for further analysis and
sense making. Signals were also sent out to various regions of the body
resulting in certain physical adjustments (e.g., sweating, elevated heart
rate, etc.). In other words, their problem situations resulted in a whole
mind-body activation. Under such conditions of high consciousness and
stress, it is likely that automatic neural processes played a prominent, if
not a dominant, role in the retrieval and organization of memories and
feelings and the subsequent construction of a solution. The demands of
the situation prompted their intuitions that, in effect, preempted the deliberative processes of the cerebral cortex.

In the second scenario, intuitions came to some principals when they
were not actively engaged in problem solving and were not highly
aroused. Some principals talked about distancing themselves consciously
from the problem at hand by taking a walk, meditating, praying, or sleeping on it. Such strategies worked particularly well with problems that did
not demand immediate solutions. In these cases, the mind seemed to be
operating on two planes—multitasking, if you will. On one plane, they
were attending to new and unrelated situations and environments (e.g.,
walking, meditating, sleeping). They had distanced themselves from the
problem physically and mentally. On a second plane, the problem and
their concerns about it continued to churn and process in background
consciousness. Although the problem was not for the moment in the foreground of conscious attention, it still captured the attention of the brain-
mind in subtle and subconscious ways. There was, in a paradoxical way, a

state of relaxation that existed within a milieu of background tension. This form of "second-tier consciousness" (our definition) provided their minds with the room they needed to play with ideas and novel constructions yet do so within a contextual framework (i.e., a focused subconscious). Their intuitions were still constructed largely through subconscious processes, but without the sense of urgency present when principals were confronted with problems in need of immediate attention.

In summary, it appears that intuitive decisions often emerge during periods of high arousal and high foreground tension or low to moderate arousal coupled with some level of background tension.

A final comment on consciousness. What strikes us as particularly important is the fact that the subconscious mind is highly active, highly creative, and constantly working to provide adaptive responses to ever-changing environmental conditions. The conscious mind is like the tip of an iceberg, but residing just below the waterline (threshold of consciousness) is a vast body of ice (the subconscious mind). There beneath the waves reside all "fully formed images to which we do not attend, all neural patterns that never become images, all dispositions acquired through experience, and all of the hidden wisdom and know-how" (Damasio 1999, 228). We recognize that for some people it is hard to understand, let alone trust, mental processes that occur beyond the realm of deliberative and rational thinking, but the reality is that much of what we know, feel, and create is assembled below the metaphorical waterline of consciousness. It is critically important for decision makers to understand this and to learn to trust their intuitions.

Whereas consciousness provides the vehicle by which we attend to and become aware of our world, emotion is the mechanism by which we make sense of it. Our expansive capacity for emotion, in concert with our powers of reason, is what makes us human. It also explains much about how and why we behave in the ways that we do. In the next section, we discuss in greater depth the role that emotion plays in human behavior and cognition, and how our intuitions are influenced by it.

EMOTIONS

Without emotion, our world would be devoid of meaning and significance. Emotion gives a direction, a focus, to our thoughts and engenders feelings about them. Devoid of emotion, behaviors, events, and objects would become sterile and meaningless phenomena about which we would have no internal compass to direct our responses or reactions. As we have noted earlier, intuitions almost always come packaged around an emotional feeling. Such feelings can include primary emotional responses like happiness, sadness, fear, anger, surprise, or disgust and a wide range of secondary emotional responses like feelings of certitude, knowingness, anticipation, discouragement, jealousy, pride, and so forth.

Emotions exist to regulate our mental and physical responses to various external and internal stimuli. Our very behaviors and thoughts are shaped by emotions. Emotions are in essence automatic evolutionary mechanisms designed to ensure individual and species survival. The activation of emotions triggers a series of complex biochemical processes in which the body releases certain hormones and neurotransmitters to raise levels of conscious attention and to prepare us for action (Dickmann and Stanford-Blair 2002).

Neurobiologically, emotions work when incoming stimuli from the external or internal environment pass through our sensory receptors (i.e., sight, sound, taste, touch, smell), or from the thinking cortical regions of the brain to the thalamus. There the signal is routed to the cerebral cortex, the limbic system, and the brain stem. As we noted earlier, olfactory signals bypass the thalamus and travel directly to the amygdala. These structures search for signal patterns and associated memories and regulate somatosensory responses to and from the body. As signal patterns are detected, they are forwarded to other areas of the brain for additional processing through the activation of neurotransmitters like serotonin, norepinephrine, and dopamine. This routing process moves the signals from the limbic system to areas of the prefrontal cerebral cortex where they are sorted and organized for deeper analysis and sense making. There, the conscious brain acts to modify limbic signals in ways that allow for an appropriate response. Left unchecked by the prefrontal cortex, highly intense emotional signals can easily overwhelm the mind and make it difficult to prioritize or adjust them to a level of intensity that better meets the needs of the situation. Under normal conditions, the cortex processes incoming signals, modifies them as needed, and sends corresponding response signals back through the limbic system for the body to receive and adjust to (Damasio 1999; Dickmann and Stanford-Blair 2002; Ratey 2001).

Emotions evolved quite early in the evolution of the human brain and preceded the development of rational/analytical capabilities. Given their primitive and subconscious origins, it is not possible to control them willfully. At best, we can educate them through conscious reasoning and practice, but to deliberately extinguish them would be exceptionally difficult. The modulation of emotion occurs primarily in the left prefrontal cortex. There, incoming signals from the amygdala are analyzed and appraised for emotional content; for example, is this an important emotion that requires an immediate and intense response, or is this an emotion that should be toned down a bit and put into its proper perspective (Goleman 1995)? Once its job is complete, the prefrontal cortex routes the refined signal back to the limbic system where it is either amplified or diminished. Extremely intense signals from the amygdala can override the ability of the prefrontal cortex to modify them. Chronic anxiety or panic attacks are extreme examples of unchecked emotional signals from the amygdala. The urge to flee a threatening situation is likewise a powerful, but temporary, condition that can defeat conscious efforts to override neural impulses.

Although the amygdala has been shown to exert a critical influence on the processing of emotions and emotional memories, several different brain sites act in concert with the amygdala in the processing of different emotions. In other words, the shaping of our emotions requires a systemwide level of cooperation between limbic, brain stem, and cortical structures. In addition, emotional memories can form without conscious thought, and some emotions never reach full conscious awareness (Damasio 1999; Goleman 1995).

Reasoning and rational/analytical thinking are strongly dependent upon emotions. Too little emotion can result in lackadaisical and half-hearted efforts. Too much emotion can overwhelm the capacity of the mind to act thoughtfully and carefully. It seems that somewhere in the middle between emotional overload and underload is optimal for critical thinking and problem solving.

It also appears that one's mood can either enhance or diminish critical and creative thinking. A positive mood coincides with feelings of pleasure, which of course occur when neurotransmitters like serotonin, norepinephrine, and dopamine are released into the neural circuitry of the brain. Such feelings improve motivation and concentration and enhance the formation of long-term memories. As a result, positive emotional states help us learn better. Positive mood may also induce automatic/intuitive processing. The mind, absent interfering levels of conflict or tension, is free to play with novel ideas, to daydream, and to remain open to the unusual. In contrast, a negative mood induces controlled, effortful processing. It constrains our mental efforts, forces upon us a narrowed field of vision, and increases the urge to regain control over our environment. Once efforts to gain control reach the foreground of our consciousness, the internal conditions for intuitive thinking become severely limited (Goleman 1995; Hogarth 2001).

Emotional responses to intuitive decisions serve us in two ways. First, an emotion is the first tangible evidence that a solution has been reached. The elements of an intuitively derived decision arrive at the surface of conscious awareness along with an emotional marker (e.g., warmth, excitement, certitude, relief, etc.). It is the feeling generated by our emotional machinery that in effect certifies that one has reached a critically important cognitive juncture. Second, emotion attaches meaning to the intuition itself and acts like a kind of directional guidance system that tells us how to proceed. The emotion of excitement, for example, energizes and spurs one on toward further action. The emotion of fear, on the other hand, prompts us to proceed with caution, if at all. Emotion also allows us to arrive at judgments about what is good and what is not, when we have succeeded or failed, and when we are on the right track. Because emotions surface before the rational brain-mind begins to analyze and modify them, we can make quick judgments about circumstances based on gut feeling alone. That is basically what an intuition is—an emotionally driven judgment about good or bad or about knowing something to be true.

As we noted above, emotions cannot be easily controlled consciously. However, they can be affected by a variety of factors such as diet, exercise, illness, culture, environment, weather, seasons, hormonal cycles, trait personality, and cognitive tasks (Damasio 1999). Finally, treating emotions as data to be examined and understood, rather than as uncontrollable phenomena, can help one to learn how to work more productively and positively within complex and often frustrating environments (Hogarth 2001).

A final word of caution about emotions. In addition to their ability to override rational/analytical judgment and modification, they can activate on the basis of similarities between current environmental stimuli and past events. Because the emotional mind is associative, even a slight correspondence between a current situation and a past experience can generate an emotional response that is identical to the response produced by the past experience. This can cause one to overreact to what most people would consider benign stimuli. Let us return to the barking dog scenario. Being bitten and terrorized by an aggressive dog as a child is undoubtedly an event of significant gravity. One's feelings of safety and security were clearly jeopardized. Feelings of fear were so profound that the amygdala and hippocampus created deep and permanent impressions in long-term memory. Even years later, when one's attention shifts toward the playful intentions of a puppy, the feelings of fear can spring forth in full bloom, as if time itself has stood still. Only through conscious mediation by the neocortex can the fear be abated. In extreme cases, phobic patterns make efforts to mediate fear very difficult.

Consciousness and emotions are critical components of the engine that drives intuitive thinking. However, without deeply seated memories, our intuitions would be mostly superfluous and highly inaccurate. In the next section, we discuss the characteristics and roles of memory in human cognition and intuitive decision making. We will also address the question of whether our memories are reliable. Can we trust them to provide the grist for useful and accurate intuitions?

MEMORY

Memories make us who we are. They allow us to revisit and reflect on past experiences and attach emotional significance to them. Memories provide the contextual framework for the self and the grist from which our deeply held beliefs, values, and dispositions are formed. Memories help us make sense of the world, interpret events, predict the future, and organize our thoughts. The quality of our intuitions depends upon the quality and integrity of our memories.

Neurologically, a memory resides in the vast neural circuitry of the brain. As we encounter new experiences or contemplate ideas and mental images, networks of neurons become strengthened, expanded, and linked to other associated neural circuits. The intensity and clarity of our memories are directly related to the strength and scope of certain neuronal networks. These networks change continuously as our life experiences shape and reshape our recollections and our perspectives. Some memories lie dormant, deeply seated within the cortex and limbic system, only to be activated through a catalytic event or thought. It is believed that most neurons actually participate in more than a single memory. The brain possesses redundant and overlapping systems that can combine in nearly infinite ways when producing mental images, thoughts, feelings, and memories (Ratey 2001).

There is no single location in the brain where memories reside or where they are formed. Instead, memory functions and structures are distributed throughout the brain. Most often, our memories are constructed from numerous submemories, pieces of information that are assembled into a comprehensive memory of an event, experience, image, or thought. These pieces can link together from areas in the temporal and frontal lobes and subcortical areas such as the amygdala and hippocampus. Take, for example, a childhood memory of a trip to Disneyland. Embedded within the memory are several submemories consisting of sounds, sights, movements, emotions, smells, and tactile experiences. Although these fragments reside in different areas of the brain, they collaborate in the construction of our recollection of what a trip to Disneyland was (Damasio 1999).

There are different types of memory, each serving a particular function. Short-term or working memory consists of the moment-to-moment memories of immediately occurring events. Lasting for only seconds at a time, working memory allows us to conceptualize and understand what is happening to and around us at any given moment. It also serves to hold especially important events, images, or thoughts long enough for them to be encoded as long-term memories. Finally, it allows us to attend to, and concentrate on, problems that need solving and decisions that need to be made.

Long-term memory, of course, consists of those memories that have been deeply imprinted upon the brain-mind. They often lie dormant for great lengths of time until activated by a catalytic event or thought process. Long-term memories exist in different forms. For example,

episodic memories contain various facts and events and their placement in time. Semantic memories, however, are cognitive in form.
They consist of categories of events and experiences, spatial knowledge, symbolic knowledge, and common knowledge needed for successful day-to-day living. Autobiographical memory consists of those
thoughts and images about ourselves, our identities, and those experiences that comprise the framework for our sense of selfhood. Implicit
memories are primarily automatic performance related memories that
require little conscious effort like walking, riding a bike, driving a car,
or any other deeply ingrained skill that becomes automatic over time
and with practice. Explicit memories are those memories about past
events or facts that are consciously retrieved from the subconscious
mind. Finally, dispositional memories are largely dormant and implicit
representations of various sensory stimuli such as shapes, sounds, or
smells. Residing in what Damasio (1999, 160) refers to as "convergence
zones" between the cortex and subcortical nuclei, dispositional memories can provoke powerful emotions and somatosensory reactions from
the body.

Memories are also embedded within a variety of sensory, motor,
visual-spatial, and language structures of the brain (Ratey 2001). For example, most of us are familiar with the term *motor memory*, which is
used to describe the deep and permanent patterning of the body in the
performance of particular physical skills. Likewise, we are impressed
with demonstrations of visual-spatial skills such as striking a fast-moving
curve ball or creatively arranging furniture in a room. Individuals with
the ability to speak more than one language or who possess a rich and
diverse vocabulary are highly valued in our society and have certain specialized areas of highly developed memories.

Our memories are malleable and can change over time. Variations in
our moods, health, cultural influences, and dispositions can cloud or al-
ter memories. So can time. Because memories reside within the complex
tapestry of brain neurons and networks, they are strengthened by use and
diminished by misuse. When we consciously recollect a past event or experience, we literally reconstruct it from the various submemory fragments that combine to form a whole memory. Since the brain is an associative organ that synthesizes submemories of similar events during the
reconstruction process, subtle changes in the shape and content of a

memory can occur. Over time, these subtle alterations may accumulate into distorted or perverted perceptions of past events (Ratey 2001).

Interestingly, as we become expert at a particular skill, our memories of that skill move deeper into the brain. Learning a new skill requires a considerable amount of neocortical effort. As we know, it is the outer executive layer of the brain that performs the bulk of cognitive tasks. New or novel situations and tasks require high levels of concentration and mental effort. As skills and tasks become increasingly familiar and routine, they require less and less cortical effort and space. Brain-imaging technology has demonstrated that with practice the memories needed to perform certain skills and tasks move deeper into the autonomic structures of the brain thus freeing up cortical space for processing other new tasks and skills. This phenomenon explains why experts can often perform tasks and skills without the same level of conscious effort required by novices (e.g., take, for example, Tiger Woods versus the typical weekend golfer or chess master Bobby Fisher versus the average player). It also helps to explain why intuitive decisions come more easily to principals who have a great deal of experience with particular tasks or job functions. It is likely that the foundation for many intuitions resides within implicit memory structures like the amygdala and hippocampus, which can activate without conscious effort.

As we noted earlier, sleep helps to sort and solidify memories. Much of this activity occurs during REM (rapid eye movement) sleep through continuous communications between the amygdala, the cingulate gyrus, and the occipital lobes. Not surprisingly, many people experience intuitive thoughts while they sleep. We interviewed a principal who recounted numerous experiences of waking suddenly from a deep sleep with an answer to a problem that had defied attempts to resolve it consciously. During sleep, the mind moves easily and without distraction between memories (recent and old) and can assemble creative links between them and a myriad of other cognitive functions that allow one to make estimations, predictions, and inferences. Unfettered by conscious distractions and impulse controls, sleep offers up the entire repertoire of mental functions and opens them for inspection and autocreative processing (Damasio 1999; Hobson 1999; Ratey 2001).

As we have seen, brain structures, neurochemical agents, conscious states, emotions, and memories work in a complex synchrony to produce thoughts, memories, decisions, and intuitions. There is another important dimension to our exploration of the brain-mind and its relationship to intuitive decision making, and that is the dimension of cognition. How the brain-mind thinks and reflects, processes information, learns, and comes to know things are critically important elements of the intuitive experience. In the following section, we discuss several key ideas relating to human cognition that will provide insights into how the thinking mind works and how one can work to refine and expand its cognitive capacities.

COGNITION: HOW WE THINK, LEARN, AND COME TO KNOW

We know that much of the information received and processed by the brain-mind is subconscious and relies on a vast array of coordinated brain structures and neurochemicals. We learn a great deal from the mere exposure to everyday events and social interactions. As we encounter stimuli from internal and external environments, the neural circuitry of our brains undergoes a continuous process of shaping and reshaping. This process occurs throughout our lives. In the absence of a pathological malfunction (such as Alzheimer's disease), the human brain can continue to evolve and change its neural patterns indefinitely. This process, called "synaptic sculpting," is stimulated by various mental activities like reading, reflecting, problem solving, and forms of creative expression. Much like the marathon runner who must combine endurance, speed, and strength training in order to maximize performance potential, the human brain responds to and thrives on various kinds of cognitive stimuli. The sculpting process can be described as both "experience-expectant" and "experience-dependent." The experience-expectant brain continuously refines, prunes, and reshapes existing neural circuits while the experience-dependent brain generates new circuits and dendritic growth through the processing of our life experiences (Dickmann and Stanford-Blair 2002, 57, 82; Ratey 2001).

The brain-mind is an associative entity that develops perceptions and thoughts by assembling chunks and bits of sensory information flavored by past experiences, memories, desires, beliefs, values, dispositions, skills, and knowledge. The brain-mind seeks out patterns and relationships in an effort to make sense of surrounding environments and stimuli. As it does this, it looks for the unusual and combines fragments of perceptions into novel constructions. It does this in a storylike fashion that is often characterized by vivid mental images. The brain-mind is driven by an innate curiosity and a creative urge to construct new knowledge. This imaginative element of the brain-mind is a uniquely human trait and serves to stimulate learning by posing alternative perspectives, scenarios, interpretations, and understandings. The brain-mind is also programmed to identify big ideas and to assemble them into broad concepts and mental schemas. It gravitates naturally toward tasks that require approximations rather than those that are laden with detailed minutia (Dickmann and Stanford-Blair 2002; Hobson 1999).

The brain-mind is especially attuned to social stimuli. According to Dickmann and Stanford-Blair (2002, 58), "Social interaction is the foil that most effectively sharpens your exotic neural circuitry." Our ability to read social situations and identify important social cues has been deeply ingrained through thousands of years of evolutionary development. Our survival as a species has, to a large extent, been the result of an inherent drive to affiliate and band together with other humans. In the absence of lethal defense mechanisms like sharp fangs, powerful jaws, or claws, humans found that social grouping was essential for survival. A sizeable portion of our ability to read and negotiate social environments has become so deeply programmed genetically that it occurs without conscious awareness.

The human brain-mind possesses an immense capacity to use and transfer neural circuits and networks to address a variety of mental tasks. For example, it has long been acknowledged that physical movement in very young children is crucial for the development of cognitive skills. In fact, from an evolutionary perspective, virtually everything the brain does is (or was) related to movement. "The brain circuits used to order, sequence, and time a mental act are the same ones used to order, sequence, and time a physical act" (Ratey 2001, 148). Likewise, the neural pathways one uses when playing a musical instrument or painting a picture overlap with those used to solve certain mathematical problems. It seems that the neural circuits employed to recognize and attend to spatial relationships can be used in a variety of contexts. The process of neural transfer occurs in many different ways and underscores what educators have known for years—that the holistic development of the mind requires exposure to and practice with numerous learning activities and subject domains.

One fascinating characteristic of the brain-mind is its ability to semanti-cally prime itself. Semantic priming occurs when certain neural circuits si-multaneously activate other related networks. This process is important for both memory formation and retrieval. We believe that semantic priming plays an important role in the development of intuition. Here is how it works. As we learn and form new memories, our minds create categories of images and mental representations. Categories are based on perceived similarities among images and representations past and present. They are also enriched by the depth and breadth of our life experiences. Take, for example, the word *fish*. For most of us, the word conjures up an immedi-ate mental image of a fish. Depending upon our experiences, fears, likes, dislikes, and so forth, one person's mental image of a fish might look like a minnow whereas another person's might look like a shark. Regardless, there are also parallel images formed when the word *fish* is spoken. For some, a mental image of the ocean appears, for others a fishing boat, and for yet others, a fishing rod and net. These multiple images serve to enrich our perceptions, memories, and mental representations. By themselves, they can easily lead to other unrelated images, but they can also be most helpful in priming our memories by activating parallel neural pathways. When you say fish, we automatically recall a morning visit to the Seattle fish market where fishermen were unloading their catch and literally toss-ing salmon, ocean bass, and other fish from the back of a truck, one fish-erman to another, all the way to the icy countertops of the vendor's booth. We also recall a recent trip to Hawaii where we had a delicious meal of mahimahi. Each of these experiences, and others like them, can trigger our memories of fish and vice versa. It is in effect a looping process whereby the brain-mind assembles seemingly disparate images and impressions in the formulation of a whole thought. Likewise, the presence of a whole thought in our minds can stimulate other parallel recollections of images and experiences (Hobson 1999).

Understanding how and why semantic priming works is particularly important for two reasons. First, it underscores the need to expose chil-dren (and adults) to a wide range of experiences and ideas. Consider, for a moment, how an impoverished and poorly educated child from the depths of the inner city might think differently about the word fish than an economically advantaged and well-educated child from the suburbs. Second, it points to a very important principle of intuitive thinking. People who have diverse and rich experiences are also likely to possess highly imaginative minds—a critical attribute of the intuitive thinker. The moral of this story is to encourage people to expand their experiences through travel, hobbies, social engagements, participation in the arts, exercise, and other activities that extend beyond the day-to-day requirements of the job.

The acquisition of knowledge comes through two primary prisms: the tacit system and the deliberate system. Tacit system knowledge includes nondeliberative, subconscious, processes like intuition (i.e., we know without knowing how we know). The deliberate system includes purposeful, consciously rational, and analytical processes to gain information or to solve problems. Within this framework, we possess many forms of knowledge, both declarative (i.e., what we know) and procedural (i.e., the tacit rules and procedures that link to declarative knowledge). Howard Gardner (1993) extends these ideas by proposing that humans possess several different kinds of knowledge, some that require pure reason and some that require highly abstract and aesthetic cognitive tools.

We know that when one becomes very knowledgeable about a certain subject, thing, or domain of ideas, he is considered to be an expert. We have talked about experts and their ability to chunk information, to think quickly and holistically, and to apply intuitive solutions to complex problems. However, there is another, neurobiological dimension to expertise described by Daniel Goleman (1995, 90) as "flow." Flow occurs when conscious awareness and actions come together. Time melts away and small preoccupations and worries are greatly diminished. There is a sense of total presence in the action being taken that is egoless, centered, and of the moment. Cortical arousal levels are quieted in a relaxed, yet focused, way. The individual in flow is highly attuned to subtle changes in the environment and can make quick adjustments when necessary. In fact, a certain level of stress is important. The task at hand must not be too easy but must stretch one's level of ability. Flow is necessary for mastery of any task. It represents the seemingly effortless actions of a highly motivated individual who, for the moment, is devoid of emotional turmoil. It is during moments of flow that one not only performs with greatest efficiency but is most open to new learning. We believe that flow can prime the subconscious mind in ways that elicit intuitive thoughts and ideas.

Although flow by itself is not an intuitive state, its neurological processes may influence what Damasio (1994, 165) calls "somatic marker signaling." This occurs when one receives a gut feeling or a somewhat ambiguous sense of knowing. It comes instantaneously and consists of feelings generated from secondary (i.e., nuanced and subtle) emotions that have been connected through various learning experiences to certain predicted scenarios. Somatic marker signaling also involves the subconscious sorting and organizing of preexisting mental schemas, images, and feelings. This process allows one to increase decision accuracy by narrowing the decision choice options and by focusing attention.

The gap between flow, somatic marker signaling, and intuition is a narrow one. But just what is an intuition? For one thing, it is a form of expertise based upon the depth and breadth of an individual's experience. Remember, intuitions can be wrong. And, people with a lot of experience may not necessarily be experts. Neurologically, intuition is produced through a process that appears to inhibit the regulatory actions of core neural circuits of the brain responsible for producing body-state changes. That is, without the overt stimuli that would normally produce feelings of fear, excitement, and so forth, the brain-mind trips the circuits that trigger body-state changes like feelings of warmth, rapid heart rate, or tingling in the stomach. Simultaneously, the brain-mind also suppresses the conscious processing of information, issuing instead an impulsive signal without conscious mediation (Damasio 1994).

Is intuitive decision making trustworthy? We would love to answer that question with an unqualified yes. But, like any form of cognition, the truth is that it depends on a number of important contributing factors such as the accuracy and quality of past experiences, the motivations of the beholder, the physical and mental health of the beholder, the attributes and characteristics of the problem, and so on.

One way to increase the accuracy of intuitive decisions is to learn how to align them with the rules and protocols of the scientific method—to become so expert in the application of the scientific method (i.e., rational/ analytical problem-solving steps) that it becomes almost automatic. Recall, that as one becomes increasingly expert at a given skill, the neurological circuitry used to process and direct the individual in the learning and application of the skill moves from the neocortex to the autonomic regions of the limbic system and brain stem. In other words, the individual no longer has to think much about the skill in order to demonstrate it. So the better one becomes at structured decision making, the greater the chances of developing well-constructed intuitions. It makes sense to us (Hogarth 2001).

SUMMARY

We have covered several important concepts about the brain-mind, its structures, functions, and its relationship to intuitive decision making. Research on the human brain, its mechanisms, and its capacity for abstract thought continues to unlock new secrets and unveil new insights about this incredibly sophisticated and complex organ. There is little question that much remains to be learned about the brain-mind. However, in recent years we have come to understand that, like an iceberg, a great deal that goes on in the brain-mind occurs below the surface of consciousness. Centuries ago, when Cartesian philosopher René Descartes uttered the comment "cogito ergo sum" (I think, therefore I am), he had no way of knowing just how powerful and important the subconscious mind was in the formulation of thoughts, the processing of memories, the management of emotions, and the creation of new ideas. Thinking is not just a conscious act. It is a phenomenon that operates at many different levels of consciousness and depends on a complex chain of neurobiological events, many of which have become deeply ingrained in the human brain-mind through eons of evolutionary development. It may be more accurate to say "I am, therefore I think."

One of our motives for writing this chapter was to dispel the attacks on intuitive decision making by naysayers and skeptics who argue that the best decisions are those that are rationally and analytically thought out, and that intuition is really a soft and unreliable way to reach good decisions. That just isn't so. As we have tried to convey throughout this book, there is a time, a place, and a context for all forms of decision making. Classical forms of analytic reasoning play an enormously important role in the processing of information and solution of difficult problems. However, intuition can play an equally important role under certain circumstances where problem attributes are not so neat and tidy that they can be effectively massaged by classical decision approaches.

As we see in the next chapter, school principals often rely upon and trust their intuitions to guide them through their most important decisions. Most of chapter 5 presents the results of research that we conducted with ninety California public school principals on the topic of intuitive decision making. The purposes of our study were to find out (a) if principals used their intuitions to solve problems and make decisions, (b) how often intuition was used in this way, (c) with what kinds of problems did they use intuition, and (d) what was the intuitive experience like at the moment of solution (i.e., at that point when an intuitive solution became conscious).

5

VOICES FROM THE FIELD: A STUDY OF INTUITIVE DECISION MAKING

Our interest in studying intuitive decision making by principals emerged about two years ago in the midst of a discussion about how public education in America has become increasingly standardized and dependent upon data-driven decisions and sophisticated computer systems. We reached the conclusion that public expectations about what principals do and how they should go about their jobs were shifting. We conjectured that the days when good judgment and common sense were the benchmarks of a good decision were rapidly disappearing. Instead, it seemed that principals were becoming data analysts and expected to be supremely rational decision makers. "Just give me the numbers, please! The data don't lie."

We remembered our own experiences as school principals (and district superintendents) and recalled that most of our toughest decisions were the ones where computer programs and lots of quantitative data just weren't very useful. We also remembered that our most difficult decisions had been made with a considerable amount of intuitive or gut feeling. We asked ourselves if times had indeed changed. Perhaps the demands and dynamics of the principalship no longer had room for less-formal methods of decision making. So, to begin our journey of inquiry, we did a couple of things. First, we talked with principals whom we knew. Second, we examined the educational administration course curricula from the top twenty schools of education in America as ranked by *U.S. News and World Report*. What we found confirmed our suspicions that principals relied very little on classical forms of decision analysis when resolving complex problems. We also found that university administrative training programs continued to place a heavy emphasis on courses that taught classical/analytical decision making. In fact, we were unable to find even one course that focused on nonquantitative forms of decision making and problem solving. We found the paradox troubling. It seemed that not only our own experiences, but the experiences of every principal we talked with, underscored the fact that formalized models of decision making really weren't used very much—particularly with the class of problems that involved conflicting values, ambiguous information, and unclear or disputed goals. After much discussion, reflecting, and reading, we developed our own study that we hoped would help us better understand the role of intuitive decision making with contemporary public school principals. In this chapter, we provide an overview of the methods, results, and implications of our research into the intuitive dimensions of administrative decision making.

Our study was designed to examine how school principals use and experience intuitive decision-making processes when solving complex administrative problems. Particular emphasis was placed on understanding the phenomenon of intuition at the moment of solution—at the point when an intuitive solution reaches conscious awareness. We also wanted to better understand how intuitive processes intersected with rational/analytical decision strategies during complex problem solving and decision making.

Our research design consisted of two phases: a mailed survey (see the appendix) and follow-up interviews with a subsample drawn from survey respondents. Data analyses for the survey consisted of descriptive and inferential statistics while a phenomenological approach was used to analyze interview data.

The survey method was used to satisfy two objectives. First, we wanted general information from a representative sample of California public school principals regarding their intuitive abilities and their use of intuition in decision making. Second, we wanted to use the survey as a vehicle for selecting a subsample of highly intuitive individuals for follow-up interviews designed to explore in greater depth the intuitive experience during administrative decision making.

THE SURVEY SAMPLE

All 221 public school principals in Contra Costa County, California, received a copy of the survey. One hundred forty three principals (64.7 percent) were from elementary schools, thirty-three were from middle or junior high schools (14.9 percent); and forty-five were from high schools (20.4 percent).

Contra Costa County is the ninth-largest county in California with a population of 930,000 (based on the 2000 census data). Within the county, there are nineteen cities with populations ranging from approximately 11,000 to 125,000. Approximately 151,000 residents live in unincorporated areas of the county. We selected Contra Costa County for its similarity to the demographic characteristics of the state as a whole.

THE SURVEY

Each principal in the sample was mailed a copy of the AIM (Agor Intuitive Management) survey. Although the survey was not designed specifically for public school principals, we selected it for use in the study for three reasons. First, according to its author, Dr. Weston Agor, much of the survey was modeled after the intuitive portions of the Myers-Briggs Type Indicator, a widely used and highly respected personality profile survey. Second, more than five thousand managers in both private and public sector jobs have taken the AIM survey under research conducted by Dr. Agor. Agor's test groups included corporate CEOs, military officers, college presidents, state health managers, city managers, state legislators, and legislative staff (Agor 1992). Third, the survey is brief and relatively easy to complete, and it assesses both intuitive ability and its use in management decision making.

Our selection of the AIM survey followed an extensive literature search for tests and measurements of intuitive decision making and correspondences with other authors in the field of intuitive management. No other intuitive assessment tool approached the AIM survey in terms of the three characteristics described above. Having said this, however, we recognize that empirically valid and reliable assessments of intuition are difficult if not impossible to devise. After-the-fact checklists and short narrative descriptions rarely capture the full depth and breadth of a highly subjective experience. Because of this, we acknowledge that any survey is limited in its ability to measure accurately and precisely an individual's intuitive ability. We believe that the AIM survey is best used for providing a look at an individual's tendencies and general orientations toward the use of intuitive decision processes rather than as a definitive diagnostic of the intuitive experience. In addition, we found the survey to be a useful tool for identifying and selecting high-scoring principals for follow-up interviews. The assumption we made was that the highest scoring principals were potentially the most intuitive principals. Given the limitations of the survey, we recognize that our subsample of six high-scoring principals could have excluded some highly intuitive principals from our follow-up interviews. With those caveats in mind, we acknowledge that the results of our study are at best suggestive and certainly not conclusive.

Before sending the survey, we made minor modifications to the demographic information section to better align its contents with educational leadership contexts. Part 1 of the survey consisted of twelve questions that provided information about the respondent's "underlying or potential intuitive ability" (Agor 1992, 9). With each question, respondents were asked to select one of two possible answers (forced choice).

Part 1 was scored according to the following criteria:

1. The total number of "a" responses for questions 1, 3, 5, 6, and 11 and the total number of "b" responses to questions 2, 4, 7, 8, 9, 10, and 12 represented an individual's intuitive score.
2. Subtracting the intuitive score from 12 (the total number of questions in part 1) provided an individual's thinking score (i.e., rational/analytical).

According to Agor (1992), if an individual's highest score is intuitive then she possesses "the ability to base decisions on unknowns or possibilities." Moreover, the individual has "the potential to apply ingenuity to problems and is more likely to prefer management situations that are unstructured, fluid and spontaneous." In contrast, an individual with a

higher score on the thinking dimension has the "ability to apply experience to problems, to bring up pertinent facts, to keep track of essential
details, and to face difficulties with realism" (11).

Part 2 of the survey consisted of fifteen questions. Some questions required short narrative responses and some required forced-choice
responses among three or more possible answers. Part 2 provided descriptive information about the problem contexts faced by respondents
as well as their experiences when using intuition to make complex decisions. It also provided information about strategies or techniques used
by respondents to develop their intuitive abilities.

Dillman's Total Survey Design Method (1978) was used as the framework for formatting and disseminating the surveys and for follow-up
mailings to nonresponders.

FOLLOW-UP INTERVIEWS

Follow-up face-to-face interviews were held with the six highest-scoring
respondents to part 1 of the survey. Four respondents (three females and
one male) scored 9 out of a possible 12 points on the rating scale. Two respondents (both male) scored 10 points. The purpose of the interviews was
to explore in greater depth the ways in which highly intuitive principals experience, use, access, and develop intuitive decision-making skills. We
were also interested in the relationship between intuitive and rational/
analytical decision processes. Using Patton's (1990) general interview guide
approach, questions were framed in ways that would allow us to probe and
examine in depth the unique perspectives and experiences of each respondent. The interview guide approach includes a general list of questions or issues that provides the interviewer with the flexibility to focus on
particular subjects and to present questions in a more conversational style.
Key questions and issues are raised without the rigidity present in a structured interview process. Below is a list of the questions we used to guide
us in shaping and implementing the interviews.

1. How do principals use their intuition to solve complex problems?
2. With what kinds of problems do principals most often use their intuition during the decision-making process?
3. How was intuition experienced at the moment of solution?

4. At what point in the decision process does intuition occur?
5. How effective are decisions made through the use of intuition?
6. How does intuition interact with rational/analytical thinking during complex decision making?
7. Do principals use any strategies or techniques to develop, enhance, or access their intuition?

DATA ANALYSIS

Responses to part 1 of the survey were analyzed by totaling the frequency of responses to each of the twelve items and calculating the percentage of responses to each item. The response totals and percentages were then compared by gender and by years of experience as a principal. Experienced principals were defined as having more than four years in the principalship. Our decision to compare gender and experience groups stemmed from research by Agor (1986) and the work of Dreyfus and Dreyfus (1986) that indicated such factors can influence intuitive thinking or the use of intuition during decision making. Finally, we used a z-test of the difference between two independent proportions to determine if differences in the responses to items in part 1 given by males and females and by experienced and inexperienced principals were statistically significant ($\geq$ = 1.96; alpha $\leq$ 0.05).

Items 13 through 27 in part 2 of the survey included questions regarding the use of intuition on the job and several demographic items pertaining to school setting, experience, gender, and ethnic background. For eight of these items, respondents could select as many answers as applied. For six items, respondents could select only one best answer. As with part 1, responses were totaled, percentage values calculated, and comparisons made using the z-test of the difference between two independent proportions to determine if significant differences occurred between male and female respondents and between experienced and inexperienced respondents. Items 14 through 22 provided space for narrative comments as well. These were transcribed and compared for thematic similarities.

Each of the six interviews lasted from sixty to ninety minutes and was tape recorded with the permission of the interviewee. Immediately following each interview, we tape-recorded our impressions and observations about the respondent and the respondent's answers to our questions. This was done privately. All tape recordings were then transcribed and analyzed using Moustakas's (1994) empirical phenomenological approach. According to Moustakas,

> The empirical phenomenological approach involves a return to experience in order to obtain comprehensive descriptions that provide the basis for a reflective structural analysis that portrays the essences of the experience. The aim is to determine what an experience means for the persons who have had the experience and are able to provide a comprehensive description of it. From the individual descriptions general or universal meanings are derived, in other words the essences or structures of the experience. (13)

SURVEY RESULTS

Ninety principals (40.7 percent) completed the surveys and returned them. Among the surveys returned, fifty (55.5 percent) were from elementary school principals, sixteen (17.7 percent) were from middle or junior high school principals, and twenty-four (26.6 percent) were from high school principals. The proportion of responses compared favorably with the total number of schools of each type in the county (i.e., 64.7 percent elementary, 14.9 percent middle or junior high, 20.4 percent high school). Thirty-three (36.6 percent) respondents were male and fifty-seven (63.3 percent) were female. Fifty-four (56.6 percent) respondents were experienced principals while thirty-nine (43.3 percent) were inexperienced. Seventy-five (83.3 percent) principals reported that they were Caucasian, seven (7.8 percent) were African American, three (3.3 percent) were Mexican American, two (2.2 percent) were Asian, two indicated Other Hispanic, and one indicated Filipino. Finally, the majority of principals worked in schools with fewer than one thousand students, fifty-nine (68.6 percent).

Part 1 of the survey consisted of twelve questions that provided information about the respondent's "underlying or potential intuitive ability." Agor's (1992) national sample of approximately five thousand managers yielded a mean intuitive score of 6.5 out of a possible 12-point rating scale. Mean scores by gender were 6.9 for females and 6.3 for males. Our results were slightly different from Agor's. Our sample had a mean score of 6.42 for all respondents, and a score of 6.58 for males and 6.33 for fe-males. In Agor's national sample, individuals with a score of 10 or above were considered "highly intuitive," and fell within the top 10 percent of all respondents. In our study, only two (2.2 percent) of the respondents scored 10 or above, while fifteen (16.7) scored 9 or above. Because of this, we adjusted the definition of highly intuitive to those who scored 9 or above. To arrive at six respondents for follow-up interviews, we took into account an individual's total score on part 1 of the survey, years of ex-perience as a principal, and the ability to describe an example of a very important decision where he followed his intuition and experienced a successful outcome (see question 16 on the AIM survey).

In our study, the proportion of males who scored 9 or above on part 1 was significantly higher than the proportion of females (27.3 percent vs.10.5 percent; $z \geq 2.05$). However, when all responses that fell within the "intuitive" rating category were analyzed, the proportion of males was not significantly different from the proportion of females (65 per-cent vs. 68 percent). Our results contradict other studies that have found females to be more intuitive than males (Hogarth 2001). We are not certain why this is so. One possibility is that in order to be perceived as competent to serve in a traditionally male-dominated profession, women have had to become more male-like, which means more direc-tive, analytical, and assertive. Of course, another possibility is that the survey does not accurately measure what it purports to measure, in which case, the results could be subject to error.

Our data revealed that the number of experienced principals who scored 9 or above on the survey was significantly larger than the num-ber of inexperienced principals. This finding is consistent with the liter-ature on expertise. Remember, as one becomes increasingly expert at a task or knowledge domain, the ability to effectively use heuristic short-cuts or intuition increases. Our study seems to support this.

Part 2 of the survey provided descriptive information about the problem contexts faced by, and experiences of, the respondents when using intuition to make complex decisions. It also provided informa-tion about strategies or techniques used by respondents to develop their intuitive abilities. There were twelve questions in this section. Each question provided several possible answers and a section for narrative comments.

First, 92 percent of the respondents reported that they frequently used intuition to guide them through their most important decisions! It was clear that with our sample, intuition played not simply a supporting role but a *primary* role in their decision making. Interestingly, there were no significant differences between males and females on this item. Nevertheless, 92 percent caught us a bit by surprise. We had no idea just how powerful intuition was in the processes of resolving complex problems.

Among our respondents, intuition seemed to be used most frequently when the problem under consideration had several plausible alternatives rather than just a few limited choices. This held true for males, females, experienced, and inexperienced principals. In addition, several respondents reported that their intuitions were called upon when problems had variables that were not scientifically predictable and where facts were limited. Again, these findings support the concept reported in the literature that intuition seems to emerge when problems are complex, nontransparent, and messy (Agor 1986; Hogarth 2001).

Table 5.1 provides a comparative look at the frequency and percentage of responses by males and females, and by experienced and inexperienced principals on the kinds of important problem characteristics or attributes where they were most likely to use intuition.

Respondents were asked to indicate the kinds of feelings experienced or signals received when they knew that an intuitive decision was right.

Table 5.1. Types of Problems Where Intuition Is Used to Make Important Decisions

Item	Total	Males	Females	Experienced	Inexperienced
A	35 (13.7%)	15 (17%)	20 (11.9%)	21 (15.2%)	14 (11.9%)
B	52 (20.3%)	15 (17%)	37 (22%)	26 (18.8%)	26 (22%)
C	52 (20.3%)	14 (15.9%)	38 (22.6%)	28 (20.3%)	24 (20.3%)
D	70 (27.3%)	24 (27.3%)	46 (27.4%)	36 (26.1%)	34 (20.0%)
E	44 (17.2%)	17 (19.3%)	27 (16.1%)	26 (18.8%)	18 (15.3%)
F	3 (1.2%)	3 (3.4%)	0	1 (.07%)	2 (1.7%)

Key: A = where there is a high degree of certainty
      B = where there is little previous precedent
      C = where variables are less scientifically predictable or where "facts" are limited
      D = where there are several plausible alternative solutions to choose from with good arguments
          for each
      E = where time is limited and there is pressure to be right
      F = other

As a group, most respondents stated that they felt peaceful and calm. Although there were slight differences in the responses by males, females, experienced, and inexperienced principals, they were not significant.

Table 5.2 provides a comparative look at the frequency and percentage of responses by males and females and by experienced and inexperienced principals on how they felt when they knew that an intuitive decision was right.

Seven respondents provided additional comments. Two stated that they "just knew" the decision was right. Similarly, another stated that he had a "gut-feeling" to that effect. Other responses included a feeling of confidence, a sense of verification, and a feeling of pride.

Respondents were also asked to give an example (or two) of a very important decision where they followed their intuition and it proved to be right. This question required a narrative response only. Sixty-four respondents provided 104 separate narrative comments. We analyzed their answers and grouped them according to nine key themes:

1. Decisions involving hiring or firing employees.
2. Decisions involving program, policy, or schedule development or changes.
3. Decisions involving conflicts or difficult situations with parents, teachers, or school board members.
4. Decisions involving student conduct or discipline.
5. Decisions involving student safety, welfare, or special needs.
6. Decisions involving communicating and sharing information.

Table 5.2. Group Comparisons of the Feelings Experienced When One Knew That an Intuitive Decision Was Right

Item	Total	Males	Females	Experienced	Inexperienced
A	40 (20.5%)	17 (23.6%)	23 (18.7%)	23 (19.5%)	17 (22.1%)
B	22 (11.3%)	9 (12.5%)	13 (10.6%)	13 (11%)	9 (11.7%)
C	47 (24.1%)	17 (23.6%)	30 (24.4%)	26 (22%)	21 (27.3%)
D	43 (22.1%)	16 (22.2%)	27 (22%)	27 (22.9%)	16 (20.8%)
E	41 (21%)	11 (15.3%)	30 (24.4%)	28 (23.7%)	13 (16.9%)
F	2 (1%)	2 (2.8%)	0	1 (.85%)	1 (1.3%)

Key: A = excitement
B = warmth
C = peaceful/calm
D = high energy
E = sudden flash of insight
F = other

7. Decisions involving personal career choices.
8. Decisions involving staffing and assignments.
9. Decisions involving employee evaluations.

Decisions involving the hiring or firing of employees was the most fre quently recorded theme. This was not particularly surprising to us since we have had many experiences in our own careers with hiring and firing employees. Personnel decisions of this sort are very difficult and are generally not effectively made through quantitative analysis. Education is a people business and, as such, judgments about an individual's professional abilities and personal qualities can be highly subjective. Other problem types that were frequently mentioned included decisions where school programs, policies, or schedules were involved, and decisions involving conflicts or difficult situations with parents, teachers, or school board members.

Although males and experienced principals were slightly more likely to use intuition when making hiring or firing decisions than females and inexperienced principals, the differences were not statistically significant.

Table 5.3 shows the frequency and percentage of the responses to the nine decision categories in descending order.

Table 5.3. Frequency and Percent of Responses to Intuitive Decision Categories

Decision Category	Total	Male	Female	Experienced	Inexperienced
Hire/Fire	30 (30.3%)	13 (34.2%)	17 (27.9%)	21 (35.6%)	9 (22.5%)
Program, Policy, Scheduling	13 (13.1%)	6 (15.8%)	7 (11.5%)	9 (15.3%)	4 (10%)
Conflicts, Difficult Situations	13 (13.1%)	4 (10.5%)	9 (14.8%)	5 (8.5%)	8 (20%)
Safety, Welfare, Spec. Needs	11 (11%)	4 (10.5%)	7 (11.5%)	9 (15.3%)	2 (5%)
Student Conduct/ Discipline	9 (9.1%)	4 (10.5%)	5 (8.2%)	3 (5.1%)	6 (15%)
Communicating, Sharing	9 (9.1%)	5 (13.2%)	4 (6.6%)	4 (6.8%)	5 (12.5%)
Career Choice	8 (8.1%)	1 (2.6%)	7 (11.5%)	4 (6.8%)	4 (6.8)
Staffing, Assignment	4 (4%)	0	4 (6.6%)	2 (3.4%)	2 (5%)
Evaluation	2 (2%)	1 (2.6%)	1 (1.6%)	2 (3.4%)	0

Not surprisingly, the majority of respondents indicated that they felt anxious when their intuitions revealed that they were heading in the wrong direction strategically. Eleven respondents provided additional narrative comments. "Fear" was cited by two respondents, as was "self-doubt." "Feeling of pressure," "uncertainty," "lack of sleep," and "discontentment" were each mentioned by separate respondents. Gender or amount of experience made no significant difference in the principals' feelings.

There were times when certain conditions obstructed the use of intuition during decision making. The most frequently noted conditions were when the respondent felt rushed, angry, or under stress. The fact that such feelings can obstruct one's use of intuition makes sense. Excessive levels of stress cause the release of cortisol in the brain and reduce levels of serotonin, dopamine, and norepinephrine. As a result, the ability of the brain-mind to function smoothly and efficiently is inhibited. As the stressed mind overflows with stimuli and suffers a dramatic shift in the work of chemical neurotransmitters, it also signals feelings of distress and discomfort. Such feelings are not conducive to good decision making, intuitive or otherwise.

Ironically, our follow-up interviews with a subsample of six principals revealed that their intuitions came to them most frequently and successfully under stressful conditions. The reason for this paradox may be due to two factors. First, our subsample consisted of the highest scoring principals on the survey. According to the survey results, they were the most intuitive of all respondents. Therefore, their minds were primed to make intuitive decisions when confronted with difficult problems. They were also highly experienced principals. All six had been principals for over four years. Since expertise appears to be related to intuitive ability, it is likely that each of the six principals possessed a vast reservoir of experiences dealing with crises and administrative dilemmas and had consciously and unconsciously created a variety of mental schemas that could be quickly drawn upon when faced with similar situations.

However, when all responses to the survey were tabulated, gender or amount of experience didn't seem to make much difference in the kinds of conditions that could obstruct a principal's intuition. A few survey respondents provided additional narrative comments such as a "lack of" or "limited information," "time pressure," "pressure from superiors," "when feeling threatened or unsafe," and "fatigue or hunger."

The survey also asked respondents if they felt comfortable sharing their intuitions with others. Our prediction was that most principals would, in fact, prefer to keep such feeling to themselves. Surprisingly, our predictions were way off. Over 90 percent of all principals indicated that they either do share or would share their intuitive decisions with others. Forty-six respondents provided additional narrative comments. We synthesized and grouped these comments into four key themes. The largest number of responses fell under the theme "Trust and belief in the value and use of intuition during decision making." For example, one respondent stated, "I believe it is a powerful tool." Another stated, "Intuition is reality and part of who I am." A third respondent noted that, "There is always a valid thought-out reason behind it, but you may not realize it at that point."

The second-largest number of responses fell under the theme "Belief in being open, honest, and sharing." There were only two respondents who commented that they did not believe in sharing. One wrote, "Colleagues don't understand." The other wrote, "When accountability is at the forefront of education today, it does not intuitively seem right to base decisions on intuition."

Nevertheless, the data from our study clearly underscore an extremely high level of comfort, if not confidence, in intuitive decision making by principals. It is our contention that the level of importance attributed to intuitive decision making by principals in the field is not widely reflected in principal preparation curricula. Again, there were no significant differences in the proportion of responses by gender or level of experience.

Understanding when intuition works best during decision making can help one know when to be especially receptive to such feelings. Equal numbers of respondents to the survey indicated that their intuitions work best at the very end of a decision process when trying to sift through and digest all the cues and information available and at various times, depending on the problem or issue at hand. As we will discuss later in this chapter, the results of our interviews with six highly intuitive principals were different in this regard than for the sample as a whole. There were, however, no significant differences in responses between genders, or between experienced and inexperienced principals.

Several respondents provided additional clarifying comments. For six respondents, the use of intuition depended upon one or more of the following factors: the complexity of the problem, the immediacy of the problem, the characteristics and needs of the participants involved with the problem, the degree of knowledge about problem facts, and the impact of

decision outcomes. One respondent stated that "Daydreaming at the beginning allows me to run through several scenarios quickly." Another said,
"Almost by definition, no two circumstances are the same, so no necessarily categorical use of intuition employed." From such statements, we
concluded that intuition is used at several junctures and in many different
ways during decision making. It does not, as many people believe, manifest itself primarily at the beginning of a decision.

Not surprisingly, the majority of respondents did nothing in particular to draw upon their intuitive abilities more effectively when making
decisions. Their intuitions simply came when they came. And, when
most principals were done with decision making, very little if any reflective thinking occurred about how they could activate or enhance
their intuitions. Even though the majority of female respondents did
nothing to draw upon their intuitions, as a group they were significantly
more likely than males to make some effort at this. This finding is consistent with long-standing stereotypes of women as being open, flexible,
and sensitive decision makers and men as being more analytical, objective, and detached (Hogarth 2001). There were, however, no significant
differences between experienced and inexperienced principals.

When we examined several additional written comments on this item,
we found that the most frequently mentioned technique used to draw
upon one's intuitive abilities was to search for, gather, and analyze as much
information as possible before making a decision. It seems as though most
principals continued to seek as much factual data as possible and to apply
some measure of analysis first. Some respondents noted that they relied
upon various centering techniques such as meditation, relaxation, reflection, and prayer while a few mentioned that they attempted to visualize
and see the problem and its possible solutions before making a final decision. We will return to these ideas later on in the chapter since they were
prominent responses among our six interviewees.

A number of comments were especially insightful. One respondent
wrote, "A bell goes off when I hear something that I feel is off. So I stop
and look for facts." Another wrote, "I try to stop thinking about facts and
try not to get too complicated—attempt not to be perfect." A third respondent wrote, "I gather data, then listen to internal indicators—heart,
guts, sense of peace or dread." And finally, one respondent wrote, "I just
always keep in mind what is best for students."

Table 5.4. Frequency and Percentage of Eight Common Techniques Used to Draw Upon Intuition

Number of Responses	Percentage	Key Theme
10	29.1%	Analyze facts, search for, and gather as much information and data as possible.
7	20.6%	Centering techniques such as meditation, relaxation, reflection, and prayer.
6	17.5%	Visualize and see the problem and its possible solutions.
4	11.8%	Personal reflection of past experiences.
4	11.8%	Personal reflection by weighing pros and cons of a solution.
4	11.8%	Talk with others about the problem.
1	2.9%	Self-talk.
1	2.9%	Ask careful questions and listen well.

The frequency and percentage of responses to each of eight themes constructed from the narrative comments are provided in table 5.4. Note that of the respondents who did report using some technique to draw upon their intuitions, over 70 percent cited approaches that were nonanalytical and qualitative.

FOLLOW-UP INTERVIEWS: METHODS AND STRUCTURES

As we mentioned above, we conducted the survey in order to get a general sense of how principals used and experienced intuition during decision making and to provide a mechanism for choosing a subsample for further in-depth interviews. Through the interview process, we hoped to uncover thick descriptions of the intuitive experience. We wanted to see if we could capture the essence of intuitive decision making and if we could construct a framework for understanding how intuition can be used to aid decision makers.

We decided to select six of the most highly intuitive principals for follow-up interviews. To arrive at six, we took into account an individual's total score on part 1 of the survey, years of experience, and the respondent's ability to describe an example of a very important decision where she followed her intuition and experienced a successful outcome (see question 16 on the AIM survey). Using this process, we selected three males (one high school principal, one alternative high school principal, one elementary principal) and three females (all elementary principals). We assigned fictitious names to each respondent in order to protect individual confidentiality.

We used Patton's (1990) general interview guide approach to outline a set of issues and topics to be explored with each candidate. Our purpose was to conduct an informal conversational interview allowing the interviewee's train of thought to flow freely. As a result, our questions were not asked in any particular order nor were they framed in identical ways with each respondent. Interviews sometimes took on a sort of circular pattern whereby certain key ideas or themes would be returned to at various times during the conversation to probe, clarify, and expand the respondent's initial answer.

We analyzed the interview data by using an adaptation of the phenomenological case analysis method described by Moustakas (1994). We were particularly concerned with capturing each respondent's experience with an actual decision event during which intuition was used in developing a solution. We began by bracketing respondents' comments. This process consisted of defining and interpreting major elements, key phrases, and statements pertaining to the various aspects of the intuitive decision-making experience. Next, the data were horizontalized; that is, the data were given equal weight and organized into meaningful and thematically similar clusters. Irrelevant, repetitious, or overlapping data were deleted. From these clusters, we then developed invariant themes and textural descriptions of the experience for each of the six respondents. We then expanded upon these themes by examining the structural or underlying factors that existed in order for the intuition to appear. For example, we looked at contextual elements, problem characteristics, cognitive/mental states, and personality attributes. Finally, we synthesized the key textural and structural elements of all six respondents in an effort to capture the universal or common essence (or essences) of the experience of intuitive decision making.

As our examination of the interviews unfolded, we identified four major categories, each of which played an important yet distinct role in the intuitive experience. The first category was "Personality Profiles." During each interview, we carefully observed and recorded the respondent's physical and expressive mannerisms, including facial expressions, tone of voice, level of energy, attentiveness, affability, intensity, locus of control, and dominance/forcefulness. During our analysis, we looked for common personality attributes or especially prominent qualities.

The second category was "Situational Factors." This category included the problem faced by each interviewee, the problem context, the decision, and the decision outcome. These factors provided a sense of perspective from which the intuitive experience could be situated and interpreted.

The third category, "The Intuition," included the intuitive experience at the moment of solution (i.e., at the precise moment when the intuitive thought surfaced into conscious awareness). Following our analysis of the interview data, we determined that at the moment of solution, the intuitive experience was for each respondent a multidimensional phenomenon characterized by five related, yet distinct, properties. The first property we labeled "Activation." This described the environmental conditions that activated or triggered the intuition. The second property, "Onset," described the temporal dimension of the intuitive experience (e.g., the chronological speed and duration of the intuitive experience once activation occurs). The third property, "Sensation," described the actual feeling generated by the intuition (e.g., emotional, physical, spiritual). The fourth property, "Representation," described the form or shape of the intuition at the moment of solution (e.g., vision, inner voice, noetic). The fifth property, "Effect," described the directional influence generated by the intuition (e.g., a sense of behavioral response potential, such as taking action, not taking action, etc.). Also under the third category, we included prominent idiographic aspects of the intuitive experience that did not fit neatly into the five properties described above.

The fourth category, "Developing Intuition," described how respondents facilitated the development of their intuitive skills in ways that were both long-term and durable.

PERSONALITY PROFILES

As one might expect, each of the six subjects possessed many similar personality attributes, but these attributes varied by degree and intensity. Martha, an elementary school principal, was a talkative, confident, and thoughtful person who was quite poised yet expressive throughout the interview. As she spoke, her hands would wave and she would, depending on the topic, routinely touch her heart, her head, or press her hands together. Martha was quite open and comfortable with her intuition and facile in her ability to express and describe the essence and meaning of intuition as an element of her decision-making processes. Martha struck us as being highly self-reflective, honest, and real. The old saying "What you see is what you get" struck us as being a particularly relevant description of Martha.

Larry was the principal of a continuation high school with over thirty years of experience in education several of which have been in the principalship. He was very direct, frank, open, and often metaphorical. Although he was not hesitant to state his opinions and beliefs, Larry did not appear to be particularly self-reflective. He was clearly action oriented and able to quickly get at the critical core of an issue or problem. His directness, however, has not always served Larry well. By his own admission, his impatience with the political nuances of the job and diplomatic approaches when dealing with supervisors and constituents often created problems for him. He described himself as "prideful." Larry had a difficult time describing the intuitive experience despite the fact that rational/analytical decision processes rarely worked for him. There was an aspect to Larry's tone that suggested he had grown a bit jaded by the "system" over the years. In fact, he firmly believed that the increasing level of state rules, regulations, and standards had so significantly constrained the decision-making prerogatives of principals that opportunities to be intuitive had been nearly extinguished.

Frank was the principal of a middle school. At the time of the interview, he was in his fifth year as principal. He immediately struck us as a youthful, bright, likeable, and passionate person. Like Martha, he was expressive with his hands as he talked. However, Frank struggled with the concept of intuition. Even though he had scored highly on the AIM survey, he was almost dismissive of the importance of intuition in his decision making. Likewise, he struggled as he attempted to articulate his experience with intuition. At one point he commented, "It feels so good to rely on data rather than intuition." Nevertheless, he stated that although his intuition "never steered him wrong," he took pride in his abilities as a rational thinker and problem solver. For Frank, intuition most often served as an ignition or catalyst for subsequent rational decision making. As the interview unfolded, we gained the impression that

Frank had some difficulty identifying with the feelings of others, almost as if he possessed a low sense of empathy. At a number of points during the interview, he made comments to the effect that being right was more important than being sensitive to the perspectives of others.

Cynthia was also an elementary principal with several years of experience. She was quite apprehensive, uncomfortable, and a bit withdrawn throughout the interview, but not unfriendly. Of the six subjects, Cynthia had the greatest difficulty providing an example of when she used her intuition when solving a complex problem. We had the impression that she rarely, if ever, thought about intuition. When she did offer an example of a time when an intuition came to her, it appeared in the form of a disturbing premonition rather than a noetic sensation. As a result of this experience, Cynthia admitted to being both confused and troubled by her intuitions. As the interview unfolded, she seemed to go in and out of the discussion. At times, she would actively engage in the conversation while at other times she would unexplainably back off. Cynthia's body language was different from the expressive enthusiasm demonstrated by Martha. Her eyes darted back and forth nervously, she played with her glasses, and she clasped her hands tightly through much of the interview.

Jack, who was the principal of a large suburban high school, was one of our favorite subjects. A large, bearded, and gregarious man with a booming voice, he eagerly delved into the topic and provided rich, insightful descriptions. Jack loved to talk and required little prompting from us. Like Larry, and even Frank to some degree, he was very direct, frank, opinionated, and confident. Unlike Larry, however, Jack possessed an almost boundless enthusiasm and passion for the job. Work for him was his recreation, and he clearly relished his role as principal. At one point he commented, "I don't go to work. I've never gone to work. I mean, I go to play and I play a lot, and I love it, and it's fun." Jack, like Martha, was extremely self-reflective. Intuition played a significant role in his decision making, and he was not hesitant to admit it. Our interview with Jack was both fascinating and energizing. We came away thinking how wonderful it would be if all principals shared Jack's commitment, compassion, enthusiasm, and creativity.

Our last subject, Karen, was also an elementary school principal. Karen was a remarkably candid, bright, and wise individual. Extremely likeable, she offered rich and penetrating views about her intuitive experiences.

Karen has a strong spiritual belief system that allows her to find mental peace when confronted with complex problems or crises. It is from this ability to ground herself when under stress that Karen is best able to activate her intuition. She was easily the most physically expressive of the subjects we interviewed. As she contemplated a point or question in our discussion, she would close her eyes and press her hands together in a way that suggested she was trying to center her thoughts. Throughout the interview, her legs would cross and uncross and, when making an important point, she would extend her arms and hands in a palms-up open gesture.

As we examined the personality profiles, we found it difficult to make generalizations about specific personality attributes that applied evenly to all six subjects. All subjects were thoughtful and serious educators who had strong feelings of professional confidence, but from there the personality profiles ran the gamut from gregarious extroversion to reticent introversion. The three male principals exhibited strong and often assertive personalities while two of the three female principals exhibited an insightful wisdom that emerged through deep and honest self-reflection based upon a strong spiritual foundation. With the exception of Larry and Cynthia, the principals were openly enthusiastic about their jobs. Jack was perhaps the most visionary of the six with a kind of fire-and-brimstone orientation to his professional mission. With the exception of Larry's cynicism and Cynthia's remoteness, the principals appeared to be well balanced emotionally and adept intellectually. We were somewhat surprised at the variations among the principals regarding their awareness of and confidence in their intuitive abilities. Although all six verified that they often relied on their gut feelings when dealing with complex problems, only three could clearly or deeply articulate their intuitive experiences and the role that intuition played in their decision making.

SITUATIONAL FACTORS

The Problem

During the interviews, we asked each principal to describe a situation in which he or she relied on intuition to solve a complex problem. In this subsection, we describe the various problems encountered by the principals.

Two of the problems described by the six principals involved employment decisions. In one case, the principal was under pressure from parents to fire a teacher. In the other case, the principal was on an interview panel and disagreed with her colleagues about the attributes of the most popular candidate for a teaching job. Two of the problems involved student decisions. In one case, the principal had to make a decision about enrolling a special education student from another school who had a history of drug-related offenses. In the other, the principal had to make a decision about how to ensure the safety of an entire class when angry parents embroiled in a heated custody case threatened to come to the classroom. One problem involved a curriculum decision where the principal was under pressure from the superintendent and school board to cancel a teacher's plan to teach a human rights lesson on gays and lesbians. Finally, one problem involved a communication decision where the principal had to decide just minutes before the start of a high school football game whether to inform the players, parents, and fans about the death of one of the football players during the team warm-up session.

Three problems required immediate on-the-spot decisions, and three required careful deliberations. Five problems were handled individually by the principal while only one required a collaborative group decision. Each of the problems contained several similar characteristics. These were:

1. Each involved human rather than technical characteristics.
2. Each possessed multiple alternatives with no one "best" solution immediately available.
3. Each contained the possibility of further conflict or controversy if a "wrong" decision was reached. Thus, the element of risk to the decision participants was high.
4. Each was nontransparent. The problem was murky, and all variables were not immediately clear or well understood by decision participants.
5. In each situation, standard operating procedures did not apply. There was no set of policies or procedural rules under which the problem could be framed or resolved.
6. Each contained nonquantifiable information. Numerical data or algorithmic decision analyses were not applicable.

7. Each involved multiple perspectives, goals, preferences, and values among decision participants.
8. In each situation, initial goals were subject to change as the decision process unfolded or additional information was acquired.

The Context

In our analysis of each problem, we tried to describe the situational context within which each problem existed. What emerged most prominently from the interview data was the fact that each problem was perceived by the principal as being quite serious. In each case, the principal felt considerable pressure to make not only a good but also the "right" decision. In only two cases were pressures being applied directly from external sources such as parents or supervisors. In the other cases, the pressure experienced was largely the product of internal forces generated by the principal's own interpretation or anticipation of the problem event. In describing problems, principals used terms like "serious," "crisis," "controversial," "crucial," "emergency," and "ugly." In each case, the problem was either novel or nonroutine and generated strong emotions.

Larry described the context of his problem by stating, "It's not anything I was ever prepared for." He also noted that the critical importance of the situation was such that he was deeply concerned about not making any decisions that could "escalate" the problem. Jack stated that his problem was one that he "cared deeply about" and one in which he felt a considerable amount of "confusion" as to what to do. In Martha's case, the pressures from parents to fire a teacher were not only serious but also "volatile," with the potential for schoolwide disruption and conflict among teachers. In Frank's case, the controversy over the teaching of gay and lesbian rights generated a "highly political" environment where "shades of gray" complicated efforts to arrive at a decision that all participants could live with. Karen was confronted with the potential of an "ugly incident" that could be extremely upsetting and even threatening to a class of second-grade students, should the warring parents come to the classroom. She perceived the problem context as a "crisis."

The Decision

For each principal, the decision consisted of some kind of action that he or she needed to take. For example, Martha's intuition led her to *meet* individually with the parents who were pressuring her to fire a teacher rather than in a group as they had requested. In Larry's case, his intuition led him to *inform* the football team, coaches, and officials that one of the players had died so that they could collectively decide on whether to play the game. He deliberately withheld that information from the cheerleaders and fans in order to defer the emotional distress that such information would cause. In Frank's case, his intuition led him to *confront* the superintendent and a board member to advocate for the teacher's decision to teach a lesson on gay and lesbian rights. For Cynthia, the intuition led her to *oppose* the collective decision by the interview panel to offer a teaching job to a candidate with whom she had serious doubts. In Jack's case, his intuition led him to *challenge* school district policy and the recommendations by his supervisor not to enroll a special education student from another school who had a history of drug-related offenses. And finally, in Karen's case, her intuition led her to *direct* a second-grade teacher to move her class to the library in order to avoid a possible classroom confrontation between two warring parents embroiled in a child custody battle.

The Outcome

Most, but not all, decisions produced positive results. In Frank's case, his protests in defense of the gay and lesbian rights lesson fell on deaf ears. Although he maintained that "in my heart, in my gut, the changes I'm making are right," his decision was overridden by his supervisors. In Cynthia's case, her opposition to the selection of a teacher candidate was likewise overridden by a majority of the members of the interview team. However, the decisions by Martha, Larry, Jack, and Karen all turned out to be positive. In each case, the principals maintained that their intuitions were an essential component of their decision-making process. Martha stated that, "It totally shifted the climate. Rather than being hostile, it became collaborative." Karen's comment captured the essence of the decision outcomes experienced by all six principals. "It was just the smartest, best decision I could have made. I couldn't have arrived at a better decision had I planned or mapped it out over time." In fact, none of the principals stated that their particular problem could have been resolved any more effectively through rational/analytical decision processes. On the contrary, all the principals stated that even though a particular decision outcome might not have turned out perfectly, they always regretted it when they failed to heed their intuitions.

THE INTUITION

For the purposes of our research, we defined intuition as an immediate, novel, and striking synthesis of what was previously unrelated or loosely related leading to direct knowledge that seeps into conscious awareness without the conscious mediation of logic or rational processes (Arvidson 1997, 43; Boucouvales 1997, 7). Or, as Mishlove (2001, 1) states, "knowing without knowing how you know." In addition, we were particularly concerned with how the principals we interviewed experienced intuition at the moment of solution; that is, at that precise moment when an intuitive impulse reaches the level of conscious awareness.

The Essence of Activation

For most principals, the intuition described in the interview activated while they were directly engaged with the problem. These were situations that required the immediate intervention of the principal as an individual decision maker. There was no time for deliberation or reflection; a sense of urgency existed that demanded an immediate response. Larry stated, "You just react"; Karen said, "It was initiated by the crisis."

Three principals stated, however, that their intuitions also surfaced while involved with group processing or decision making. Three principals also noted that their intuitions most often surfaced when they distanced themselves from the problem. According to Jack, intuition "can't happen without some true quiet times. I never make significant decisions on the spot. I want to run it by myself. I want to wake up tomorrow and ask myself the same question and make sure I get the same answer." They described a range of activities during which their intuitions frequently arose. Two mentioned being awakened in the middle of the night with an intuitive revelation. Frank's description of the 3 A.M. arrival of a sudden voice mail, "Oh my God, I've figured out this problem, and I didn't know it was a problem," aptly describes this nocturnal phenomenon. Two found that walking often produced intuitive insights. One prayed, one daydreamed, and another silently contemplated at home. In fact, even though Karen's example required an immediate response, she stated that more often than not, her intuition came to her when she was experiencing "stress in the midst of relaxation and insight in the midst of relaxation."

The Essence of Onset

All but one of the principals reported that the intuition occurred very rapidly. Martha stated, "It was quick. Just like that. All of a sudden, something inspired me. It was like an inspiration." According to Larry, "Your brain immediately kicks in; I can't tell you how it happens." Frank noted that his intuitions came in a "flash," while Karen's came "all at once. It was just there." Jack, however, had a different experience. For him, the intuition developed over time, incrementally, as he sorted through the issue and gave himself time to contemplate. Jack's intuition was often the product of his feelings of "discomfort" or while he was "in confusion" over a problem.

There was, with each principal, the sense that when the intuition surfaced they were cognitively neutral. That is to say, at the moment of solution they were not consciously processing data, sorting through environmental cues, and weighing alternatives. They were, for the moment, completely open, completely receptive, and in a state of nonjudgmental thinking. This state of open awareness occurred both during on-the-spot crises and during times when the individual had some time and distance from the problem. In fact, it was Larry who stated, "If you have to think about it; it's no longer intuition."

The Essence of Representation

The most common form taken by an intuitive thought was a mental picture or vision that represented in a holistic way what the solution actually looked like. According to Martha, "I begin to sort of see pictures of solutions. It's almost like seeing a movie." Similarly, for Frank and Karen, a "mind's-eye" vision appears that shows them what needs to happen. For Larry and Cynthia, the intuition came to them in the form of a cognition, a knowledge of what to do. As Cynthia stated, "I just know." And according to Larry, "There is something in your brain that says here is what we have to do." In Jack's case, the intuition came to him in the form of an emotional feeling. This was not surprising since Jack was easily the most passionate of the six principals.

The Essence of Sensation

Interestingly, most principals reported feeling more than one sensation. The most commonly shared sensation among the six principals was a feeling of certainty. The sense that they really understood what it was that needed to happen. There was no equivocation, no debate, no second thoughts. Frank stated, "I just know in my gut the changes I'm making are right." According to Larry, "I knew I was doing the right things, not a wild guess." For most, a feeling of calmness and clarity accompanied their feelings of certainty. For example, Jack said, "I feel a kind of power through peacefulness" and Larry commented, "It is not necessary to calm yourself; you are calm." Frank added that he felt a sense of "passion" at the moment his intuition kicks in.

Few of the principals commented on feeling any physical sensations beyond calmness. Although Karen did note that when her crisis arose she could "feel the stress in her body" and Jack described a general feeling of "discomfort," these were sensations that preceded the intuition and were quickly extinguished once they had arrived at a decision. Larry had an interesting experience in that his feelings of stress didn't arrive until after he had used his intuition to solve the problem. He stated that, "After it's over, I'm the worst basket case in the world."

The Essence of Effect

For all six principals, the intuition provided a guide to action, a kind of catalyst that both mapped the decision terrain and stimulated them to take action. According to Frank, when an intuition occurs, "I will push. I will move." Karen stated that, "I didn't flash on the facts. The action was apparent." And Larry indicated that, "You just react." In Jack's case, the intuition caused him to check for confirmation with others before making a final decision. For each principal, the effect of the intuition described in the interview was a stimulus for what to do rather than for what to avoid. However, both Karen and Jack explained that, depending on the situation, their intuitions also served to inhibit or delay action. For Karen, when her intuition acts to ward off a particular course of action, she begins to "feel a sense of anxiety and confusion" and she will "pull the chain and stop the train." The key point, however, seems to be that the intuition was an energizing phenomenon that both increased awareness and focused attention.

Rationality and Intuition

During the interviews, we also asked each principal to describe how and when during the decision event their rational/analytical decision-making skills came into play. Martha stated that she only uses rational/analytical decision approaches when long-term planning is involved or when she seeks consensus among teachers. Larry indicated that, "I really don't follow rational decision processes because I spend so damn much time trying to figure out what is the best solution that usually the situation is just over—it's gone." In Frank's case, rational/analytical processes came into play immediately after the initial gut response. At that point, he attempts to focus on the long-term consequences or outcomes of a decision rather than "what is right at the moment." He went on to say that, "the thinking part often is, 'okay, slow down, how do I get there?'" Frank's intuition provided the broad outline of a solution while his deliberative thinking filled in the details. For Cynthia, the rational/analytical process works together with her sense of intuition as the decision unfolds. The same was true for Karen, who explained that her rational/analytical thought process "weaves in and out" alongside her intuition. With Cynthia and Karen, decision making was a nonlinear process in which they moved back and forth through a problem, visiting and revisiting its various parts. Like Jack, Karen often felt a need to bounce an intuitive decision off another person "to see whether it is going to work or not." This supports the theory that our minds are especially attuned to social stimuli. Through social contact, we actually sharpen our ability to interpret cues and process information with little, if any, conscious effort (Dickmann and Stanford-Blair 2002). We chuckled when Karen admitted that from time to time she had to go back after an intuitive decision and "make up the facts to inform others how I got to a decision."

Karen, Jack, Martha, and Larry each admitted to being very reliant upon their intuitions when dealing with complex problems. Jack estimated that his intuition guided his most important decisions about "99 percent of the time." In contrast, Karen estimated the ratio of intuitive versus rational/analytical decisions made during a typical day at "70 percent analytical and 30 percent intuitive." She noted, however, that the percentages also reflected the ratio of routine versus complex decisions on any given day. For complex decisions, Karen almost always used her intuition.

Larry and Karen were quite troubled by what they perceived as diminishing opportunities for principals to use their creative/intuitive decision-making skills. They attributed this to the increasing amount of district, state, and federal laws, regulations, and standards that have narrowed the principals' zones of indifference. By zones of indifference, we mean those opportunities for executive decision making that are unfettered from potential challenges by interest groups, coalitions, supervisors, and coworkers. According to Larry and Karen, there is an inverse relationship between the growth of externally imposed standards and regulations and the use of intuitive decision making by principals.

Idiographic Aspects of the Intuitive Experience

As one might expect, several aspects of the principals' intuitive experiences did not always fit neatly into our analytical framework. We attempted to distill from each interview a particularly pertinent element or insight that helped to define the intuitive experience for that principal.

For Martha and Jack, the intuitive experience was filtered through a deeply established philosophical perspective about schools and children. Martha described it as "doing what's best for kids." This philosophy acts like a cognitive template from which to gauge and weigh problem attributes and potential solutions. It also acts to focus, narrow, and simplify attention when confronted with complex problems. Similar to an advanced organizer, Martha's philosophy presets her mind on her most deeply held value, or as Jack commented in his interview, a "core value." This allows them to quickly evaluate problems, divergent points of view, and possible solutions while providing a cognitive framework that helps to guide intuition.

Frank was an information processor. For him, the act of managing, sorting, coding, decoding, and contemplating the various problem attributes provided the basis for his intuitive experience. Processing information was the mechanism that ignited his intuition. When Frank processed, he was in a heightened state of awareness and vigilance. His sensory and perceptual skills were both highly stimulated and primed for action. Frank described his intuition as "a flash," an apt description for someone in a heightened state of awareness.

Larry was the compartmentalizer. His intuition came to him when he had essentially isolated himself emotionally. He described it as being "in a bubble." For Larry, the ability to compartmentalize and isolate allowed him to neutralize his emotions. It provided him with a way to greatly reduce the emotional clutter, distress, and distractions that accompanied the crisis event. It was, in a way, a coping mechanism that protected him from losing control, objectivity, and emotional balance. As a result, Larry's intuition came to him in a way that resulted in "just knowing." It was not the sort of spine-tingling eureka sensation so often described in the literature on intuition. Free from clutter and emotional "resistance," Larry's neural circuitry provided a quick and efficient pathway for intuitive decision making.

Cynthia, the most reticent of the six principals, was also the most fearful and distrustful of her intuitive experiences. These feelings appeared to be the result of a highly upsetting premonition about the death of a colleague. Cynthia had kept her premonition to herself, and when the colleague in fact died, she harbored deep feelings of guilt for not sharing her fear with him. It was therefore not at all surprising that she indicated her intuition was most intense when issues relating to "self-preservation" arose: the greater the danger to her own sense of professional safety and security, the greater the intensity of the intuitive experience.

Finally, Karen described herself as being "attention enriched," a state of conscious awareness that allows her to constantly scan the environment for information and decision opportunities. In fact, Karen admitted that this characteristic periodically created difficulty for her, especially when she became involved in tasks and issues beyond her zone of professional experience and competence. At one point during the interview, she described a rather painful experience where her intuition led to an involvement in a parent club fundraising dilemma, an area in which she had little experience. Nevertheless, Karen's state of attention enrichment belies a highly inquisitive mind and a wide-angle vision of the organization. At times, Karen's openness and curiosity lead to information overload. Karen's intuition allows her to manage large chunks of information and to navigate quickly and efficiently through what she describes as the "myriad of factoids" that envelop her typical workday.

Developing Intuition

Only two of the six principals made any concerted or consistent effort to nurture and develop intuitive skills. Similarly, only 22 percent of the respondents to the AIM survey indicated that they regularly practiced techniques to improve their intuitive skills. Of course, this is hardly surprising given the lack of training or coursework available through administrator preparation programs. Karen indicated that she regularly practiced the Chinese art of Tai Chi to bring balance and peace into her stressful life as a principal. She also relies heavily on song to help calm and center her mind. These kinds of activities, according to Karen, allow her to both open and quiet her mind, thus providing a receptive mental state for the generation of intuitive thoughts. Similarly, Martha found that her spiritual faith and moments of prayer provided an avenue for the use of intuition when solving complex problems.

Another theme that surfaced among some principals was the idea of putting distance between themselves and the problem by sleeping on it, walking, or talking things over with another person. These kinds of strategies make sense when compared with the factors that frequently obstructed a principal's intuition (i.e., a rushed decision, when angry, or when highly stressed). Of course, creating distance between oneself and a problem is not always possible, as evidenced by the various on-the-spot crises described by the interviewees. This paradox raises an important question of whether intuitions raised under fire are less reliable or accurate than intuitions raised through distancing strategies.

SUMMARY

Ninety-two percent of all respondents to the AIM survey indicated that they almost always used their intuitions when making difficult decisions. In our sample, the most highly intuitive principals were males, not females, but when the total spectrum of scores on the AIM survey was examined, there was virtually no difference between males and females in terms of intuitive ability. Although most principals did little if anything to draw upon or develop their intuitive skills, they placed a great deal of trust and confidence in them as evidenced by their willingness to share their intuitions with others. Intuitions most often produced feelings of peacefulness and calm followed by high energy and excitement. Most intuitive decisions involved situations where there were many possible alternatives or where problem variables were not scientifically predictable. Situations involving hiring and firing employees most often seemed to invoke intuitive decision making. However, survey respondents also noted that their intuitions were frequently used when dealing with conflicts and difficult situations with parents or when trying to handle changes in policies, programs, and schedules. Feelings of anger or stress were the most frequently mentioned barriers or obstructions to intuitive decision making. Among survey respondents, intuition seemed to come most often after they had applied analytical thought processes or intermittently as a decision unfolded. In general, there were very few differences between the response patterns of males, females, experienced, and inexperienced principals.

Three of our six interviewees were able to provide rich and detailed descriptions of intuitive decision making. The other three struggled a bit to describe how they used their intuitions. Only three admitted to being thoughtfully and reflectively aware of their intuitive ability and its role in complex decision making. We found all six principals to be highly confident and dedicated professionals. Beyond that, there were no defining personality characteristics of the highly intuitive principal.

Each principal had a unique style and orientation to decision making. There was a sense among some principals that the trend toward standardization in education has reduced opportunities for principals to use intuitive thinking. The proliferation of policies, rules, and regulations has reduced the principal's range of independent decision making, thus constraining the use of intuitive thinking.

The kinds of problems that most frequently required the use of intuition described by the interviewees paralleled those reported by survey respondents. They were messy, contentious, often ambiguous, and laden with emotional content. Moreover, they were problems that required immediate action and that gave principals little, if any, time for reflection. Most interviewees described intuition as a sudden flash of insight that came to them relatively early on in the decision-making process. For most, their intuitive decisions were most frequently correct. Although there were times when intuitions proved wrong, each principal always regretted it when he or she failed to follow an intuition.

Through the analysis of interview data, we discovered five common elements of the intuitive experience at the moment of solution: activation, onset, representation, sensation, and effect. For most interviewees, intuition provided a guide to action, a kind of catalyst that both mapped the decision terrain and stimulated them to take action. Rational thinking and intuition were used in different ways by different principals. For some, intuition always preceded rational analysis. For others, intuition and rationality were intertwined. For one principal, rationality always preceded intuition. It was clear from the data, however, that intuition and analysis operated on a continuum and in nonlinear ways. Only two of the six interviewees described strategies and techniques used to access or develop their intuitive skills.

In the next chapter, we discuss and interpret the findings of our research and several key concepts from the literature. Importantly, we show how these ideas can help principals develop and use their intuitions to become more effective decision makers.

6

TYING IT ALL TOGETHER: USING INTUITION FOR BETTER DECISION MAKING

We begin this chapter with a discussion of the major conclusions from our study and how they correspond to other research in the field of intuitive decision making. We also discuss several common intuitive experiences shared by all six of our interview subjects. The question of whether intuition can be developed and enhanced is a particularly important element of this book. We think it can, and we provide several practical suggestions and insights framed around our research findings and those found elsewhere in the empirical literature on the topics of decision making, intuition, and the brain-mind. We conclude by providing several suggestions for further research in the field of intuitive decision making.

CONCLUSIONS FROM OUR STUDY

The survey and interview data provided a number of important and useful clues about intuition as a decision-making tool for school principals. First, it is clear that intuition is a widely used but little understood phenomenon. The fact that 92 percent of all respondents to the survey indicated that they frequently used intuition to guide their most important decisions while few respondents could clearly articulate or describe the experience underscores this point. Of course, each of our interview subjects was selected precisely because of his or her high scores on the AIM survey. And, although each of the principals interviewed testified to the power and utility of intuitive skills when making complex decisions, several had trouble articulating the experience, and only one could describe in any depth the kinds of activities used to nurture and develop intuitive ability.

Importantly, however, most respondents to the survey (92 percent) and all of the interview subjects reported that they had few qualms about sharing their intuitions with others. There were two primary reasons why they felt this way. First, they trusted their intuitions and believed in the value of intuitive decision making. This is a very important point in view of the fact that few researchers in the field of leadership behavior attach much credence to intuition as a subject worthy of serious study. Second, they tend to see themselves as being fundamentally honest and open individuals with nothing to hide. This, of course, reflects a degree of confidence and self-assurance that one would expect to find in any leader. A sizeable number of respondents to both the survey and interviews noted that their willingness to share was situational depending upon the intended audience and its receptivity toward this kind of decision-making approach.

We were also struck by the reported accuracy and effectiveness of the respondents' intuitive decisions. Admittedly, our research relied entirely on self-reported data and did not attempt to triangulate or compare data from other sources that could verify such perceptions. However, with this caveat in mind, it is safe to say that principals place a great deal of faith in their intuition as being a reliable and often indispensable decision-making tool when confronted with the myriad of ambiguities, uncertainties, and complexities of the job. Cynthia made an interesting comment in this regard. "I think people make it too hard on themselves. And then I see them get bogged down and not have any fun and enjoy their job. I think if they were to rely more on their intuition it could be easier for them, more enjoyable, and just as productive." Jack stated "that if any of us were honest, we would all recognize we use our intuition a lot, but we hide behind other people's reasoning in laws and books and policies."

A closer look at the kinds of decisions made by principals that most frequently required an intuitive approach found that such decisions closely paralleled the findings by Agor (1986), Cappon (1994), and Rowan (1980). These decisions often contained unclear goals or solutions, multiple alternatives, conflicting perspectives, ambiguous information, a limited time frame, high risks, and qualitative rather than quantifiable elements. There was a decidedly subjective rather than objective quality to virtually all of the decision events described by our respondents.

There was also a decidedly nontechnical aspect to the types of decisions described in both the survey and interviews. These were not the kinds of number-crunching problems that involved budget figures, test score data, or other kinds of student/school performance data. Nor were they problems involving clearly delineated rules, policies, or procedures. Rather, these were messy human relations problems involving employment decisions, student issues, communication issues, or curriculum controversies. All of the problems were quite serious and in some cases described as "crises" or "emergencies." Of course, we know that these are precisely the kinds of situations that occupy a principal's time and, if not handled well, can precipitate his demotion or even dismissal (Davis 1998).

As our analysis of the interview data unfolded, it became apparent that the experience of intuition during decision making consisted of five distinct yet related properties: activation, onset, representation, sensation, and effect. Although as a set these properties do not parallel the findings from any one study done in the past, their elements can be found among the research conducted by Agor (1986), Brown, (1990), Cappon (1994), Landry (1991), and Morris (1990). What seems clear is that the intuitive experience is multidimensional with several closely linked attributes that combine in various ways to give it depth, texture, and meaning.

Intuition during decision making can appear at any time in the process. The largest proportion of survey respondents reported that their intuition most often appeared at the very end of a decision when they were trying to sift through and digest all the cues and information available. In contrast, our interview respondents more often found that their intuition appeared at the beginning of a problem or crisis event. Moreover, it served not as a reflective mechanism used to weigh and consider the products of rational analysis but as a guide to action, a precursor to some kind of affirmative behavior by the principal to accelerate and implement a course of action. Several interview respondents, however, explained that their intuitions periodically came to them incrementally, in bits and pieces, as a decision process unfolded. In essence, they would use a form of limited rationality to acquire and scan information, weigh that information against past experiences, values and beliefs, policies and procedures, and so forth, and then incrementally check for internal credibility. These internal credibility checks often took on the form of an intuitive feeling.

We believe that such differences in the temporal placement of intuitive thinking during decision making may have less to do with the attributes of the decision maker than with the attributes of the problem. For example, five of our six interviewees described problems that required on-the-spot resolution. There was no time to carefully sort through data or to analyze facts. As a result, their intuitions arrived early on in the decision-making process. With less immediate problems, principals had time to think through the problem elements and possible solutions. When their intuitions arrived, they had already contributed a great deal of cognitive effort toward finding a resolution.

Our research verified what has long been known about the intuitive experience at the moment of solution—it happens quickly. It is not a process that oozes up from the subconscious mind and slowly constructs new insights. Rather, as Laughlin (1997, 11) describes, it "springs into consciousness wholecloth, seemingly out of nowhere." Even those who experience intuition incrementally as a decision unfolds describe the process as little flashes of knowledge that literally pop into consciousness. Intuition is not a wild guess, nor any kind of guess for that matter. Neither is it the same as a primordial survival instinct—a process that lies far deeper in the reptilian brain than intuition does. It is a form of consciousness, a noetic awareness, that informs and guides behavior through the "intrusion of unconscious content into conscious apperception" (Landry 1991, 17).

Most respondents to both the survey and interviews described the intuitive sensation at the moment of solution as one of calmness and peacefulness. Virtually all respondents also experienced a clarity that provided a sense of the whole as if all of the missing pieces to a complex puzzle suddenly appeared and aligned themselves in a perfect way. And with the calmness and clarity came a sense of certitude that what needed to happen was right and correct.

We were particularly interested in determining whether gender or years of experience on the job would influence a principal's use of intuition when solving complex problems. Among all of the comparisons done, we found only two statistically significant differences. First, we found that female principals were more likely than males to use techniques that help them draw upon their intuitions during decision making. Although this suggests that females may be more aware of or tuned into their intuitive skills, we were surprised to find that the proportion of males who scored 9 or above on the AIM survey (rated as highly intuitive) was significantly higher than for females. This finding contradicts previous research on managers that found females to be more intuitive than males (Agor 1986). Even when all scores on the survey were calculated, the average scores for males and females were not significantly different. In fact, when our survey results were compared with the results of Agor's study of 5,000 managers, female principals scored lower while male principals scored higher than their gender counterparts in other occupations (although these differences were not statistically significant). We hesitate to speculate as to the reasons for this finding except to say that from the results of our study it appears that in general intuitive decision-making skills are fairly evenly distributed between male and female principals.

We were surprised to find no statistically significant differences between experienced and inexperienced principals in the use of intuition when making complex decisions. Our findings contradict other research in this regard (Dreyfus and Dreyfus 1986). One possible explanation is that experience makes the most difference by enhancing intuitive accuracy and quality rather than frequency during decision making. It may also be true that the kinds of problems where principals are likely to draw upon their intuitions are so complex, messy, and ambiguous that no amount of "practice" in the field can develop the kind of skill and performance precision found among experts in other fields such as sports, medicine, engineering, law, and so forth. We suspect that a principal's core personality plays a large role in how difficult problems and dilemmas in schools are conceptualized and processed (undoubtedly more so than it would in performing a skill like shooting a basketball, gall bladder surgery, or designing a bridge). As such, experience may have less to do with the quality of a principal's intuitions than maturity, common sense, emotional balance, stress tolerance, feelings of efficacy, and locus of control.

From the interview data, we were able to develop the following list of common experiences shared to one degree or another by all six interview subjects. This list provides important insights into the context and dynamics of the intuitive experience for these principals. Granted, a sample of six is not enough for us to make broad generalizations, but it is important to note that eleven of the twelve items on our list are supported by the literature on intuitive decision making. Only with item 11, which covers gender and experience, do our findings depart from the norm.

1. All principals experienced intuition during complex decision making.
2. Intuition was used primarily with qualitative issues where subjective judgment and human rather than technical issues were at stake.
3. A principal's intuition rarely led to a bad decision.
4. Principals struggled to articulate or describe the intuitive experience.
5. The principals' intuitions served as guides to action and typically informed them of what they needed to do instead of what they needed to avoid doing.
6. Intuition most often surfaced early on in the decision-making process rather than at the end. In some cases, it appeared incrementally as the decision unfolded.
7. At some point in the decision process, principals used rational/analytical thinking in concert with their intuition. Rational/analytical thinking was used to verify an intuition or as a precursor to an intuitive thought.
8. The intuitive experience was, for most principals, an emotional experience and evoked as Daniel Goleman (1995) states "feelings about feelings."
9. Principals rarely exercised, trained, or otherwise used any particular techniques to develop their intuition. It just happened, and it happened quickly.
10. The more self-reflective a principal was, the more likely he or she was to rely on intuition during decision making.

11. Neither gender nor experience made any significant difference in how principals used or experienced their intuitions.
12. There did not appear to be any uniform personality characteristics that predicted a principal's ability to use intuition during decision making.

DEVELOPING THE INTUITIVE DECISION MAKER

Can intuitive decision making be taught or enhanced? Are there ways to increase one's ability to access intuition when faced with complex human service-related problems? These are critical questions for administrators and university professors of educational administration. Most of our interview respondents were not sure. Karen expressed a belief that if principals could look at their lives holistically and "really reflect on who they are as a whole in the present," they would open themselves to intuitive thoughts. Cynthia also believed that self-reflective people were more receptive to intuitive thinking. Martha, Larry, and Jack felt that having a clear focus on doing what is best for kids helps to structure if not develop intuitive thinking. Larry and Frank did not think that intuition could be taught. Rather, from their perspective, intuition only comes with experience. As Larry commented, "You just have to experience stuff."

However, recent insights into how the brain functions and develops suggest a number of ways in which principals can enhance their intuitive skills. There is no question that the human brain is a marvelously complex organ that operates on many levels of consciousness. In fact, most of what the brain-mind does, it does subconsciously. Not only does the subconscious brain continuously process various sensory stimuli, memories, emotions, and thoughts, it does so powerfully and in ways that shape how we think, what we think about, and what we know and understand about ourselves and the world around us. That well-developed intuitions can provide decision makers with very reliable and efficient ways to resolve complex human service problems is not at all surprising in view of the growing body of scientific knowledge about both the structure and function of the brain-mind. And although unsettling to some, the fact that with certain types of complex problems intuition can compete very successfully with more formalized, rational, methods of decision making is no less surprising. Of course, the key is to help principals learn to trust their intuitions and to find ways to enhance their intuitive skills. What we propose below is not, by any means, intended to be a recipe for developing intuitive decision makers. Rather, we provide a range of ideas that may prove useful in ways unique to each individual. We believe that even if the following ideas do not improve intuitive decision making, they can at the very least help to enhance basic mental functions and suppleness during decision making.

As we know, the human brain-mind is incredibly plastic. Its capacity to change and grow is immense and continuous throughout our lifetimes. Much of the work of the brain-mind occurs on the subconscious level through subcortical structures designed to prime the body for quick and efficient responses to external stimuli (particularly those deemed threatening). A great deal of information from the environment is received, processed, and often acted upon before the conscious mind has had time to deliberate and respond. Intuition is a quick reaction form of cognition that responds especially well to problems that arise within domains of personal expertise. Although the gestation of an intuitive thought occurs subconsciously, there are a number of ways in which we may be able to stimulate its development through the application of conscious exercises or thought processes.

First, and most important, one can't force intuition. Once conscious thought processes have taken over, our thinking is no longer intuitive. At best, we can only create conditions that enhance our capacity for intuitive thinking, the quality of our intuitive thoughts, and the accessibility of our intuitions during complex decision making. It is also important to remember that the brain-mind prefers to work with large concepts and chunks of information rather than with minutia and highly detailed bits of information. Similarly, our intuitions usually provide only approximations rather than precise formulations of how to resolve problems and dilemmas. In light of this, principals would be well advised to spend time thinking "big" when addressing problem attributes. They should focus on finding large patterns and themes rather than pouring over every little detail. Once the contours of a solution are established, the rational/analytical mind can provide the details of an action plan. Thinking heuristically can help to facilitate this process (Rowan 1986).

Principals should attempt to visualize possible solutions and create mental images, or schemas, that provide a "mind's-eye" view of how a decision would look in finished form. You will recall that when the brain-mind visualizes, it facilitates the development of new neural connections and strengthens old ones. In essence, visualization changes the way we think and expands the repertoire of possible response options to complex problems. In this vein, tasks that contain strong visual components tend to stimulate intuitive thinking (Hogarth 2001; Kouzes and Posner 1987; Morris 1990; Ratey 2001).

In a similar fashion, the process of mentally rehearsing certain behaviors, actions, or decisions stimulates thinking through the strengthening of certain neural circuits (Rowan 1986). By mentally playing out possible scenarios, the brain-mind tests and assesses novel combinations of ideas and images. Even though many such ideas are never acted upon, the very exercise of mental rehearsal and visualization trains the brain-mind to become more agile, plastic, and responsive. Since intuitions are constructed from our vast reservoir of experiences, memories, thoughts, and cognitions, it seems reasonable that visualization and mental rehearsal will provide our intuitions with a deep and rich pool of information to draw from.

In a similar vein, finding ways to strengthen memories may lead to better intuitions. By strengthen, we mean two things. First, practice ways to help commit important information into long-term memory. Second, practice ways to efficiently and quickly access long-term memories. Mnemonic devices are good examples of this. Clear and vibrant memories are the grist for intuitive thinking. Without them, our intuitions would be seriously flawed, inconsistent, or fragmented.

Learning how to observe both the foreground and background elements of our environment and the people within it may enhance the development of intuition by expanding our field of attention (e.g., field of vision) and our ability to read social situations. In doing so, we become more attuned to the fine-grained characteristics of our external surroundings and the subtle forces acting upon it. The act of observation can be enhanced through efforts to find dissimilarities as well as similarities among environmental cues and stimuli. Similarly, looking for novel connections between environmental images, objects, or stimuli can stimulate our ability to find relationships to apparently unrelated phenomena.

We also need to learn from what we do *not* observe. For example, are there elements of a problem or situation that should be present but are not? Is what we see consistent with what we expect to see? If not, why not? What are the gaps, the missing pieces? What elements should be included to fill out the contours of the problem? Paying attention to what we do not see stimulates our ability to extrapolate, predict, think critically, and think imaginatively.

Finding ways to stretch one's imagination by daydreaming, brainstorming, speculating, and lateral (unconventional) thinking is an important way to train the brain-mind and expand its pool of mental resources for intuitive thinking. Imaginative thinking allows us to transcend linearity, rigid analysis, and conventionality in how we approach problems. It stimulates creative, out-of-the-box solutions to what often seem to be intractable problems. Highly imaginative people are also curious people who regularly look for the novel or unique attributes of a situation or problem. Again, by looking for novelty and uniqueness, the decision maker expands her range of options while focusing the mind on what's different or important. Neurologically, this type of thinking stimulates the growth of capillaries to the brain and the number of glial cells that provide the nutrients for neuronal health (Brown 1990; Cappon 1994; Dickmann and Stanford-Blair 2002; Glaser 1995).

Play is another way to stimulate imaginative thinking. Play can be verbal, nonverbal, or some combination of the two. Play is often associated with childlike properties of spontaneity, fancifulness, joy, and the uninhibited release of personal expression (physical and mental). Playful people typically possess a metanoetic perception of the world as an interesting and challenging place that stimulates creative ideas and behaviors (Laughlin 1997). Similarly, look for the humor in life. Take time to laugh at the absurdities in life. Take periodic time-outs from serious endeavors. On a neurobiological basis, highly joyful and satisfying experiences are both the result and activators of the release of neurotransmitters like serotonin, dopamine, and norepinephrine. These chemicals serve to improve mood, concentration, feelings of well-being, and motivation—all important elements to good thinking (intuitive or otherwise) and decision making.

Other approaches to expanding our imaginative powers include the use of analogies, metaphors, and synectic thinking. We think metaphorically when we describe problems and situations through the use of parallel yet unrelated images of common experience. For example, the statement "she can get to the heart" of a problem uses the imagery of a heart to represent the core life force of the issue. Likewise, the phrase "she is a wellspring of information" conjures up images of a well bubbling over with water to communicate the point that this person possesses a great deal of useful information. Or consider the phrase "he's sharper than a tack" as a metaphorical representation of high intelligence. These kinds of descriptive yet fanciful statements are tremendously useful ways to distill the complex properties of a problem into an image that can be understood by most people quickly and effectively. In a similar way, the use of analogies (where an attribute or characteristic of one entity is compared with an attribute or characteristic contained by a different entity) can be quite useful in conjuring up rich and novel images and ideas. For example, the term "she's got a mind like a steel trap" is commonly understood to mean she's exceptionally bright and mentally agile. The use of metaphors and analogies allows us to chunk problem elements into a rough, but colorful, storyboard that portrays the problem in a uniformly understood context. They also provide the brain-mind with a robust collection of preselected and creative images that can serve as effective heuristics thus allowing one to avoid (or reduce) the painstaking process of rational/analysis.

Synectic thinking is similar to metaphorical thinking in that the decision maker makes use of creative imagery to address a complex problem. The synectic thinker conceptualizes the inanimate elements of a problem as being animate or visa versa. By giving lifelike properties to a concept, an image, or an object, one teases the brain-mind into generating unconventional and novel associations between problem elements and possible solutions. Synectics, metaphors, and analogies all serve as ways to stretch our powers of creative thinking and enhance the subconscious processing of intuitive thoughts. Our brain-minds thrive on such novelties and unusual ways of thinking and perceiving.

Another important way to stimulate intuitive ability involves actively redefining and reframing problems. In doing so, the decision maker pauses to consider a problem from another point of view or to consider variations in the weighting of certain problem elements. What might appear to be the core element of the problem on the surface might, in fact, be viewed as peripheral by someone else. Recall our story about vice principal Dan Charles and his decision dilemma over how to deal with Darla Campbell who had acted out in Mr. Colt's class. Had Dan not redefined the problem from being an act of disobedience to an act of extreme personal distress, he would have thought less about helping Darla through a horrifying personal crisis and focused more on how to punish her for breaking school rules.

Bolman and Deal (1996) offer four ways in which managers can frame any given problem: structural, human relations, political, and symbolic. Each frame provides a unique set of perspectives and assumptions about what happens in complex organizations and why. A manager's behaviors and actions may vary considerably depending on which frame he uses to think about and address organizational issues and dilemmas. The point here is not to advocate for a particular set of problem frames, but to illustrate how reframing and redefining problems opens up new and unanticipated possibilities and ideas. Moreover, reframing shapes our own beliefs, values, and motivations (Glaser 1995).

Leaders who can reframe problems are by necessity reflective individuals. The ability to reflect allows us to examine past behaviors, values, thoughts, beliefs, feelings, motivations, and decision outcomes with a critical eye. Through reflection, we shape our perspectives about what we do well and not so well and how our behaviors relate to important social conventions and professional standards. Effective leaders reflect forward as well as backward. By reflecting forward, we examine and test our past and current behaviors, beliefs, and feelings against an imagined (or predicted) future. Reflecting forward not only helps to build rich and textured mental schemas but it enhances the mind's ability to quickly size up unconventional situations and challenging problems without a great deal of deliberative processing (Hogarth 2001).

Reflection, of course, is focused thinking, but not all such thinking is good or correct. The highly effective reflective thinker employs what Hogarth (2001) calls "mental circuit breakers." Mental circuit breakers are conscious efforts to periodically catch and interrupt inaccurate, biased, or counterproductive thoughts. We do this by questioning longstanding assumptions and beliefs and seeking out disconfirming information about them. As we noted in chapter 5, our memories fade over time as do their accuracy and content. Likewise, deeply ingrained feelings about past events may bias the way in which we feel and think about current events, even if the events are only approximately similar to past encounters. In effect, the fallibility of human memory and emotion may take what was once a kind environmental feedback loop and twist it into a wicked one. Recall that intuitions that are derived from wicked environments are usually wrong, whereas those that are derived from kind environments are more likely to be right (Hogarth 2001). Mental circuit breakers, then, serve as diagnostic checkpoints that help us to make more accurate decisions.

The likelihood of encountering kind environments and learning structures increases as we become experts at a given task or tasks. Of course, expertise tends to be domain specific. It makes sense, then, that people who work at developing expertise in particular domains will find that their intuitions tend to be more frequent and useful within those domains. In addition, regular practice reinforces and strengthens certain neural circuits within the brain and reduces the demand for deliberative thinking. The point is that our intuitions work better when we focus on being very good at a few important task domains than on being moderately competent in several (Hogarth 2001).

We know that the brain-mind is especially sensitive to social stimuli. Reading social situations and various physical cues (like facial expressions, tone of voice, body language, etc.) is a deeply ingrained mental process that is almost automatic in nature and requires little, if any, deliberative thinking. In addition, building social relationships allows us to test, evaluate, and modify our beliefs, values, thoughts, and attitudes. In essence, social stimulation has a powerful impact on the shaping and reshaping of neural circuits. It literally changes how we think. Because of this, activities that involve social interactions may prove beneficial to the development of intuition.

There is also evidence that verbalization stimulates and enhances certain neural circuits in the brain. Moreover, verbalization makes our thoughts explicit, which in turn reinforces ideas or helps to reveal errors in our thinking. Of course, verbalization often results in verbal responses from others, thereby providing fresh perspectives and feedback about our ideas. A number of principals who took part in our study explained that their intuitions were both activated and enhanced when they talked problems and issues over with other people. For many people, talking is especially useful in helping them to clarify and reinforce thoughts and ideas and construct new ones. Once again, we return to the principle that activities that stimulate our thinking, even when conscious and overt, increase the brain-mind's capacity, efficiency, and quality of thoughts. As the brain does its job better, so do cognitive processes like intuition.

It is important to point out, however, that the usefulness of verbalization may be context specific. Attempting to verbalize while actively engaged in problem solving may actually extinguish intuitive thinking. Whereas verbalization as part of an exploratory dialogue conducted away from the immediate problem situation may actually stimulate intuitive thoughts (Schooler, Ohlsson, and Brooks 1993).

Movement and exercise appear to be quite important in the development of a supple and agile mind, and, we suspect, intuition. All deliberate movements are products of directions sent from neocortical structures to the body. In essence, movement is the acting out of our cognitions. Like verbalization, movement makes our thoughts explicit and helps to reinforce ideas, skills, and memory. Exercise, done regularly, provides the added benefit of triggering the release of various hormones and neurotransmitters such as endorphins, dopamine, serotonin, and norepinephrine. We know that such chemicals increase feelings of well-being and pleasure, which are precursors to effective thinking. A common comment shared by principals in our study was that various forms of exercise (e.g., jogging, walking, yoga, Tai Chi) seemed to stimulate and often trigger intuitive thoughts. Clearly, there is a neurobiological basis for this.

We should add, however, that various forms of relaxing and mind-centering techniques also seem to be very helpful in activating and enhancing intuition. Often, sleep itself can help the brain-mind organize thoughts and stimulate novel constructions of seemingly disparate ideas, memories, and thoughts. It is also believed that during sleep the brain restores and balances the neurotransmitters necessary for proper cognitive functioning. Because fatigue is such an especially powerful constraint to intuitive thinking, we recommend that principals find ways to rest periodically throughout the day. Even a short five-minute catnap can help to refresh and clear the mind.

Of course, we know that meditation can provide people with a kind of open and uncluttered state of consciousness. The results of our research and that of others suggest that intuitions frequently come to people when they are in a state of focused relaxation. Goleman (1995) refers to the concept of flow in his description of activities where the mind reaches a state of deep focus, clarity, and effortless efficiency. Flow comes when one is deeply engaged in a pleasurable activity that is not too easy and not too hard. Examples of flow producing activities include working in the garden, solving a jigsaw puzzle, drawing, practicing a golf swing, playing a musical instrument, and doing needlepoint. Like meditation, activities that generate feelings of flow act to reduce highly deliberative thoughts and render the mind more receptive to spontaneous and creative ideas.

Meditation, flow, and relaxation also serve to distance oneself from the immediacy of the problem at hand. A number of participants in our study indicated that their intuitions often came to them when they were able to get away from the problem for a while. Of course, with problems that require immediate attention, like Marsha's three dilemmas described in the introduction, creating distance is impossible. However, for difficult problems that do not require on-the-spot decision making, creating distance allows the problem to shift from foreground consciousness to background consciousness. The mind relaxes, reduces the level of attention and cognitive activity directed at the problem, and frees the subconscious mind to play with ideas. The problem never completely disappears from the mind's "radar screen." It simply moves from the center of the screen to the periphery.

We spoke above about the power of personal reflection. An important element of reflection includes the way in which we think about and respond to our emotions. Remember that emotions are precursors to feelings and largely the product of subconscious processing. That is, various subcortical structures such as the amygdala receive and process emotionally charged stimuli before the neocortex has had time to properly identify, process, and mediate the emotional signal. As Daniel Goleman (1995) explained, it is often exceedingly difficult to take conscious control of highly intense emotional stimuli. He refers to the term emotional hijacking to describe the power held by the amygdala over the neocortex when emotional signals are especially intense.

Hogarth (2001), however, suggests that by treating our emotions as data, rather than instructions, we can become more self-reflective and self-aware. Both qualities are important to the process of thinking reflectively and intuitively. When emotions become data, they become contextualized and subject to conscious reflection and investigation as opposed to being unharnessed triggering mechanisms that can evoke an emotional hijacking.

Oftentimes, the way in which one goes about addressing complex problems overwhelms the mind's rational and intuitive capacities. Especially difficult and large problems (e.g., wicked dilemmas) may be better resolved by taking only a "corner of the problem" and peeling the elements of the problem away incrementally (note the metaphor). Because the brain-mind innately seeks ways to reduce cognitive demand, the peeling process allows the brain-mind to both conserve effort and direct attention toward manageable chunks of information.

As we discussed earlier in the book, there is a prevailing attitude among managers that good decision making follows a linear trajectory. Likewise, managers put a great deal of time and effort into structuring problems in ways that allow for sequential and orderly solution finding. Intuitions, however, rarely emerge under such effortful and deliberative contexts. Learning to accept nonlinearity and being able to consider multiple alternatives simultaneously can help to open the mind to unconventional, novel, and intuitive channels of thinking. By accepting the principle of nonlinearity, one reduces the frustrations of attempting to maintain absolute control over complex problems and decision processes and creates conditions where imaginative thinking can lead to innovative solutions. Nonlinearity acknowledges that in complex organizations like schools it is difficult, if not impossible, to link causes and effects. It also acknowledges that the most challenging and important problems are rarely well structured or clearly understood and that decision-making processes zigzag toward final solutions. The effective decision maker understands that preconceived notions of rationality rarely work in complex organizations and that attempts to oversteer decision-making processes not only reduce intuitive thinking but also constrain the environmental conditions where creative solutions might be found.

We believe, however, that Hogarth's (2001) recommendation is right—becoming proficient in the scientific method can help to develop better intuitions. When our analytical skills become highly developed, they become less mindful and deliberative and more automatic and subconscious. The whole idea behind developing our intuitions is to orient the brain-mind in ways that reduce cognitive demand while preserving decision accuracy.

Hobson's (1999) explanation of semantic priming offers important insights as to how the brain-mind links seemingly disparate thoughts and images. Rich and diverse life experiences stimulate the formation of thoughts and images that enrich our memories and perspectives and facilitate the development of parallel neural circuits in the brain. As we described in chapter 4, when we say fish, the experientially endowed individual conjures up not only images of fish but also parallel images that are only indirectly connected to the image of a fish. Indirect images like this help to stimulate and enrich our memories and expand the way in which we comprehend or come to know the world. The moral of this story is this: rich and diverse life experiences enhance the reservoir of thoughts and images available for intuitive construction. Similarly, we should add that becoming aware of and competent in interacting with different cultures are vitally important ways to endow one's reservoir of life experiences with rich and diverse perspectives, images, and ways of thinking.

We have covered a great deal of ground in offering ideas for developing, enhancing, and activating intuition. As we stated above, intuition can't be forced. We can only create the conditions conducive to its emergence and effectiveness. Our suggestions were derived from both our research and the research of others. However, we openly admit that there are no formulas for success. What works for one individual may not work for another. Moreover, we can't think ourselves into being intuitive decision makers. However, we believe that we can educate and train our brain-minds to be more receptive to intuitive thoughts and to be more effective in applying our intuitions toward resolving real-world problems. We have one final comment: trust your intuition. The chances are that your gut reaction is going to be right much of the time. Remember, intuition is highly influenced and shaped by one's experiences, reflections, and core values. Certainly, it can be wrong—but so can rational approaches to decision making.

Table 6.1.   Thirty Key Ideas for Developing, Enhancing, and Activating Intuitive Decision Making

1. Focus on large concepts and big ideas.
2. Practice ways to organize information into manageable chunks. Practice heuristic thinking.
3. Visualize possible solutions. Create mental images of desired outcomes.
4. Mentally rehearse intended or desired behaviors.
5. Practice ways to enhance memory skills.
6. Observe both foreground and background elements of the environment.
7. Look for novel or unexpected connections between objects and images.
8. Learn from what you do not see.
9. Practice imaginative and divergent thinking.
10. Play.
11. Seek and appreciate the humor in life.
12. Think metaphorically and synectically.
13. Learn to redefine and reframe problems.
14. Reflect backward and forward. Be self-reflective and self-aware.
15. Apply mental circuit breakers.
16. Seek out kind learning environments and structures.
17. Develop domain-specific expertise.
18. Seek out avenues for social interaction.
19. Verbalize your thoughts and ideas.
20. Exercise regularly. Move your body.
21. Practice ways to relax and center the mind.
22. Rest! Get ample sleep and take short naps when possible.
23. Distance yourself from the problem physically, temporally, mentally, and emotionally.
24. Practice activities that induce "flow."
25. Treat your emotions as data rather than instructions.
26. Tackle only one corner of the problem.
27. Accept nonlinearity.
28. Consider multiple alternatives simultaneously.
29. Become proficient in the scientific method.
30. Find ways to become experientially endowed.

In table 6.1, we provide an outline of thirty key ideas expressed in this chapter for developing, enhancing, and activating one's intuitive decision making.

RECOMMENDATIONS FOR FURTHER RESEARCH

We have four major recommendations. First, intuitive administrative decision making needs to be studied through the lens of experimental psychology. More accurate and scientific ways need to be used to assess the intuitive experience of principals while in the act of making complex decisions. Surveys and self-reported phenomenological analyses can only capture individual perceptions and interpretations, some of which may become blurred or distorted over time. Although we are not cognitive or neurophysiologists, we wonder if there might be ways to measure certain brain structure characteristics, brain wave characteristics, or neurochemical characteristics of intuitive principals, or principals who are in the midst of an intuitive decision-making experience. By better understanding the neurobiology of intuitive thinking, we may find new and effective ways to stimulate and enhance its use during complex decision making.

Second, we recommend that additional research be conducted to improve the validity and reliability of surveys used to assess the intuitive self-perceptions of principals. Attempting to assess intuitive ability through the use of an ex post facto survey under the best circumstances is questionable. However, we believe that a well-designed survey might provide useful information about tendencies and general orientations toward intuitive decision making. Survey results could be used to help researchers identify individuals with intuitive tendencies and to help decision makers better understand their own decision-making styles.

Third, the effectiveness of intuitive decisions by principals merits additional research. Case-study methods should be used to examine and triangulate multiple perspectives and other evidence that corroborate the self-perceptions of principals that their intuitions rarely lead to bad decisions. And finally, we recommend further research on how varying conditions of emotional stress and task complexity influence the use and quality of intuitive decisions.

AIM SURVEY

Directions: Complete the survey as quickly as you can (10–15 minutes should be sufficient). Be honest with yourself. In Part I, questions 1–12, select the response that *first* appeals to you. Circle the letter to the left of that response. In Part II, respond to each question as indicated.

PART I: YOUR INTUITIVE ABILITY

1. **When working on a project, do you prefer to:**
    A   Be told what the problem is, but left free to decide how to solve it?
    B   Get very clear instructions about how to go about solving the problem before you start?

2. **When working on a project, do you prefer to work with colleagues who are:**
    A   Realistic?
    B   Imaginative?

3. **Do you admire people most who are:**
   A   Creative?
   B   Careful?

4. **Do the friends you choose tend to be:**
   A   Serious and hard working?
   B   Exciting and often emotional?

5. **When you ask a colleague for advice on a problem you have, do you:**
   A   Seldom or never get upset if he/she questions your basic assumptions?
   B   Often get upset if he/she questions your basic assumptions?

6. **When you start your day, do you:**
   A   Seldom make or follow a specific plan to follow?
   B   Make a plan first to follow?

7. **When working with numbers, do you find that you:**
   A   Seldom or never make factual errors?
   B   Often make factual errors?

8. **Do you find that you:**
   A   Seldom daydream during the day and really don't enjoy doing so when you do it?
   B   Frequently daydream during the day and enjoy doing so?

9. **When working on a problem do you:**
   A   Prefer to follow the instructions or rules when they are given to you?
   B   Often enjoy circumventing the instructions or rules when they are given to you?

10. **When you are trying to put something together, do you prefer to have:**
   A   Step-by-step written instructions on how to assemble the item?
   B   A picture of how the item is supposed to look once assembled?

11. **Do you find that the person who irritates you the most is the one who appears to be:**

A Disorganized?

B Organized?

12. **When an unexpected crisis comes up that you have to deal with, do you:**

A Feel anxious about the situation?

B Feel excited by the challenge of the situation?

PART II: DO YOU USE YOUR INTUITIVE ABILITY TO MAKE IMPORTANT DECISIONS?

13. **Do you believe that you use intuition frequently to guide your most important decisions? (Check one.)**

NO_____ YES_____

14. **If yes, in which circumstances or situations do you use your intuition to make your most important decisions? (Circle the letter(s) of all choices that apply.)**

A Where there is a high degree of certainty.

B Where there is little previous precedent.

C Where variables are less scientifically predictable or where "facts" are limited.

D Where there are several plausible alternative solutions to choose from with good arguments for each.

E Where time is limited and there is pressure to be right.

F Other (specify) _____

15. **What kinds of feelings or signals do you get when you "know" that a particular decision is "right?" What do you rely on for cues? (Circle the letter(s) of all choices that apply.)**

A Excitement

B Warmth

C Peaceful/calm

D High energy

E Sudden flash of insight

F Other (specify) _____

16. Give an example (or two) of a very important decision where you followed your intuition, and it proved to be the "right" decision. _____

17. What feelings or signals do you get when you "know" you are heading in the wrong direction or should delay your decision for a while? (Circle the letter(s) of all choices that apply.)

   A   Anxious
   B   Upset stomach
   C   Mixed or conflicting signals
   D   Other (specify) _____

18. What kinds of conditions have obstructed the use of your intuition in important decision-making situations? (Circle the letter(s) of all choices that apply.)

   A   When angry
   B   Under stress
   C   Too much ego involved in the decision
   D   Rushed my decision
   E   Lack of confidence
   F   Other (specify) _____

19. Do you intend to "keep it a secret" that you use intuition to make decisions, or do you feel comfortable sharing this fact with other? (Check one.)

   Keep it a secret   _____
   Share with others   _____
   Please explain: _____

20. When using your intuition to make a decision, where have you found it functions best? (Circle the letter of the choice that applies.)

   A   At the very beginning when I am trying to assess the future or the options available to me.
   B   At the very end when I am trying to sift through and digest all the cues and information available to me.
   C   It really varies depending on the problem or issue at hand (specify) _____

21. When making a major decision, do you use any particular technique or method(s) to help draw on your intuitive ability more effectively? (Check one.)

YES _____
NO _____
If yes, please describe: _____

22. Do you use or regularly practice any particular technique or method(s) to help develop further your intuitive ability? (Check one.)

YES _____
NO _____
If yes, please describe: _____

23. Please indicate your current work environment. (Circle the letter(s) of all choices that apply.)

A   Elementary school
B   Junior high/Middle school
C   High school (regular/comprehensive)
D   High school (alternative)
E   Enrollment: 1–250
F   Enrollment: 251–500
G   Enrollment: 501–750
H   Enrollment: 751–1000
I   Enrollment: 1001–1500
J   Enrollment: 1501–2000
K   Enrollment: over 2000

24. Please indicate the number of years that you have worked as a principal. (Circle one.)

A   Less than a year
B   1–4 years
C   More than 4 years (specify) _____

25. I like my occupation and feel it is right for me. (Check one.)

YES _____
NO _____

26. **Please indicate your gender**

   A   Female
   B   Male

27. **Ethnic background. (Circle the one with which you identify most closely.)**

   A   African American
   B   American Indian, Alaska Native
   C   Asian American, Asian Indian, Oriental, Southeast Asian
   D   Filipino
   F   Mexican American
   G   Middle Eastern, Northern African
   H   Pacific Islander
   I   White Non-Hispanic, Caucasian, European
   J   Other (specify) _____

Thank you for your time and assistance. Your responses are a vitally important element of this research project and will be included in the data analysis and final results. Please be assured that your responses will be treated with complete confidentiality. Your name, district, or school will not appear in any way on any document, report, or article that may be published as a result of this research.

Please don't hesitate to contact us if you have questions or comments related to this survey or research project.

REFERENCES

Agor, W. H. 1986. *The logic of intuitive decision making: A research-based approach for top management.* New York: Quorum.

———. 1989. The intuitive ability of executives. In *Intuition in organizations: Leading and managing productively*, edited by W. H. Agor. Newbury Park, Calif.: Sage.

———. 1992. *Intuition in decision making: How to assess, use, and develop your intuitive powers for increased productivity.* El Paso, Tex.: Global Intuition Network.

Arsham, H. 1996. "Applied management science: Making good strategic decisions" at ubmail.ubalt.edu/~harsham/opre640 (accessed June 24, 2001).

Arvidson, P. S. 1997. Looking intuit: A phenomenological exploration of intuition and attention. In *Intuition: The inside story*, edited by R. Davis-Floyd and P. S. Arvidson, 39–56. New York: Routledge.

Aul, L. E., Sr., and J. A. Johnson. 1987. *Tacit knowledge, social insight, and personality.* Paper presented at the annual meeting of the Eastern Psychological Association, 9–12 April, at Arlington, Va.

Bargh, J. A., and T. L. Chartrand. July 1999. The unbearable automaticity of being. *American Psychologist* 54, no. 7: 462–79.

Baron, J. B. 2000. *Thinking and deciding.* 3rd ed. Cambridge: Cambridge University Press.

Beach, L. R. 1997. *The psychology of decision making: People in organizations.* Thousand Oaks, Calif.: Sage.

Beach, L. R., M. Chi, G. Klein, P. Smith, and K. Vincente. 1996. Naturalistic decision-making and related research lines. In *Naturalistic decision making*, edited by C. E. Zsambok and G. A. Klein, 29–35. Mahwah, N.J.: Lawrence Erlbaum.

Bennis, W. 1989. *On becoming a leader.* Reading, Mass.: Addison Wesley.

Bennis, W., and B. Nanus. 1985. *Leaders: The strategies for taking charge.* New York: Harper and Row.

Bergstrand, B. 1998. "Situating the estimate: Naturalistic decision-making as an alternative to analytical decision-making in the Canadian forces" at www.cfcsc.dnd.ca/irc/nh/nh/9798/0021.html (accessed June 14, 2001).

Bolman, L. G., and T. E. Deal. 1997. *Reframing organizations: Artistry, choice, and leadership.* 2nd ed. San Francisco: Jossey-Bass.

Bombardi, R. 2001. How rationalists construe "clear and distinct ideas" at www.frank.mtsu.edu/~rbombard/RB/Spinoza/cnd.html (accessed June 21, 2001).

Boucouvales, M. 1997. Intuition: The concept and the experience. In *Intuition: The inside story*, edited by R. Davis-Floyd and P. S. Arvidson, 3–18. New York: Routledge.

Bower, B. July 1998. Seeing through expert eyes. *Science News* 154, no. 3: 44–46.

Brown, C. 2001. "Rationalism-Plato & Descartes" at www.csus.edu/indiv/m.mccormickm/IEPKantArt.htm (accessed June 21, 2001).

Brown, E. 2002. How can a dot-com be this hot? *Fortune* 145, no. 2: 78–84.

Brown, R. A. 1990. *The use of intuition in the decision making process of public school superintendents.* Ph.D. diss., Texas A&M University.

Busenitz, L. W., and J. B. Barney. Jan. 1997. Differences between entrepreneurs and managers in large organizations: Biases and heuristics in strategic decision-making. *Journal of Business Venturing* 12, no. 1: 9–30.

Cappon, D. 1993. The anatomy of intuition. *Psychology Today* 26, no. 3: 40–94.

———. 1994. *Intuition and management: Research and application.* Westport, Conn.: Quorum.

Cohen, M. D., J. G. March, and J. P. Olsen. 1972. A garbage can model of organizational choice. *Administrative Science Quarterly* 17: 1–25.

Cuban, L. 2001. *How can I fix it? Finding solutions and managing dilemmas: An educator's road map.* New York: Teachers College Press.

Daft, R. L. 2001. *Organizational theory and design.* 7th ed. Cincinnati, Ohio: South-Western College Publishing.

Damasio, A. 1994. *Descartes' error: Emotion, reason, and the human brain.* New York: Avon.

———. 1999. *The feeling of what happens: Body and emotion in the making of consciousness.* San Diego: Harcourt.

Davis, S. H. 1998. Superintendents' perspectives on the involuntary departure of public school principals. *Educational Administration Quarterly* 34 (February): 58–90.

Davis, S. H., and P. A. Hensley. 1999. The politics of principal evaluation. *Journal of Personnel Evaluation in Education* 13 (November): 383–404.

Deal, T. E., and K. D. Peterson. 1994. *The leadership paradox: Balancing logic and artistry in schools.* San Francisco: Jossey-Bass.

Dickmann, M. H., and N. Stanford-Blair. 2002. *Connecting leadership to the brain.* Thousand Oaks, Calif.: Corwin Press.

Dillman, D. 1978. *Mail and telephone surveys: The total design method.* New York: Wiley.

Drake, T. L., and W. H. Roe. 1999. *The principalship.* 5th ed. Upper Saddle River, N.J.: Merrill.

Dreyfus, H. L., and S. E. Dreyfus. 1986. *Mind over machine: The power of human intuition and expertise in the era of the computer.* New York: Free Press.

Dunne, B. J. 1997. Subjectivity and intuition in the scientific method. In *Intuition: The inside story*, edited by R. Davis-Floyd and P. S. Arvidson, 121–28. New York: Routledge.

East, B. W. 1997. Decision-making strategies in educational organizations. *Journal of physical education, recreation and dance* 68, no. 4: 39–45.

Elwell, F. 1996. "Verstehen: Max Weber's home page" at www.faculty.rus.edu/~felwell/theorists/weber/whome.htm (accessed June 1, 1999).

Fullan, M. 1997. *What's worth fighting for in the principalship?* New York: Teachers College Press.

Funke, J., and P. A. Frensch. 1995. *Complex problem solving research in North America and Europe: An integrative approach.* Unpublished manuscript, Max-Planck Institute for Human Development and Education. Berlin, Germany.

Gardner, H. 1993. *Frames of mind: The theory of multiple intelligences.* New York: Basic.

Gaynor, A. K. 1998. *Analyzing problems in schools and school systems: A theatrical approach.* Mahwah, N.J.: Lawrence Erlbaum.

Gigerenzer, G., and P. M. Todd. 1999. *Simple heuristics that make us smart.* Oxford: Oxford University Press.

Glaser, M. 1995. Measuring intuition. *Research Technology Management* 38: 43–46.

Goldstein, W. M., and R. M. Hogarth. 1997. Judgment and decision research: Some historical context. In *Research on judgment and decision making: Currents, connections, and controversies*, edited by W. M. Goldstein and R. M. Hogarth, 3–65. Cambridge: Cambridge University Press.

Goleman, D. 1995. *Emotional intelligence: Why it can matter more than IQ.* New York: Bantam.

Gopnick, A., and E. Schwitzgebel. 1998. Whose concepts are they anyway? The role of philosophical intuition in empirical psychology. In *Rethinking intuition,* edited by M. R. DePaul and W. Ramsey, 75–91. Lanham, Md.: Rowman & Littlefield.

Green, C. D. 2001. "The principles of psychology: William James (1890)" at www.psychclassics.yorku.ca/James/Principles/prin24.htm (accessed June 22, 2001).

Greenberg, J., and R. A. Baron. 1997. *Behavior in organizations: Understanding and managing the human side of work.* Upper Saddle River, N.J.: Prentice Hall.

Hanson, E. M. 1996. *Educational administration and organizational behavior.* 4th ed. Boston: Allyn & Bacon.

Harbort, B. 1997. Thought, action, and intuition in practice-oriented disciplines. In *Intuition: The inside story,* edited by R. Davis-Floyd and P. S. Arvidson, 129–44. New York: Routledge.

Harvey, T. R., W. L. Bearley, and S. M. Corkrum. 1997. *The practical decision maker: A handbook for decision making and problem solving in organizations.* Lancaster, Pa.: Technomics Publishing.

Hobson, J. A. 1999. *Consciousness.* New York: Scientific American Library.

Hocker, R. 2001. "Greek philosophy = Aristotle" at www.wsu.edu.8080/~dec/greece/artist.htm (accessed June 21, 2001).

Hogarth, R. M. 2001. *Educating intuition.* Chicago, Ill.: University of Chicago Press.

Hogarth, R. M., and H. Kunreuther. 1997. Decision making under ignorance: Arguing with yourself. In *Research on judgment and decision making: Currents, connections, and controversies,* edited by W. M. Goldstein and R. M. Hogarth, 482–508. Cambridge: Cambridge University Press.

Hoppe, H. H. 1997. On certainty and uncertainty, or: How rational can our expectations be? *Review of Austrian Economics* 10, no. 1: 49–78.

Howard, P. K. 1996. *The death of common sense.* New York: Warner.

Internet Encyclopedia of Philosophy, s.v. "continental rationalism," at www.utm.edu/research/iep/r/rat-cont/htm (accessed June 29, 2001).

Jarris, C. 2001. "Functions and principles of management" at www.sol.brunel.ac.uk/~jarvis/bola/competence/fayol.html (accessed July 6, 2001).

Johnston, J. H., J. E. Driskell, and E. Salas. 1997. Vigilant and hypervigilant decision making. *Journal of Applied Psychology* 82, no. 4: 614–22.

Jones, R. A. 1986. *Emile Durkheim: An introduction to four major works.* Beverly Hills, Calif.: Sage.

Jones, S. 2001. "The philosophy behind ordinary consciousness" at www.culture. com.au/brain_project/phil_pt1.htm (accessed June 23, 2001).

Kahneman, D., and A. Tversky. 1982. Intuitive prediction: Biases and corrective procedures. In *Judgment under uncertainty: Heuristics and biases*, ed ited by D. Kahneman, P. Slovic, and A. Tversky, 414–21. Cambridge: Cambridge University Press.

Kenneth, R. H., R. M. Hamm, J. Grassia, and T. Pearson. 1997. Direct comparison of the efficiency of intuitive and analytical cognition in expert judgment. In *Research on judgment and decision making: Currents, connections, and controversies*, edited by W. M. Goldstein and R. M. Hogarth, 144–80. Cambridge: Cambridge University Press.

Klein, G. 1996a. An overview of naturalistic decision making applications. In *Naturalistic decision making*, edited by C. E. Zsambok and G. A. Klein, 49–60. Mahwah, N.J.: Lawrence Erlbaum.

———. 1996b. The recognition-primed decision model. In *Naturalistic decision making*, edited by C. E. Zsambok and G. A. Klein, 285–292. Mahwah, N.J.: Lawrence Erlbaum.

Kouzes, J. M., and B. Z. Posner. 1987. *The leadership challenge*. San Francisco: Jossey-Bass Publishers.

Krabuanrat, K., and R. Phelps. 1998. Heuristics and rationality in strategic decision making: An exploratory study. *Journal of Business Research* 41: 83–93.

Landry, L. 1991. *A study of the experience, use, and development of intuition*. Ph.D. diss., University of Massachusetts.

Laughlin, C. 1997. The nature of intuition: A neuropsychological approach. In *Intuition: The inside story*, edited by R. Davis-Floyd and P. S. Arvidson, 19–37. New York: Routledge.

Lipshitz, R., and O. Ben Shaul. 1996. Schemata and mental models in regognition-primed decision-making. In *Naturalistic decision making*, edited by C. E. Zsambok and G. A. Klein, 293–303. Mahwah, N.J.: Lawrence Erlbaum.

March, J. G. 1994. *A primer on decision making: How decisions happen*. New York. Free Press.

McCormick, M. "Immanuel Kant" at www.csus.edu/indiv/m/mccormick/ IEPKantArt.htm (accessed June 19, 2001).

Microsoft Encarta, s.v. "Hegel, Georg" at www.connect.net/ron/hegel.html (accessed June 19, 2001).

Miller, S. J., D. J. Hickson, and D. C. Wilson. 1999. Decision-making in organizations. In *Managing organizations: Current issues*, edited by S. R. Clegg, C. Hardy, and W. R. Nord, 43–62. London: Sage.

Mintzberg, H. 1973. *The nature of managerial work*. New York: Harper and Row.

———. 1976. Planning on the left side and managing on the right. *Harvard Business Review* (July/August): 57–62.

———. 1980. Managerial work: Analysis from observation. In *Readings in organizational behavior and performance*, edited by A. D. Szilaggi and M. J. Wallace Jr., 158–74. Santa Monica, Calif.: Goodyear.

Miranda, T. 2001. "Rationality and critical education" at www.educaco.pro.br/rationality-critical.htm (accessed June 21, 2001).

Mishlove, J. 2001. "Intuition: A link between psi and spirituality" at www.intuition.org/revision.htm (accessed June 24, 2001).

Morris, L. E. 1990. *Strategies and tactics to access intuition: A look at the moment of solution.* Ph.D. diss., Virginia Polytechnic Institute and State University.

Moustakas, C. 1994. *Phenomenological research methods.* Thousand Oaks, Calif.: Sage.

Owens, R. G. 1995. *Organizational behavior in education.* 5th ed. Boston: Allyn & Bacon.

Pashiardis, P. 1994. *Problem and dilemma identification and formulation as the most critical element of the decision-making process: Behavioral biases and characteristics.* Paper presented at the International Intervisitation Programme in Educational Administration, 15–27 May, Toronto, Canada.

Patterson, J. L. 1993. *Leadership for tomorrow's schools.* Alexandria, Va.: Association for Supervision and Curriculum Development.

Patton, M. Q. 1990. *Qualitative evaluation and research methods.* 2nd ed. Newbury Park, Calif.: Sage.

Payne, J. W., J. R. Bettman, and E. J. Johnson. 1997. The adaptive decision maker: Effort, and accuracy in choice. In *Research on judgment and decision making: Currents, connections, and controversies*, edited by W. M. Goldstein and R. M. Hogarth, 181–204. Cambridge: Cambridge University Press.

Peters, T. J., and R. H. Waterman Jr. 1982. In *search of excellence.* New York: Harper and Row.

Philosophical Dictionary. 2001. s.v. "rationalism" at www.philosophypages.com/dy/r.htm#ratm (accessed June 21, 2001).

Planck, M. 2001. "Freedom's nest" at www.freedomsnest.com (accessed October 16, 2001).

Pondy, L. R. 1983. Union of rationality and intuition in management action. In *The executive mind*, edited by W. Bennis, R. O. Mason, and I. I. Mitroff, 169–91. San Francisco: Jossey-Bass.

Ratey, J. J. 2001. *A user's guide to the brain.* New York: Pantheon.

Razik, T. A., and A. D. Swanson. 2001. *Fundamental concepts of educational leadership.* Upper Saddle River, N.J.: Merrill Prentice Hall.

Robbins, S. P. 1997. *Managing today.* Upper Saddle River, N.J.: Prentice Hall.

Rowan, R. 1986. *The intuitive manager.* Boston: Little, Brown.

Schooler, J. W., S. Ohlsson, and K. Brooks. 1993. Thoughts beyond words: When language overshadows insight. *Journal of Experimental Psychology: General* 122: 166–83.

Sergiovanni, T. J. 1000. *Leadership for the schoolhouse.* San Francisco: Jossey Bass.

Shafir, E., and A. Tversky. 1997. Reason based choice. In *Research on judgment and decision making: Currents, connections, and controversies,* edited by W. M. Goldstein and R. M. Hogarth, 69–94. Cambridge: Cambridge University Press.

Simon, H. A. 1986. Decision making and problem solving. In *Research Briefings 1986: Report of the research briefing panel on decision making and problem solving,* 1–24. Washington, D.C: National Academy Press.

Smith, G. F. 1997. Managerial problem solving: A problem-centered approach. In *Naturalistic decision making,* edited by C. E. Zsambok and G. A. Klein, 371–80. Mahwah, N.J.: Lawrence Erlbaum.

Smith, S. C., and P. K. Piele. 1997. *School leadership: Handbook for excellence.* 3rd ed. Eugene, Ore.: ERIC Clearinghouse on Education Management.

Sorokin, P. A. 2001/1941. "The integral theory of truth and reality" at www.intuition.org/sorokin.htm (accessed June 22, 2001).

Stanford Encyclopedia of Philosophy 2001. s.v. "Historicist theories of rationality" at www.plato.stanford.edu/entres/reationality-historicist/ (accessed June 21, 2001).

Sternberg, R. J., and P. A. Frensch. 1991. Solving complex problems: Exploration and control of complex systems. In *Complex problem solving: Principles and mechanisms,* edited by R. J. Sterberg and P. A. Frensch, 185–222. Hillsdale, N.J.: Lawrence Erlbaum.

Tannenbaum, R., and W. H. Schmidt. 1958. How to choose a leadership pattern. *Harvard Business Review* 36: 95–101.

Taylor, T. 2001. "Aristotle, rationality, and the sophron" at www.its.uidaho.edu/ngier/_disc4/0000007f.htm (accessed June 21, 2001).

Tenbrunsel, A. E., T. L. Galvin, M. A. Neale, and M. H. Bazerman. 1999. Cognitions in organizations. In *Managing organizations: Current issues,* edited by S. R. Clegg, C. Hardy, and W. R. Nord, 63–87. London: Sage.

Ubben, G. C., and L. W. Hughes. 1997. *The principal: Creative leadership for effective schools.* 3rd ed. Boston: Allyn & Bacon.

Vroom, V. H., and A. G. Jago. 1978. On the validity of the Vroom-Yetton method. *Journal of Applied Psychology* 63: 151–62.

Wagner, R. K. 1991. Managerial problem solving. In *Complex problem solving: Principles and mechanisms,* edited by R. J. Sternberg and P. A. Frensch, 159–84. Hillsdale, N.J.: Lawrence Erlbaum.

Weick, K. E. 1995. *Sensemaking in organizations.* Thousand Oaks, Calif.: Sage.

Wozniak, R. H. 2001. "Mind and body: René Descartes to William James" at www.serendip.brymawr.edu/mind/James.html (accessed June 21, 2001).

Yukl, G. 1994. *Leadership in organizations.* 3rd ed. Englewood Cliffs, N.J.: Prentice Hall.

Zsambok, C. E. 1996. Naturalistic decision making: Where are we now? In *Naturalistic decision making,* edited by C. E. Zsambok and G. A. Klein, 3–16. Mahwah, N.J.: Lawrence Erlbaum.

INDEX

act-think phenomenon, 63
administrative decisions in
schools: themes and
dimensions, 45
administrative training programs,
136
Age of Enlightenment, 2, 87–88;
philosophers of, 2–4, 87–88, 97
Agor, W., xii, 11, 21, 76, 80, 84,
89, 90, 94, 97, 99–100,
139–140, 142–144, 171
Agor Intuitive Management
(AIM) Survey, 100, 139–141,
166–167, 173, 189–194
amygdala, 84, 121, 123, 126; and
arousal, 115; emotional
hijacking, 115, 183; emotional
memory, 115–116; emotional
stimuli, 183; feelings of
passion, 114; intuitive
foundation, 129; long-term
memory, 126; neuronal

clusters, 116; role in intuition,
117; signals from, 112, 124;
social cues, 115
analogies, 179
analysis: errors of, 95; use in
decision making, 43
anterior cingulated gyrus, 84
arational thinking, 63
Aristotle, 2
Arsham, H., 3, 9–11, 46, 99
Arvidson, P. S., 76, 81, 100

Bargh, J. A., 25, 59, 63, 96
Barney, J. B., 58, 65
Baron, J. B., 91, 94, 96
Baron, R. A., 6, 11, 18, 43, 46, 51,
56, 67, 69, 71
Bazerman, M. H., 35, 41, 53, 55,
60, 65, 71
Beach, L. R., 34, 44, 46, 49,
54–56, 58, 63, 65, 69–70
Bearley, W. L., 41, 44, 65

ABOUT THE AUTHORS

Stephen H. Davis is an associate professor (teaching) of educational leadership at the Stanford University School of Education. In addition to teaching graduate courses in school leadership, he directs the Stanford Prospective Principals Program. Dr. Davis has been an associate professor of Educational Administration at the University of the Pacific, a school district superintendent, director of personnel, high school principal, high school dean, and high school teacher. Dr. Davis received an Ed.D. in educational administration and policy analysis from Stanford University, an M.A. from San Jose State University, and a B.A. from Stanford University.

Patricia B. Davis is currently the superintendent of the Ross Valley School District in San Anselmo, California. During her thirty years in public education, Mrs. Davis has been a superintendent in two school districts, an assistant superintendent, a deputy director of instruction, an elementary school principal, a district staff development coordinator, and an elementary teacher. She has also served as a Learning Support faculty member in the California State University's CalStateTEACH program. Mrs. Davis received an M.A. in educational supervision from Chapman University and a B.A. from the University of California, Davis.